Shura Cherkassky

The Piano's Last Czar

Elizabeth Carr

The Scarecrow Press, Inc.
Lanham, Maryland • Toronto • Oxford
2006

SCARECROW PRESS, INC.

Published in the United States of America
by Scarecrow Press, Inc.
A wholly owned subsidiary of
The Rowman & Littlefield Publishing Group, Inc.
4501 Forbes Boulevard, Suite 200, Lanham, Maryland 20706
www.scarecrowpress.com

PO Box 317
Oxford
OX2 9RU, UK

British Library Cataloguing in Publication Information Available

Library of Congress Cataloging-in-Publication Data

Carr, Elizabeth
Shura Cherkassky : the piano's last czar / Elizabeth Carr.
p. cm.
Includes bibliographical references (p.), discography (p.), and index.
ISBN 0–8108–5410–4 (hardcover : alk. paper)
1. Cherkassky, Shura. 2. Pianists—Biography. I. Title.
ML417.C45C37 2006
786.2′092—dc22 2005016897

™ The paper used in this publication meets the minimum requirements of American National Standard for Information Sciences—Permanence of Paper for Printed Library Materials, ANSI/NISO Z39.48–1992.
Manufactured in the United States of America.

For Shura

"He has totally tamed that large black animal, the grand piano, and has for the last half a century traveled round the world with it in his pocket. It obeys the master's slightest command; it tiptoes on velvet paws; it cascades with lightning speed, and at the slightest signal from its master it alters its speed, changes color and appearance, and goes on to perform a feather-light somersault."

—*NRC Handelsblad*, 28 January 1988

Contents

~

Preface

Shura Cherkassky played a remarkable role in my life. We were two strangers who became friends and ended up soulmates. Still, the story of Shura Cherkassky is not an easy one to tell. His innate shyness was coupled with a fierce aversion to speaking about the past, which left storytellers little material with which to weave their tales. Reporters and interviewers fared not much better. Over the course of my long and treasured friendship with Shura Cherkassky, I would often sit quietly by, secretly amused, as an unsuspecting journalist posed the first question in a long-sought interview. More often than not there would be a very long pause followed by the response, "Why do you want to know *that*?" And so it would go: the world-renowned pianist parrying questions from an increasingly perplexed reporter, and skillfully and wittily avoiding giving information unless the subject turned to travel (after music, the other great passion of Shura Cherkassky), at which time he became as excited as a child, asking endless questions and bubbling with enthusiasm as he recounted the minutiae of airline schedules and tour itineraries. That his life, his thoughts, and his experience might be of interest to anyone never appeared to cross his mind. He was how he was; he played how he played. For him it was as simple as that. But for others he was as complex as a prism, ever inviting scrutiny while ever preventing discovery of his secrets. Concerning the future he was continuously enthusiastic and optimistic. When questioned about the past he was unequivocal: it did not interest him in the least and he refused to talk about it other than in some oblique way. One positive result of this resistance was that, when he did speak, he told only the truth and nothing but the truth. He could no more spin the facts of his life than change the harmony of a Chopin ballade, and any recollections he did share with the outside world were as precise and reliable as his memory for his vast piano repertoire.

At the time of his death in 1995 at age eighty-six, Shura Cherkassky was universally recognized as one of history's greatest pianists as well as the last link to the romantic piano tradition of Chopin, Liszt, and Anton Rubinstein. Born in Russia, trained in America, domiciled in London, and constantly traveling throughout the world, Cherkassky began his concert-playing life in Ukrainian Odessa at a time of lethal civil strife in Mother Russia. When he was a small boy standing on the balcony of the family apartment, a stray bullet from the street fighting below whistled just inches above his head and lodged in the wall behind him. That incident, coupled with near starvation, led his parents on a valiant struggle to escape unsustainable hardships. Permission was finally obtained in 1922 to immigrate to America, where the family was taken in by relatives who had immigrated earlier in the century to Baltimore, Maryland. Subsequently, the child prodigy came under the tutelage of famed pianist Josef Hofmann at the Curtis Institute in Philadelphia. Hofmann's unfailing personal and professional assistance continued for more than twenty years and was a crucial ingredient in the persistence that finally earned Cherkassky the acclaim that otherwise might have eluded him.

From his sensational 1923 American debut season, which included a command performance at the White House for President Harding, to appearances with Walter Damrosch and the New York Symphony, through sold-out concerts in the music capitals of six continents, Cherkassky's pianistic brilliance remained virtually undiminished until his death, arguably an unprecedented achievement in the history of music. His active international solo and orchestral career, which lasted more than seventy-six years, was unmatched in its duration. And his commercial recording career continued for seventy-two years, a longer time span than any performer in music history.

The story of Shura Cherkassky merits telling not only for the sake of these musical achievements but also for the inspiration the character of the man provides. In the face of adversity he demonstrated tenacity, integrity, common sense, and uncommon courage. Though his was one of the most promising careers of the twentieth century, it nearly came to a halt as war blighted Europe. Few engagements, near poverty, and overwhelming concern for his beloved mother were a given in Cherkassky's life from 1939 until 1949, when an invitation came for him to perform in Hamburg, Germany. Ignoring all the warnings from his friends not to accept because of his Jewish origins, Cherkassky followed his instincts and went ahead with the engagement. With that one concert he exploded on the European musical scene, and for the next forty-six years he trekked tirelessly around the globe playing recitals and orchestral engagements. He also became one of the music world's most interesting personalities offstage, generating intense emotional responses from many who knew him, responses that resulted in personal peaks and valleys and often deep unhappiness for Cherkassky until the day he died. That unhappiness never once interfered with Shura Cherkassky's commitment to his art, however. If anything, it drove him harder, as did his ambivalence about his homosexuality.

Although the artistry of many great pianists of the twentieth century is amply preserved through recordings and videos, the details of their lives, outlooks, problems, setbacks, work habits, and techniques (details meaningful to students, scholars, and music lovers in general) too often receive only the sketchiest documentation. Books contain facts, but more often than not readers are left with a glass of facts half-full. In Shura Cherkassky's case the situation is even more extreme. Away from the stage, he left friends and observers with the glass of the facts of his life and his psyche (both of which were key to the performances he delivered on stage) not half-full but empty. This silence, rather than quelling curiosity, served to intensify it, almost guaranteeing that the interest in Cherkassky as a man and the fascination with his pianism while he was alive would not abate with his death. Compounding the researcher's problem created by Cherkassky's silence was the fact that he outlived the colleagues and friends of his youth, friends like William Harms and Abram Chasins, and had neither close family nor students, each of which would otherwise have been a principal source of biographical and personal data. The problem was only exacerbated by his frequent changes of concert managers and recording companies, leaving many of these potential biographical sources with fractured and incomplete information.

Tracing the motivating forces behind Cherkassky's achievements was an intriguing challenge. I first met the pianist backstage at Hunter College in 1976 upon his return to the American concert scene after an absence of fourteen years. That evening a solid friendship began that lasted until his death in 1995. To unravel the mystery and circumstances of Cherkassky's past and to show how they shaped his unique artistic temperament became my compelling interest. And coincidentally, I had a connection to Cherkassky prior to ever meeting him. As a piano major in college I studied with William Harms, a student of Hofmann and close friend and contemporary of Cherkassky at the Curtis Institute. Following graduate school, I also coached with world-famed authority on the music of Charles-Valentin Alkan, Raymond

Lewenthal, who in his youth in Los Angeles studied with Shura Cherkassky's mother, Lydia Cherkassky.

As the closest of friends for the last twenty years of his life, I on occasion traveled with him on tour, attended recording sessions in London, observed numerous hours of practice and rehearsal sessions, watched him learn new pieces and relearn old ones, and saw how he planned programs and coped with pianos, acoustics, conductors, and orchestras. I visited at length with him in Europe and the United States, received over 160 letters and faxes from him as well as innumerable telephone calls from around the globe, and served as his confidante in troubled as well as happy times. Through this relationship it was possible for me to gain a vivid understanding of Shura Cherkassky as both a human being and a performer. What he did, how he thought, what he said, who he knew, who he liked or disliked, where he went, how he reacted to triumph or disappointment—all these provided precious insight into what made him a unique artist.

These personal observations have been supplemented by extensive, carefully documented, and never before published research conducted in the United States, Austria, France, Great Britain, Germany, Holland, Italy, and Russia. Of major significance was the discovery of seventeen years of correspondence between Cherkassky, Josef Hofmann, and Mary Louise Curtis Bok, founder of the Curtis Institute. These letters contain revelatory information concerning Cherkassky's relationship to Josef Hofmann, the personal pain the young Cherkassky suffered during his years in America, and Hofmann's continuing and unconditional support of his student well into adulthood.

Further evidence used to trace Cherkassky's life and career was culled from private documents, including, in addition to Cherkassky's letters to me, a large collection of additional letters and communications to friends, managers, and acquaintances, as well as close to two thousand articles and concert and record reviews published worldwide between the years 1923 and 2004. Other sources of important information were the 1935 Cherkassky letters in Henry Steinway's private files, personal letters between the conductor Artur Rodzinski and the pianist, contracts citing fees and unusual details, divorce filings, White House documents, and Cherkassky's last will and testament. Documents have been scanned into the text in their original form except when blurred ink or faded print made it necessary to transcribe them.

Personal testimony in addition to mine I derived from extensive interviews of conductors, managers, critics, colleagues, recording engineers, archivists, curators, lecturers, and major figures in the piano world. Of particular importance in gathering this testimony were trips to Moscow where I met and spoke at length with Shura Cherkassky's first cousin, Tanya Peltzer, and to Odessa, the Ukraine, where I visited Cherkassky's birthplace and interviewed friends of the Cherkassky family who knew them at the time of their residence there from 1909 to 1922. Cherkassky family descendants in Baltimore gave information concerning the child prodigy's debut years, and illuminating information was contributed by Anton Hofmann and David Saperton, the respective sons of Josef Hofmann and David Saperton, Shura Cherkassky's mentors.

My discussion and appreciation of Cherkassky's playing, repertoire, and style are the result of a careful study of his commercial recordings, as well as of other recordings not available to the public, and from vivid recollections and contemporaneous notes of his live performances, more than eighty of which I attended. In an effort to avoid the possibility that my close relationship with Cherkassky might skew my judgment in relation to his piano playing, contemporary critical sources are quoted to provide an objective basis with which to view the public perception of Cherkassky's artistry. Anyone with an opportunity to read the copious commentaries devoted to Cherkassky and written over a period of eighty-one years (1923–2004) would be obliged to conclude that the criticism lavished on Cherkassky's playing was overwhelmingly favorable. Indeed, the most striking feature of these documents is their unanimity of voice. For this reason, and because of the scarcity of any disagreement with this unanimity, a significant number of the few negative or personal criticisms Cherkassky attracted have been included or referred to in the text.

Shura Cherkassky's story, as his piano playing, is a provocative and seductive one. It was my intent in writing this narrative of his life and career to provide as intimate an understanding as possible of this singular artist who was among music history's most intriguing and complicated personalities.

~

Acknowledgments

The enthusiasm of the following individuals for the writing of this book and their generous sharing of knowledge made my task even more of a pleasure. For their gracious response, special thanks are extended.

To Maestro Vladimir Ashkenazy, pianist and conductor, NHK Symphony; Maestro Daniel Barenboim, pianist and music director, Chicago Symphony Orchestra, and general music director, Deutsche Staatsoper, Berlin; Henry Z. Steinway, president of Steinway and Sons, 1955–1976; Richard Rodzinski, president, Van Cliburn International Piano Competition; Timothy Day, curator, British Library National Sound Archive, London; Jonathan Summers, curator, British Library Classical Music Division, London; William Lyne, director, and Pamela Best, archivist, Wigmore Hall, London; Thomas Frost, record producer, Columbia Masterworks; and Franz Mohr, for thirty years chief piano technician, Steinway and Sons, New York.

To pianists Martha Argerich, Van Cliburn, Leonid Hambro, Murray Perahia, Gyorgy Sandor, Abbey Simon, and Ruth Slenczynska.

To concert managers Harold Shaw, Lee Lamont, John Gingrich, and Sheldon Soffer of New York City; Pim Broere of South Africa; and Christopher Axworthy of Rome.

To Elizabeth Walker, head librarian, Curtis Institute of Music; and Joanne Seitter, archivist, Curtis Institute of Music.

To the librarians of the Peabody Institute in Baltimore; the Musikverein in Vienna; the British, Westminster, and Barbican libraries in London; the Performing Arts Library at Lincoln Center in New York; the Slavic and Baltic Division of the New York Public Library; the International Piano Archives at College Park, Maryland; the Los Angeles Public Library; and the Osterville Free Library, Osterville, Massachusetts.

To William Allman, White House curator; Elise Kirk, author and research specialist on music at the White House; Gerard Kimelkis, Moscow music critic and personal friend of Shura Cherkassky; Arthur Weiner, Army War College graduate and U.S. Intelligence Officer.

To Larissa Mamaev of Moscow, translator of Russian documents; Ilse Rixen of Krefeld, Germany, translator of German documents; pianophiles Caine Alder, of Salt Lake City, Utah; and Steven Heliotes of Chicago; Yonah Gershator, Columbia Artists assistant; and Roy Kehl, organist and scholar.

To Anton Hofmann, son of Josef Hofmann, for sharing recollections of his father.

To Judy Bender of Arnold, Maryland, daughter of Sadie Dashew Ginsberg, first cousin of Shura Cherkassky, for sending precious family photos and documents relating to the early years of the Cherkassky family in America.

To Chloe Curtis Cherkassky of Keene, New Hampshire, Shura Cherkassky's cousin through marriage, for information on the genealogy of the Cherkassky family.

To Julian Kreeger, for his splendid photograph of Shura, reproduced on the cover.

To Richard, my husband, whose insight and great good humor made him an authentic hero throughout it all.

Finally, to Shura Cherkassky, who urged me to write this book even though he never quite grasped the need for him to provide the answers that he alone knew. How he would have delighted in the merry chase that he led me. It was my privilege to play detective on Shura Cherkassky's case!

Permission to use materials in this book has been received from Summy-Birchard Music, a division of Summy Birchard, Inc.; Warner Brothers Publications U.S. Inc.; the International Piano Archives at the University of Maryland, College Park; the Hearst Corporation; Nimbus Records, Wyastone Leys, UK; the Curtis Institute of Music; Vladimir Ashkenazy; Thomas Frost; Richard Rodzinski; and Henry Steinway.

CHAPTER ONE

Mother Russia

I think Odessa has some sort of inner magic.

—S. C.

"*Whooooosh.* I can still hear it today." With these words Shura Cherkassky described the sound of a bullet sailing just over his head before crashing into the wall behind him as he stood, a small boy, on the balcony of the family apartment in Ukrainian Odessa. Had the child been one inch taller there would be no reason to tell the story of Shura Cherkassky for his life would have ended then and there, one more brutal consequence of the civil strife raging in the streets of Odessa.

Like Milstein, Gilels, Barere, Oistrakh, de Pachmann, and Moiseiwitsch, Shura Cherkassky was born in Odessa, a sun-drenched city caressed by the sea. There is a romance about this place, where harmonious architectural ensembles combine with shady lanes and cozy squares, imparting an air of intimacy to what became known as the Pearl of the Black Sea region. Founded like St. Petersburg to be a "window on Europe," its history dates back to the late eighteenth century when a small settlement called Khadzlibei grew up on the shores of the Black Sea in the vast steppe wilderness reclaimed by Russia from the Ottoman Turks, who had been the controlling force there from 1526 to 1789. Renamed Odessa by Catherine the Great, in a feminized version of the ancient Greek colony of Odessos, the city grew rapidly, becoming a crossroads of cultures, languages, and trade, and ranking third in population after St. Petersburg and Moscow. Early in the nineteenth century, a theater, city hospital, cathedral, and post office were constructed, followed somewhat later by the residence of the city governor, St. Michael's Church, and the Palais-Royal trading rows. Many famed persons in arts and letters strolled Primorsky Boulevard, a pleasant, tree-lined expanse running parallel to the sea, which was designed to be the compositional pivot of the city. Statues of the poet Pushkin and of Armand-Emmanuel du Plessis, Duc de Richlieu (a nobleman who fled to Russia from the French Revolution and governed Odessa from 1803 to 1814), stand prominently on the boulevard, its leafy elegance interrupted only by the steep descent of the *Potemkin* stairs. Immortalized in Eisenstein's 1925 film *Potemkin*, the 192 steps were bloodied in the 1905 massacre by czarist troops of innocent civilians as they stood in a peaceful show of support for the reforms demanded by sailors aboard the battleship *Kynaz Potemkin Tavrichestii* anchored in the harbor. Grigori Aleksandrovich Potemkin, the Russian prince for whom the battleship was named, had chosen the site of Odessa's port, which he recognized for its strategic importance. He was also the lover of Catherine the Great, and according to Potemkin's biographer, Sebag Montefiore, "Their love affair and political alliance was unequaled in history by Anthony and Cleopatra, Louis XVI and Marie Antoinette, Napoleon and Josephine, because it was as remarkable for its achievements as for its romance, as endearing for its humanity as for its power."[1] As the two toured southern Russia in 1787, the prince, described by his enemies as a notorious master of deception, allegedly kept one step ahead of Catherine and her entourage by arranging to have built at each of the designated stops along the way façades of prosperous-looking villages inhabited by temporarily well-fed serfs, all for the purpose of reflecting well on his beloved mistress. This widely circulated apocryphal story endured, and the relationship between Catherine and her prince is one that intrigued Shura Cherkassky.

As Odessa grew, the Peresyp quarter with its railroads and warehouses was built north of the city center on the lower sandy shoreline. Southwest of the city a district called Moldavanka was founded, and no book on old Odessa can do without a description of the colorful lifestyle of Moldavanka residents. With time, however, industrial enterprises took over the streets of this lively quarter, and the once refreshing steppe airs became mixed with soot and grime from nearby factories, greatly tempering the once carefree atmosphere.

Later in the nineteenth century, a number of the significant monuments of Odessa architecture, including the Theatre of Opera and Ballet, the buildings of the New Stock Exchange, the pawnshop, and the public library were erected, many of which were built of shell limestone that had been quarried from the sandstone on which Odessa stands. One by-product of this process was the formation of a labyrinth of a thousand kilometers of underground tunnels, the winding passages of which gave birth to numerous legends associated with the activities of the contraband dealers of old Odessa. When the Great Patriotic War, 1941–1945, was fought, Odessa partisans conducted operations from these underground passages, which were inaccessible to the enemy.

During the first half of the nineteenth century, numerous landowners who had moved to Odessa, attracted by its profitable grain trade, started constructing their private residences. It was their practice to build what amounted to palace compounds containing two-storied mansions with forecourts, wrought iron grilles, porticos indicating the entrance, and strikingly opulent formal rooms. Wealthy merchants and factory owners also constructed mansions to the designs of the best Odessa architects, and in accordance with their fortunes they decorated their homes using various ornaments and architectural details borrowed from different styles and epochs. Each owner attempted to trump his neighbors by using increasingly more lavish embellishments, resulting in a stunning array of arresting and whimsical edifices. Alexander Kuprin (1870–1938), a prominent anti-Bolshevik author of Russian birth who was considered by Tolstoy to be one of the best writers he ever encountered, wrote of Odessa in his *Autumnal Flowers*:

> Flashing on the left and on the right are enchanting glimpses of Odessa millionaires' villas with extravagant openwork grilles, decorated with dragons and coats-of-arms; brightly lit terraces in the depth of the gardens adorned with Chinese lanterns; a kaleidoscope of colors in the fore gardens and on the flowerbeds, and rare plants with intoxicating aromas filling the air.

True to Kuprin's description, during springtime the entire city is redolent with the scent of flowers in bloom.

It was in the idyllic setting of Odessa on October 7, 1909, that Lydia Cherkassky at the age of thirty-seven gave birth to what would be her only child, during a year in which tension and turmoil raged in the Balkans. Russia invaded Persia; Tolstoy's publisher was jailed for publication of Tolstoy's article, "Thou Shalt not Kill"; Maxim Gorky was expelled from the revolutionary party for bourgeois hedonism; Diaghilev took the Ballets Russes to Paris; and Rachmaninoff made his American concert debut at Smith College and premiered his Third Piano Concerto in New York under Walter Damrosch. Elsewhere Count Ferdinand von Zeppelin flew his dirigible a record twenty-two hours from Friedrichshafen to Berlin; Commander Robert E. Peary planted the American flag at the North Pole; London publishers accused Mark Twain of plagiarizing Shakespeare; Orville Wright soared to an unprecedented height of sixteen hundred feet over Potsdam; the liner *Mauretania* shaved fifty minutes off her voyage from New York to Southampton; the World's Fair opened in Seattle; and the first permanent waves were given by London hairdressers. Meanwhile, the music world heard the premiere of Strauss's *Elektra*, Rimsky-Korsakov's *The Golden Cockerel*, Ralph Vaughan Williams's *Fantasia of a Theme of Tallis*, Schoenberg's *Three Piano Pieces*, Wolf-Ferrari's *Il Segreto di Susanna*, and Lehar's *The Count of Luxembourg*; and the art world saw the first abstracts of Kandinsky.

The birthday of Lydia Cherkassky's newborn child, if calculated by the Julian calendar, which Russia followed until 1918, would have been September 24 because the Julian system was thirteen days behind the Gregorian calendar instituted by Pope Gregory XIII on October 4, 1852. But after seizing power on January 30, 1918, Lenin had ordered that Russia convert to the Gregorian calendar, and this changed the young Cherkassky's birthday from September 24 to October 7. Available documents therefore consistently give October 7 as his day of birth. During his early childhood Cherkassky's parents also altered the year of his birth to 1911 in order to prolong his prodigy years. October 7, 1911, is the date that appears on his passport and on his parents' immigration papers.

Isaak and Lydia Cherkassky named their son Alexander but his mother chose to call him Shura, a Russian diminutive for his given name. And so it remained throughout his life. The child adored his mother, a fact that puzzled many who viewed her as cold, domineering, and smothering. Born Lydia Schlemenson in Tulchin, an agricultural community on the Selnitsa River in southwest Ukraine, she listed her date of birth in her petition for naturalization in 1928 as June 31, 1872, an apparently faulty conversion from the Russian calendar. Her actual birth date was July 19, 1872. On the same document Odessa, not Tulchin, is listed as her place of birth, an error contradicted by Shura Cherkassky's postcard (from the Ukraine) to me in which he identifies Tulchin as the site of his mother's birth. A graduate of the Imperial Conservatory of Petrograd where she once played the *Tchaikovsky Variations* for its composer, she studied with Karl van Ark, a student of Leschetizky and distinguished professor of piano at the conservatory. She continued her studies with another Leschetizky student, Annette Essipova, who went on to a highly successful concert career and was an exponent of the Leschetizky method, which placed great emphasis on a beautiful singing tone. The term *Leschetizky method* is one that had wide currency in the piano world for many years and will still have meaning to many readers. Others will dispute that there was such a thing as a Leschetizky method, citing Leschetizky's own disclaimer on the matter. In spite of this refutation, however, Leschetizky allowed a book to be published in 1902 bearing the title: *The Groundwork of the Leschetizky Method, issued with his approval by his assistant Malwine Bree*—a book that most obviously would perpetuate the idea of a specific method. (Malwine Bree was one of Leschetizky's teaching assistants, and inside her book can be found the personal endorsement of Leschetizky over his signature.) Edwin Hughes, a pupil of Leschetizky who became a distinguished piano pedagogue in America, often said, "Yes, there was a Leschetizky method. It was the remarkable ability for taking pains." There is no dispute that the latter was a dominant characteristic of Lydia Cherkassky's teaching and Shura Cherkassky's playing.

Upon her marriage to Isaak Cherkassky, a dentist by profession and violinist by avocation, Lydia Schlemenson Cherkassky settled in Odessa. Soon she began teaching piano at the conservatory as well as in the family apartment. Her frequent appearances on the concert stage, until health problems forced her withdrawal, further prepared her for the role of mentor to her son. When Cherkassky the boy pianist startled the music world in general and Paderewski and Rachmaninoff in particular, the accolades were as much for his mother as for the young prodigy himself.

Cherkassky was steeped in music from the time of his birth. His mother recalled,

> When he was three months old he used to lie in his cradle by the piano while I teach my pupils. Every time I stopped playing he cried and cried until I play some more. When he was three years old he would say to my pupils, "No, that is wrong," when they play wrong note. We took him to the opera at Odessa where we live, when he was seven. Then he cut little dolls of wood and put them on the table, then he move them about and sing right through the operas. He wrote four operas of his own when he was seven. They are childish, of course, but some of the music, it is good.[2]

As a toddler Shura Cherkassky was taught to read music by his father, a skill he grasped immediately. Isaak Cherkassky listed October 13, 1859, as his day of birth on his passport, while October 14 is given in his naturalization papers. The naturalization papers list Zlotopol, a village in the Ukraine, as his place of birth, although descendents report that he was born in Bila Tserkva near Kiev. As a father he was particularly proud of his son's dog-eared notebook in which the child scribbled music over every inch of space, just as he scrawled notes on the walls and furniture of the family apartment. The young Cherkassky would also run to the piano in those early years and perfectly reproduce the pitches of bells on the trams that ran in front of the family's home. Located in a graceful pale green building with a curving façade at 61 Pushkinskaya, the apartment was just down the street from 13 Pushkinskaya where Alexander Pushkin lived and wrote during his Odessa exile of 1823–1824.

Brought up in an atmosphere of music, the child was never forced to study the piano, except for a very brief period when he had to practice scales. "In my earlier childhood I did not like to practice. In fact, it was not until I was eight that I really wanted to practice." From the time he could walk he was permitted to enter the room where his mother played or taught her best pupils, retaining in his memory the notes of all the masterpieces he heard. "My mother, when she had other pupils at the house used to let me listen to them play. I loved to listen to them, but did not want to do the work myself." As an adult he often said he heard the Chopin *F-minor Fantasy* so often that he felt it was born in him. It is said that Lydia Cherkassky, busy one day in another room of their apartment, heard the piano being played in the living room. Thinking one of her advanced pupils had arrived early for a lesson she entered the room to find not a student but her tiny son playing the Chopin *F-minor Fantasy*. In an interview given to *Etude* magazine in 1927, Shura Cherkassky verified his ability to play music he had never studied, telling a reporter, "A great deal of the music I had heard played by my mother's pupils seemed to come to me at my fingertips, as soon as I got a technic. In other words, I listened to the music and absorbed it. . . . When I have once mastered a piece, I do not have to bother playing it much. I just seem to know it from that time on."

When Cherkassky was four, piano lessons began with his mother but soon were discontinued and the child was taught only to absorb music until serious study began at the age of seven. Lydia Cherkassky remained his only teacher until he began working with Josef Hofmann in America in 1925. During an Australian tour in 1928, the young artist recounted to a reporter how he had thought of himself as a very lucky boy. "Children do not want to practice when they are forced to. It is much better to get them to listen and learn to love music. Then if they have talent and a lot of energy they will want to practice."

By all accounts Shura Cherkassky was a delightful child with a gurgling laugh and a wonderful sense of humor, two characteristics he kept throughout his life. In his childlike innocence he would gleefully imitate the discomfort of his dentist father's patients as the good doctor practiced his profession in the family apartment without the benefit of anesthesia. Surrounded by relatives who wanted to keep adulation away from him as long as they possibly could, Cherkassky was not told that the critics had proclaimed him a genius but was instead allowed to go happily along in his small boy ways as if there were nothing extraordinary about his precocity. Modesty remained one of Shura Cherkassky's charms throughout his life. As a child he had a marked penchant for candy, cherished deeply a small mongrel dog named "Brownie," and loved to run and play ball in the streets with other boys. In his jacket pocket he carried a treasured penknife and, as his mother has related, once after hearing a performance of *Aïda* and another one of *Faust* at the Odessa Opera House, he went home and carved the figures and the settings almost as easily as he sang the scores from memory. However nothing, not candy, shaggy dogs, or playing in the streets was enough to distract the child when he was at the piano. It was the focus of his being, a source of delight that stayed with him to the end of his life.

Shura Cherkassky's Odessa debut, playing a program that included the Schubert *Impromptus*, Op. 90 and the Beethoven *Tempest* Sonata, Op. 31, No. 2 caused a sensation and should have brought great good fortune. Instead the Russian Revolution savaged the life of the Cherkassky family and of those around them, causing goods to become scarce, prices to skyrocket, and famine to threaten larger cities. A tide of discontent spread across the country as strikes were held in Petrograd, and increasingly violent encounters took place between civilians, police, and the dreaded Cossack troops. From 1917 to 1920 Odessa was alternately controlled or occupied by Ukrainian nationalists, Bolsheviks, Germans, Austrians, the French, the British, the Bolsheviks again, and the Whites, a party that opposed the radical socialism of the Bolsheviks, and many of whose members favored the return of the czar. Brought to the brink of starvation by the famine of 1921–1922 and suffering intensely from numbing cold, the Cherkasskys bartered household goods for food and fuel. When they were unsuccessful in their trading attempts they burned pieces of furniture to provide warmth. A chilling account of the misery suffered by the Cherkassky family is found in a letter dated September 18, 1921, and written to Isaak Cherkassky's brother by B. Zeltman, a musician, neighbor, and close friend of Isaak. In June of 1921 Zeltman had escaped from the turmoil in Odessa by smuggling himself across the border to Poland where he remained in Warsaw before trying to pass over the Romanian border to Kishineff to meet relatives there. In the process he was caught, arrested, and jailed. Upon his release he carried out a promise he had made to contact Isaak's brother living in America, using the address he had been given by Isaak and had sewn into the lining of his coat when fleeing Odessa. This extremely long letter, translated by the American Classical Company of Park Row in New York, gives a sobering account of the effects of the Bolshevik regime.

> Bessarabia, Roumania, Kishineff, Roumania, Sept. 18, 1921
> Dear Mr. Tcherkassky [*sic*],
> . . . In spite of the fact Isaak is known in the city as an excellent dentist and Lydia as one of the most excellent music teachers, they are without work and have been for a long time. It is to be explained in a very simple way as normal life has been completely destroyed by the Bolsheviks and everybody in the city, even the former millionaires, are without funds and cannot afford to attend to their teeth or to take music lessons. This is now considered a luxury. In such a way, they are compelled to do exactly the same as everyone else is doing in Odessa: to go daily into a market and try to get rid of some household article, a sheet or tablecloth, a bed sheet, a skirt or something similar perhaps and to try to exchange some of these articles against flour, sugar and potatoes. The articles are exhausted little by little and the end of it is that I. and L. are near starvation. Anything they can get they are first of all giving to the child as he is in poor health and needs special treatment. The doctors are of the opinion, after careful examination, that he needs special food treatment, but there can be no question about special treatment good enough if they can afford to keep him alive and to save him from starvation. He requires specially good food as in spite of his 9–10 years he is working very hard.[3]

The letter contains firsthand documentation of the child's talents and Zeltman asks if Isaak's brother is acquainted with the fact that his nephew, according to the opinion of the most prominent musical representatives of the city of Odessa, is a genius and that they are unanimous in saying that a brilliant future and worldwide reputation are in store for him as a pianist, conductor, and composer. He writes of the child's musical accomplishments:

> He has quite a reputation now in our city and is quite famous among the musical circles of Odessa. A famous Russian composer, Glière, director of the Conservatory in Kieff [Kiev] happened to be sometime ago in our city and Shura, naturally, was presented to him. The verdict of this famous musician, after hearing Shura, was most favorable. Three years ago, in 1918, when this infant prodigy was only seven years old, he had to pass an examination at the Conservatory in Odessa. The subject treated was Theory of Music. . . . The class is composed of 20–25 grown-up pupils, age 20–25 years, who are waiting their turn. The director of the Conservatory, Professor Malishensky, takes Shura on his knees and is testing his musical abilities by questioning him most complicated musical formulas. Shura gives his

> answers in a very concise way, half smiling, with an ease and grace, and naturally gets the highest mark, while half of the grown up pupils failed in passing the examination. A year later, in the same brilliant manner, he passes elementary harmony and last year, he passed the course of higher harmony. In the meantime the boy has contributed his share to a benefit concert especially arranged for the starving pupils. He conducted an orchestra of fifty musicians and interpreted one of the symphonies of Haydn. The result surpassed even the expectations, and when Shura last year had to pass his examination at the same conservatory in the superior course of piano, there was confusion and a hard fight among the teachers. . . . Finally they were compelled to take him from the conservatory and at present he is studying with L., his mother. Three or four years ago he showed remarkable abilities as a composer of an opera, and what is even more astonishing he wrote the words. You could notice the spark of genius, something that happens very seldom and that few possess and that one cannot buy and even a king cannot command. . . . He is really the world genius. There is no doubt about it.

Zeltman states that since he is not acquainted with Isaak's brother, he is ignorant of his financial situation, but wants to know in what way he might help the family, for Isaak had repeated to him many times that his brother remained his only hope in the disastrous situation in which he found himself. He goes on to describe the pathetic physical condition of the little Schurochka:

> This remarkably gifted boy is pale, thin, livid and is seldom satisfied with his meals, being most of the time hungry. Atrocities of this kind are only possible under the Bolshevik regime. Of course if the parents would consent to confine his education in the hands of the Bolsheviki, a change would happen. The Bolsheviki would place him in a special children's boarding house, but there of course his companions would be poor neglected children, among whom criminals could be found and in this way the boy might be lost. Little matters if his hunger would be satisfied, his morals would be destroyed. Under such circumstances who would take care of his education and his musical development? The situation of his parents who adore him and who would gladly do anything they could for him is disastrous. They cannot do much for him and are witnessing the way he is getting weaker physically and is hampered in his development. It is a tragic case. The only way out of this dreadful situation, to save themselves from these cannibals, is to escape to Europe or America, where the parents as professional people could find work and the child might get into the hands of a real professor in the conservatory who would take the necessary care of his further education and would make him the happiest man in the world.

Zeltman next muses on ways to make this happen:

> To sneak through is very hard and in case they will decide to risk it where are they going to scrape up the necessary amount of money required for the purpose? At least 25 to 30,000 leis are required for the purpose. Naturally if the Bolsheviki quit and they could travel in an official way, the amount would be considerably reduced. But who knows when this will happen?

There is no record of a written response to this ardent plea for help, but soon care packages from relatives in America began arriving with powdered milk, considered by the child prodigy to be a special treat, along with chocolate candy bars he found tucked in the packages.

The stray bullet that almost ended their beloved child's life was the breaking point that led Lydia and Isaak Cherkassky to begin their struggle to obtain an exit visa from Russia. In the ensuing months prominent musicians came to their aid and petitioned Soviet officials to take pity on the child. A plan was made to allow the family to go to Germany for two years where Shura could perform, providing the Bolsheviks with favorable propaganda. For lack of funds, however, the scheme fell through, and instead a visa for travel to America was finally granted in 1922. After waiting three days in Odessa for a train to Moscow, and then ten days for a train to Riga, during which time they had practically nothing to eat, the family boarded the ship *Estonia* at the port of Libau and embarked on a two-week ocean voyage to America. They arrived at the port of New York on December 22 and were promptly deloused along with their fellow passengers. Jubilant family members greeted them, then Lydia, Isaak, and Shura Cherkassky settled in Baltimore, Maryland, to begin their American odyssey.

Notes

1. Sebag Montefiore, *The Life of Potemkin* (New York: St. Martin's, 2001), 5.
2. *Times* (London), 1929.
3. Curtis Institute of Music, archives, RG 20.5 Cherkassky, Shura.

CHAPTER TWO

Baltimore, 1923

> Theosophists might call this boy pianist the reincarnation of a Carl Tausig or a Franz Liszt. I call him the greatest child artist I ever met.
>
> —Theodore Stearns, *New York Evening Telegraph*

The happy bustle of Baltimore with its lamp-lit streets, park-like squares, and neat row houses provided much needed and appreciated relief for the Cherkassky family. Embraced by a variety of relatives who had immigrated from Russia earlier in the century, the Cherkasskys settled in with Julius Bloom, an uncle of Shura's through marriage to Jenny Cherkassky, sister of the child's father. The Baltimore telephone directory of 1922 listed professions along with telephone numbers, and Bloom is identified there as treasurer of the Brown and White Taxicab Company. Away from his daily work he was also a very savvy promoter of the child prodigy, and rumors of the boy genius spread rapidly. Before striking a single key in public, the rambunctious child with black curly hair, soulful eyes, and a gurgling laugh met the press on February 14, 1923, in the living room of the Blooms' home at 3503 Morris Avenue.

When the reporter from the *Baltimore Evening Sun* was introduced, the boy put out his right hand, doubled the other across his breast and bowed while shaking hands. "How do you do?" he said, but after that, his knowledge of English exhausted, he sat on the arm of his mother's chair as his uncle translated into Russian the reporter's questions. Sometimes Mr. Bloom forgot and spoke to the boy in English. "Shura, the gentleman wants to know what kind of music you like best." The child would burst into a merry peal of laughter followed by an excitable correction in Russian—"Americanski, Americanski." So the question was repeated in Russian. The interviewer heard "Chopin, Chopin," followed by "Rachmaninoff, Rachmaninoff," and the boy's uncle reported that of the old masters this boy genius liked Chopin best, while among his contemporaries he leaned toward Rachmaninoff.

When queried by the reporter about what pleased him most in America, the child responded that he liked to see a bathtub in every house and thought that Americans must be very rich to have them. Since so many American homes had a piano, Shura also believed that Americans were musically inclined because, as his uncle made clear, in his untrained mind and judgment he took the form for the substance. Bloom added that the child had never seen so many music stores before and thought that Americans did nothing but buy musical instruments.

As the interview continued the subject turned to jazz music, and it was evident that the child had already expressed himself on that score because his uncle laughed as he translated the question, saying that the boy had asked what jazz was the first time he heard it. The reporter later wrote that Shura spoke with his features as well as his tongue and lips, and even before he had finished shaking his head, the questioner knew that he had no great love for the American school of musical expression. Julius Bloom explained that Shura thought it was too rough. "There's no word in English for what he says, but that's what it means—rough."

As to whether Shura would rather play music than play with other boys, his uncle responded that he liked to sit at the piano, but "when he's through he likes to play in the streets and have fun. He's just like any other boy. He likes to tear about the house and have a good time."

Shura protested loudly when his father suggested that the interviewer be shown an opera Shura had composed while still living in Odessa. "No good, no good!" he shouted. (As a seven-year-old he had written this opera, complete with score, cast, and libretto; and at eight he was composing orchestral music.) "See," said Bloom, producing the opera, "all written in Russian, there's the clarinet; here's the violins, and then comes the bells." Shura then reiterated his point of view, vehemently saying, "No good; no good."

He also communicated that he liked America better than Russia after the Bolsheviks rose to power because they took all the furniture out of the opera house in Odessa and closed it. Mr. Bloom emphasized, "Shura did not like that."

At the conclusion of the interview the boy's parents declared it was their intention to send the boy to the best teacher in America when he was older. The reporter in turn predicted that the child was destined to immortality in the world of music.

It was Julius Bloom who made arrangements for the child prodigy to play for Harold Randolph, director of the Peabody Conservatory, and who along with Frederick R. Huber, municipal director of music for the city of Baltimore, figured prominently in the first year of the boy pianist's life in America. Harold Randolph had entered the Peabody Institute at the age of thirteen where he was a piano student of Annette Falk Auerbach, a teacher who, according to Randolph, believed in making people stand on their own two feet and develop technique through personal effort. In 1890 he joined the faculty of the Peabody Institute, becoming director in 1898 when enrollment stood at 180. During the 1922–1923 season, when Shura Cherkassky arrived in Baltimore, enrollment at the Peabody was in excess of 2,500—a record. One of the first decisions Randolph made as director was to reorganize a concert series that had engaged local artists at a charge of twenty-five cents per ticket and instead to bring in out-of-town performers at a new price of fifty cents per ticket, thereby creating a rich menu of many world-class artists to perform for Baltimore audiences.

The Peabody Institute's scrapbook for the 1922–1923 season records that Randolph returned on September 18 from vacationing in Colorado, California, and Minnesota to take up his duties at the school, at which time he engaged Arthur Schnabel for the upcoming school year and also booked Feodor Chaliapin, Mary Garden, Maria Jeritza, and Fritz Kreisler for the 1923–1924 concert series at the Peabody. That same season the Lyric Theatre also heard William Jennings Bryan expounding against Darwinian theory, and Eugene V. Debs, the American Socialist.

Baltimore, alone in the United States, placed a music department within the framework of agencies that normally make up a city government. Frederick R. Huber created this position, and having been appointed to it by a Democratic mayor, he held the office for many years, becoming a dominant force in the musical life of Baltimore. Everything relating to music was referred to Huber who had previously been a teacher of piano and organ at the Peabody Institute.

Life-altering events followed Shura Cherkassky from the moment he climbed on the piano stool to play for Randolph, a few music lovers, and a round of Baltimore music critics in Randolph's room at the Peabody Institute in February of 1923. Dressed in blue serge, with an Eton collar, knickerbockers, rumpled socks, and scuffed shoes, the child astonished his listeners. The program included Beethoven's Sonata, Op. 31, No. 2; Daquin's *Le Coucou*; Chopin's C-sharp Minor Etude and his *Fantasie Impromptu*; Rachmaninoff's C-sharp Minor Prelude, Barcarolle and Polka; and the child's own composition, *Prélude Pathétique*. In addition, he played numerous other compositions at the request of Mr. Randolph who reported that he almost fell over and called Frederick Huber and asked him to come down and listen to this wondrous child. "I almost fell over too," said Mr. Huber. "In all my years in music, I've never experienced such a thrill." His enthusiasm was such that he told the *Baltimore Evening Sun* on February 13, 1923, that although over the past several years he had confined his musical management to civic affairs, he was so convinced of the genius of this youth that he felt he owed it to the public to make an exception, and therefore arranged an appearance in recital at the Little Lyric Theatre on Saturday March 3 at 8:30 p.m. He added that he was confident young Shura's extraordinary gifts would attract the widest attention at the Baltimore recital and that the recital would turn out to be the outstanding individual event of many seasons. Huber also commented that the great basso Feodor Chaliapin had told him that although Shura Cherkassky was a child, "He plays like a man who has experienced every emotion."

Shortly thereafter newspapers were filled with stories of the boy wonder and preparations were made to introduce him to the Baltimore stage as "The greatest musical genius since Josef Hofmann and possibly greater than he." Critics commented that it was no exaggeration to state that this child was one of the very few real prodigies in the history of performing music, adding that it is only when we happen to meet real genius that we appreciate how rare and wonderful it is. The whole picture added up to an abnormal precocity, and his playing in Mr. Randolph's room was described as astounding, both technically and interpretatively, not simply because of his age but because in very few of the best and most experienced pianists did one find so perfect a sense of rhythm, phrasing, and shading, or so fine a grasp of compositions as a whole and in their broader divisions. Special attention was called to his ability to make repetitions sing out convincingly, and yet with a subtle difference that gave fresh flavor to each return. His pianissimo was described as "delicate," his fortissimo as "pregnant with splendor." The maturity of Cherkassky's playing and his modest self-confidence were striking, leading one critic to write, "Indeed, there was the atmosphere of a miracle about the entire performance, so incredible did it seem that this little child could be doing what he was doing. In short so great was his genius, so far beyond anything with which we ordinarily come in contact, that one felt it almost impossible to believe that his ears heard truly."

It was strongly recommended that anyone who had the opportunity to do so should attend the child prodigy's debut recital at the Little Lyric Theatre, for the citizens of Baltimore would then have an opportunity—that would not come again for many generations—of hearing one whose name would go down to posterity with those of the greatest pianists in the world. At this time the myth begun by his parents that the child prodigy was born in 1911 and not 1909, his true birth date, was being widely circulated. Additionally, during the nearly two years he lived in Baltimore he was always billed as being eleven years old, the reason for this being an oversupply of posters made in 1923. Once the boy plaintively asked Mr. Huber, "When can I be twelve?"

Shura Cherkassky's formal American debut took place at Baltimore's Little Lyric Theatre on Saturday March 3, 1923, at 8:30 p.m. For his initial performance the child prodigy chose a varied program, but one that was also rich in nineteenth-century Romanticism:

RECITAL
SHURA CHERKASSKY, Pianist
(First American Performance)
"LITTLE LYRIC"
Saturday, March 3, 8:30 P.M.

G. F. HANDEL	ARIA CON VARIAZIONI, in D minor
L. van BEETHOVEN	SONATA in D minor, Op. 31, No. 2
	Largo-Allegro
	Adagio
	Allegretto
C. DAQUIN	LE COUCOU
SCARLATTI-TAUSIG	PASTORALE
	CAPRICCIO
S. RACHMANINOFF	PRELUDE in C sharp minor, Op. 3, No. 2
	PRELUDE in G sharp minor, Op. 32, No. 12
	BARCAROLLE
	POLKA
F. CHOPIN	ETUDE in C sharp minor, Op. 25, No. 7
	FANTASIE-IMPROMPTU
F. LISZT	AU BORD D'UNE SOURCE
SHURA CHERKASSKY	PRELUDE PATHETIQUE
M. MOSZKOWSKI	LIEBESWALZER

STEIFF PIANO USED

"I can see Shura now," recalled Huber of the debut recital. "He came on stage, bowed jerkily to the left and right and sat down. Someone in the crowd tittered. Then he began to play Handel's *Aria con Variazoni* and the audience was spellbound."[1] It was generally agreed that the opinion of the musicians and critics who had heard him in Mr. Randolph's room was more than justified, and newspaper critics found themselves groping for superlatives adequate to describe the public debut of the child prodigy. On March 5, 1923, John Vandercook wrote in the *Baltimore Evening Sun*, "When Shura rushed from the stage after his final encore the audience beat its hands frantically, stamped, roared, cheered—completely forgot its dignity before the child who is without question one of the greatest living pianists." He concluded that the young pianist's serenity and poise of interpretation, coupled with his purity of tone, brilliant technique, and vigor of phrasing and execution marked Cherkassky as a finished musician, rather than simply a prodigy. Particular note was made of his own composition, the *Prélude Pathétique*, which reinforced for the listener the intellectual grasp of his genius. The piece, which was published by G. Fred Kranz of Baltimore and dedicated by the child to his friend Harold Randolph, was described as a masterly bit of musical construction with expert harmonics and singularly mature meaning.

So great was the success of this initial concert that a second was arranged for the following Saturday March 10. However, preempting the furor over the March 10 concert was an even more intense uproar created by concern for the child prodigy's future. The future development of the child pianist became a matter of heated discussion among his parents, Mr. Randolph, Mr. Huber, Julius Bloom, and musicians everywhere, resulting in an editorial published in the *Baltimore Evening Sun*, the week of March 4, philosophizing on the possibilities for the future of the young Shura Cherkassky, whose discovery was seen as not only adding to the list of musical celebrities, but also extending the fame of Baltimore musical culture. The editorial read in part:

> The fond, young hope of the Peabody Conservatory, this Shura Cherkassky, comes from Russia, a country in which genius buds in the one extreme, just as stupidity and the swinishness grows in the other; where a Tolstoi or a Dostoievski breathes the same atmosphere of unbelievably stolid and sodden neighbors. . . . But what will happen to him will very likely depend upon the manner in which he is handled, the method and care of his instruction, together with his own adaptability.

It was obvious that Peabody authorities had thrust upon Baltimore a golden, if difficult opportunity, and for its own sake as well as for the sake of a great art, all hoped that a complete fulfillment would come to pass.

Shortly after the appearance of that editorial, Frederick R. Huber, Harold

Randolph, various musicians, and Shura's uncle, Julius Bloom, who acted as Shura's adviser, labored over a plan that would assure the boy's proper development. The arrangement as formalized through an agreement between Mr. Huber and the boy's parents determined that the child would be trained by "safe and sane methods," and it put the entire musical activities of the boy in the hands of Mr. Huber for the coming year. In all probability, that term would be extended, but for at least twelve months there would be no performances except for those arranged by Mr. Huber, and even those would not exceed two per month. The boy's instruction would remain exclusively in the hands of his mother, cited as the painstaking guide who was solely responsible for Shura's phenomenal technique. Time not spent in practice and in preparation for these few concerts would be spent in cultural education and, Mr. Huber and Mr. Bloom alike insisted, in "American boys' play" so that the young genius would grow into normal manhood. For the present, by arrangement with the school board of Baltimore, Shura would attend a public school for certain courses and a tutor would aid him in the rapid acquisition of English and other languages. To further his cultural education, the agreement provided that a fixed percentage of receipts from the concerts would be dedicated to Shura's education. The remainder would be used as his uncle wished, with most of the money going to aid Lydia and Isaak Cherkassky, whose lack of professional standing in America caused major financial difficulties.

"I feel greatly relieved over the assurance that the boy will develop soundly," said Mr. Huber, adding that both he and Mr. Bloom were fearful that in a misguided moment the child might get into the hands of a vaudeville promoter who would lure the boy with promises of quick money and ruin his entire artistic future.[2] With his mother solely responsible for his musical education, the two men felt he was sure to develop in the best possible way, and the arrangement for his cultural education and healthy play life would make of him a man as well as a great artist. Huber pointed out that Josef Hofmann actually was barred from the stage for ten years (an error on Huber's part) but that he and his colleagues did not favor doing this with Shura, who responded so eagerly to the chance for public performance. According to Huber, limiting Shura's appearances to two concerts a month would protect him from exploitation without depriving him of the encouragement that an occasional recital gives a young artist. He stated with absolute authority that he didn't have the slightest doubt that if this arrangement could be prolonged, Baltimore would one day witness in Shura the greatest pianist of the day.

With the problem of the future temporarily resolved, the second public program of Cherkassky's American career took place and met with the same phenomenal success as the first. An announcement of the concert was placed in the local papers.

> As the limited seating capacity of the
> *"Little Lyric"*
> was insufficient to accommodate the great demand
> to hear the phenomenal young pianist
> *Shura Cherkassky*
> at his first American recital, the PEABODY INSTITUTE
> announces a second recital to be given in its Concert
> Hall on Saturday, March 10, 1923, at 8:30 o'clock.
> Tickets $1.50 and $1
>
> NOW ON SALE AT (tax-exempt) ALBAUGH'S AGENCY

The program consisted of works by Beethoven, Busoni, Weber, Chopin, Mendelssohn, Grieg, Paderewski, Glinka, Liszt, and the child's own *Prélude Pathétique*. Once again the public and the press roared their approval, and a third concert was scheduled for Sunday evening, April 8, this time at the larger Lyric Theatre. The outstanding feature of the playing, as before, was the child's perfect control, guiding everything as he wished, technically and interpretively. Just as he did full justice to compositions by Beethoven, Schubert, Mendelssohn, and Brahms, so he did equal justice to the moderns, for one of the marvels of his playing, even at that early age, was his insight into both the old and the new. Doubts as to whether his playing would be as effective in the vast space of the Lyric Theatre as it had been in the more intimate space of the Little Lyric were immediately dispelled. All reports agreed that his tone carried to the farthest reaches of the hall and that his intense little personality drew his listeners into a charmed circle. On April 9, 1923, Grace Spofford, a reviewer for the *Baltimore American* noted that the Beethoven *Moonlight* Sonata does not fall within the understanding of the usual eleven-year-old boy, but the child pianist fully caught the spirit of the work, playing the first movement with serenity, the second with gracefulness, and the third with impetuosity. She summed up the recital, writing, "A miracle if you will; a reincarnation if you wish. Explain it as you may, but something so precious that one can only hope that this joy and exuberance may not be crushed, but brought to complete fruition in a master pianist."

Other qualities came forward and were duly appreciated in this third recital, among them his unconcern over an audience of more than two thousand, and a tonal volume far greater than would have been expected from his light physique. The Strauss-Schutt *Die Fledermaus* paraphrase, which ended the program, was learned in a week. It was generally acknowledged that, while diminutive in stature, Shura Cherkassky, even at this tender age, was a giant at the piano.

Of all the writings and musings on and elucidations of this child prodigy, perhaps the essence of his being was best caught in a *New York Times Magazine* report of 1923.

> It is as if he is two separate persons. One of them is a normal little boy with awkward gestures and something very sweet and appealing in his manner, vastly interested in anything around him, quick to pick up anything new that crosses his path, unspoiled, unaffected, unconscious of his gifts. The other person springs into being as soon as he touches a piano. It is a public performer with a repertoire of 200 pieces. It is a composer whose work is said to show mature understanding of the technique of composition. It is an artist with skill and insight that seem strangely placed in the awkward little boy.[3]

By now Baltimore was "Cherkassky mad," and a fourth recital was scheduled for May 1, once again at the Lyric Theatre. On April 17 at 7:00 a.m., an hour and a half before the ticket sale began, a line two blocks in length formed at Albaugh's Ticket Agency located at 3 East Fayette Street. The two-thousand-seat hall was sold out by 11:30 a.m. for what was billed as Shura Cherkassky's final concert of the 1923 season.

Before the May 1 performance, however, a glitch arose concerning a permit to work, which was required by the state of Maryland. Under Maryland's child labor laws, a child prodigy, born in Baltimore, could not make his professional debut in his home city. It was required that he first go to some city outside of Maryland, obtain a permit, and perform there. Although Shura was not born in Baltimore, the law was applicable to any child under sixteen giving a professional performance. Huber produced a permit from the authorities in Washington, D.C., after a phone call to Harry A. LeBrun, inspector of street trades in that city. It was reasoned that the three previous concerts in Baltimore had not violated the law because they did not count as professional, having been benefits for the theater in which they had been held. The permit from the Washington authorities was therefore granted on the basis that a concert would take place in Washington, D.C., at Poli's Theater on Friday afternoon, May 11. Billed as Shura Cherkassky's "Last Appearance in America This Season," the concert was to be presented by Mrs. Wilson Greene's Concert Bureau, with a 10 percent war tax added to the price of each ticket. Maryland authorities accepted this permit as valid for the May 1 concert in Baltimore, and all proceeded on schedule.

The same month saw one more stellar event in the career of Master Shura Cherkassky when, on Thursday evening May 17, 1923, he performed on the gold piano at the White House for President Warren G. Harding and Mrs. Harding and their guests at a dinner honoring George Harvey, ambassador to the Court of St. James's, and Mrs. Harvey. The distinguished group included Chief Justice William Howard Taft and Mrs. Taft, the Speaker of the House and Mrs. Gillett, the Secretary of State and Mrs. Hughes, Senator Henry Cabot Lodge, the Honorable and Mrs. Robert Woods Bliss, the Honorable and Mrs. Henry White, Mr. John Hays Hammond, Mrs. Eugene Hale, Mrs. Stephen B. Elkins, Mr. and Mrs. Charles C. Glover, and the Honorable and Mrs. Chauncey M. Depew. Well known for his oratory, his colorful political career, and his ability as an after-dinner speaker, Depew was ninety-four at the time of Shura Cherkassky's White House appearance. White House documents do not show a record of the dinner menu for the evening of May 17. They do list the table decorations as pink roses, bridal wreath, and maidenhair fern.

With Shura to Washington, D.C., went Julius Bloom, Frederick Huber, and his parents, all delayed in their arrival at the White House by a late train. The child prodigy didn't know he was to play for the president of the United States until he was on his way to Washington. He simply had been told, "We are going out this evening." Included in the program were the Rachmaninoff Prelude, Polka, and Barcarolle; the *Ecossaises* of Beethoven; Mozskowski's *Liebeswalzer*; Shura's own *Prélude Pathétique*; and works by J. S. Bach, Handel, Weber, Mendelssohn, Grieg, and Scriabin. After playing several numbers, Shura was asked by Mrs. Harding to play something from Chopin, and in response he performed the C-sharp Minor Waltz. The president then asked him to play a work of Strauss, and the young pianist rendered the Strauss-Schutt *Fledermaus* paraphrase. In spite of the tardy starting time, Shura recalled that the president and Mrs. Harding accorded him a most gracious reception, which he thoughtfully described.

> They were so kind to me. If I had been playing in Russia I would have expected to see soldiers and police all around the room. But at President Harding's home they made me feel just as if I were playing right here in my own home.
>
> Mrs. Harding sat beside me at the piano and it was difficult for her to understand how I could reach an octave with my small hands. Several times she took my hands in hers and looked at them so closely. But I really can cover nine notes, you know.

> But the President—well, when he shook my hand with such a hard grip and told me how much he hoped for my success—well, it just all seems like a dream to me and I never, never shall forget it.
>
> I wasn't nervous; I was too happy for that and the President and Mrs. Harding made me feel so much at home. I never felt nervous but once in my life when playing, and that was in Odessa. But in the White House I tried so hard to please and they had such a wonderful gold piano that I forgot about being afraid.[4]

The gold piano of which the child prodigy spoke was a Steinway concert grand, the 100,000th instrument made by the Steinway firm, which had been presented to the Theodore Roosevelt White House in January of 1903. When the White House was extensively renovated in 1902–1903 by the architectural firm of McKim, Mead and White, the instrument became the first piano to be placed in the East Room, and in its early years was played by such luminaries as Paderewski and Rachmaninoff. Created by architectural designers Joseph Hunt and Richard Hunt, the case was made of cherry intricately carved and inlaid with gold. At the request of President Theodore Roosevelt, the decorations on the underside of the lid represented a national theme. American painter Thomas Wilmer Dewing was engaged to execute the task, and according to curators at the National Museum of American Art, "Dewing really showed his mettle as an artist by cleverly shaping his composition to fit into the irregularly shaped lid." America, depicted as a "languidly seated female," received the Nine Muses represented by ladies in colonial dresses. The design was finished off with scrolls of green acanthus vines linking medallions of the thirteen original states. Steinway and Sons paid Dewing $7,000 for his work, equivalent to over $150,000 in 2005 dollars.[5]

"Shura's playing gave the biggest thrills since I've been at the White House," said Mrs. Harding who was responsible for the invitation to the child prodigy to perform for the president. Married to Warren G. Harding in 1891 she was an unusually cultured woman and a professionally oriented musician who had studied at the Cincinnati Conservatory of Music. During her tenure as First Lady she arranged for a mahogany Baldwin grand piano, on which she practiced daily, to be delivered to the mansion where it was placed in the second-floor Oval Room. Following Shura's performance, a letter was sent to Julius Bloom by Miss Laura Harlan, secretary to Mrs. Harding: "Mrs. Harding wants you to know how much the President and she and their guests enjoyed the wonderful little Shura Cherkassky. He really seems beyond belief and one wonders what he will be when he is a grown man. I am sending him, in your care, a photograph of the President and Mrs. Harding."

While the biggest thrill for the First Lady was certainly the playing of the curly haired prodigy, for the prodigy the biggest thrill was not performing for the president of the United States on the gold piano at the White House but rather the surprise planned especially for him by Mrs. Harding. Before the recital the First Lady had been told that at his home in Baltimore Shura had a much-loved Airedale called Brownie. When the concert ended, the doors of the ballroom were thrown open and through them ran "Laddie Boy," the White House dog. And to Laddie Boy ran little Shura. The two romped and played, oblivious to the assembly of distinguished guests, and it was for Laddie Boy that the prodigy had the biggest hugs and fondest caresses. His attachment to his own Airedale, Brownie, was so deep that the dog was his constant companion, and on one occasion it accompanied its young master to a movie where the manager indulgently allowed the dog in. All went well until a dog in the film being shown started barking and Brownie responded in kind, causing havoc in the theater.

Following the White House performance, an editorial in the May 19, 1923, edition of the *Baltimore Sun* rhapsodized on the event: "Deathless art and temporal might, self-contained genius and the wielders of organized power—these two were in the same room. But did they meet each other? It is doubtful. None of the great men could understand any more than the rest of us, the fire that is in little Shura's soul; and as for Shura, he hurried to play with 'Laddie Boy.'"

Press comments of the day attest to the stunning success of Shura Cherkassky's first season in America, which rivaled that of another great piano prodigy, Josef Hofmann, his mentor-to-be. What is most striking is the unanimity with which eight diverse music critics spoke when they recounted what they heard when Shura Cherkassky made his debut on the American stage:

> It is no exaggeration to state that this child is one of the very few real prodigies in the history of the performing of music.
>
> —Francis Fielding Reid, *Baltimore American*, February 14, 1923

> It can only be said that the child's performance is indeed astonishing. He is so evidently a genius that after it was all over it left one rather limp. It was as if one had been worshipping a shrine.
>
> —John Oldmixon Lambdin, *Baltimore Sun*, February 16, 1923

> Not since the days when Josef Hofmann was a child prodigy has an American audience been enthralled by a stripling in knickerbockers, as was the

throng which last night packed the Lyric for Shura Cherkassky's first public appearance in America.

—Mark S. Watson, *Baltimore Sun*, March 5, 1923

Genius is the only word one thinks of after hearing Shura Cherkassky play as he did last night at the Lyric, when he made his America Recital debut.

—Warren Wilmer Brown, *Baltimore News*, March 5, 1923

It is genius, that is all there is to it. His technic is amazing. His knowledge of music, his depth of interpretation of music, his uncanny adaptability—ah, all place the boy in a class of himself. He is marvelous. That is the word.

—Victor Herbert, *Baltimore Sun*, April 9, 1923

Shura Cherkassky, the eleven-year-old pianist, coming to Washington comparatively unheralded yesterday, won a remarkable triumph at Poli's. This remarkable boy received a volume of applause hardly surpassed at any Recital this year, excepting that of the great Chaliapin, and the recognition accorded him was richly deserved.

—*Washington Times*, April 14, 1923

Is it reincarnation? Shura Cherkassky, the Russian boy pianist, is not merely a musical marvel, a prodigy. His amazing genius needs further explanation of the phenomenon of his playing that first astonished and then completely enthralled his audience at Poli's Theatre yesterday afternoon.

—Jessie MacBride, *Washington Herald*, April 14, 1923

Once again Musical Baltimore bent down before the uncanny wizardry of little Shura Cherkassky who gave his fourth and final Concert of the season at the Lyric last night. The house was packed to the doors; standing room was at a premium.

—Gustav Klemm, *Baltimore Evening Sun*, May 2, 1923

As can be imagined, the ability of a child in knickerbockers to present four arresting programs of remarkable variety in so compelling a manner stunned and electrified the public.

In sum, within the space of less than three months the Russian émigré child, a fugitive from war, numbing cold, and near-starvation astounded and conquered the music world, and left it besotted with his brilliance.

Notes

1. *Baltimore Sunday Sun Magazine*, 2 January 1955.
2. *Baltimore American*, 2 April 1923.
3. *New York Times Magazine*, 18 March 1923.
4. *Baltimore Evening Sun*, 19 May 1923.
5. The piano has a metallic action frame patented August 10, 1869; a repetition action patented November 30, 1875; a Capo D'Astro bar patented November 30, 1875; and a duplex scale patented May 14, 1872. On December of 1938, the piano was transferred to the Museum of History and Technology, Smithsonian Institution.

CHAPTER THREE

Shura and the Palmist, the 1923–1924 Season

> He will be staunch in his affections, and with a friend will always be a friend.
>
> —article in the *Baltimore American*, about S. C.

Significant events of Shura Cherkassky's 1923–1924 season in America were his orchestral debut, twelve recitals on the East Coast and in the Midwest, readings by a palmist, meetings with Paderewski and Rachmaninoff, and a deep rift between Frederick Huber and the child's parents that led to the Cherkasskys' departure from Baltimore.

In August of 1923, prior to the opening of the concert season, one of the more unusual of a series of unusual events that marked Shura Cherkassky's life occurred when a palmist in Baltimore read his hands. Those readers who knew Cherkassky will quickly see that the details of the reading and the forecast that it made for his life were uncanny in their precision, for the palmist predicted that Shura would always be staunch in his affections, would be plagued by "blue devils" that would cause him to be dissatisfied with himself, would increase in strength and vitality as he grew older, would always retain a simple boyish spirit, and would have only one deep lasting love in his life (which turned out to be the piano). The reading, which gives special resonance to Shura Cherkassky's belief in extrasensory perception and intuition, was published in the *Baltimore American*.

> Here is one pair of hands that thousands of music lovers watched scintillate over the keys of the piano last season, producing effects that made them "sit down and take notes."

It is the hand of Shura Cherkassky the eleven-year-old boy pianist who created such a furor when he was introduced to the local public and whose talent is so marked that no less a person than Rachmaninoff offered to oversee his training for the next two years. It is the hand of a child who is undoubtedly a musical genius as well as a child prodigy.

When you have seen little eleven-year-old Shura's hands flying over the keyboard, mastering technical difficulties that you feel sure would be the despair of your very much larger digits, you have perhaps wondered just what it is in that hand—what it holds—what it looks like at close range.

Well, here it is—and here are some of the things that if you are a palmist you will learn from the mounts, the shape of the hand and the way in which it is posed. In the first place, little Shura's hand tells you that he is both imaginative and sensitive. The line which for some time merges with the headline, indicates sensitiveness to a great degree, and it is evident encouragement and appreciation are very necessary to the young genius. A study of his hand also indicates the heart line gouging more deeply into the hand than any other line.

Much may be read from this heart line—a deep capacity for affection, and a great desire for love is one of the characters thus shown. That it rises to the mount of Jupiter indicates that its owner is a great lover of beauty, that he has the heart of a poet, ambition, and adores the brilliant things in life. Little Shura's artistic impulse is not limited to his music, but includes as well an appreciation of all things artistic. He is away now in the mountains, and while there is no doubt that he is enjoying all the good times that a boy on a vacation enjoys, there is also the certainty that the beauties of nature are making a strong appeal to a mind that loves and understands them. That he has a brilliant future in store for him is promised by the line that leaves the heart line, it is a branch of the heart line, in fact—and continues further on to the mount of Jupiter—which, as you know, is the mount under the index finger.

Little Shura's heart line being the stronger line and shaped as it is gives him a love of truth as well as of beauty. He will be staunch in his affections, and with a friend will always be a friend. His tendency to idealize will perhaps bring him unhappiness, as he will see nothing but good in those he loves and when the fact that there is dross mingled with gold is forced upon him it will always cause pain.

Strange to say, Shura Cherkassky's hand is not the hand of the "temperamental" person. While the fingers are shorter than the palm, which indicates that he will always be guided by instinct and intuition rather than reason and logic, the fingers are more square than pointed. The square or round fingered person will perhaps always have his head in the clouds, but his feet will be firmly planted on the ground, and the outbursts of temper that one usually associates with the genius will be with him very few and far between. These rounded fingers also indicate a great capacity for application—an attribute at times lacking in artists.

Notice the way the little finger branches off from the remainder of the hand.

This formation is often found in people who have something to give the public—actors and musicians are noted for it, and photographs of the hands of Sarah Bernhardt often show this tendency.

Now notice the way the little thumb bends backward—Shura's thumb tells us quite a lot about him. In the first place that bending thumb says that he is instinctively generous. Shura will never be a miser and wealth to him will be something that he will enjoy dispensing. The rounded phalange at the end of the thumb indicates his intuitive determination, and the long second powers, to which reference has been previously made.

Then crossing the hand to the Mount of the Moon—ah, here is where the high gods of the Imagination are to be found! Here we read of the dreams of the boy prodigy—the hopes and the ambitions. Here we find that there will be times when he is not satisfied with himself, when he will feel discouraged, and when perhaps the "blue devils" will gain a hold on him for a short time. But, fortunately, the mount of Venus, at the base of the thumb, is equally strong, and the "blue devils" will have only a short sway. The love of living, of all that is cheerful, is here to balance an imagination that might sometimes threaten the happiness of the owner of the little hand. Here, on the Mount of the Moon there is the promise of much travel in the life of Shura. Many times he will cross the ocean, and many miles on land will he cover. Already the small laddie has come from his home in Russia to find a resting place in Baltimore, but this is by no means his last voyage. The future holds for him many flittings and he will see many strange lands.

Will he live long?

Yes, the life-line is strong and well etched. Shura's strength and vitality increase as he grows older and what is best, this life-line indicates that age will not be for a state of decrepit dependence, but a hearty and hale accumulation of years.

And what of romance?

The type of heart line that the little genius reveals as he holds out his hands promises that there will be much romance, for there is much sentiment and much love of beauty, but there will be only one deep, lasting love—and this is as it should be, isn't it?

Shura has a double line of fate—this is the most unusual feature of this palm, and its promise is a wealth of worldly good fortune. He will see brilliant people, his achievements will be brilliant, his ambitions will soar always.

This might indicate that he will be "spoiled" but the rounded fingers deny that, and it is probable that as the years go on and Shura Cherkassky mounts higher on the ladder of fame he will still retain the simple boyish spirit that made a romp with "Laddie Boy" one of the principal features of the visit he paid last season to the President of the United States at the White House.[1]

One is led to wonder about readings of other subjects by this palmist because she produced in 1923 a summary of Shura Cherkassky's life looking forward that scarcely needed alteration at the end of his life looking backward.

Before starting his scheduled performances of the 1923 concert season, as *Music Trades Magazine* of New York reported, the child prodigy came to the Charles Street store of Sanders and Stayman Companies in Baltimore on September 29, 1923, where he edited the Duo Art recording of his own *Prélude Pathétique*, the *Polka* of Rachmaninoff, and the *Liebeswalzer* of Moszkowski. Three months later in the Duo Art bulletin of December 23 the Rachmaninoff *Polka*, as recorded by the child pianist, was described as "dainty, graceful, cheery and deliberate in a prankish manner." On September 30, 1923, the child prodigy made his Boston debut at Symphony Hall where at the end of the program not only the audience but also at least three of the critics remained for the encores, an act deemed by the *Boston Globe* to be "a fact which to the initiated will seem a remarkable proof of the boy's ability to interest people." His musical imagination was judged to be far more rare and precious than just the finger technique that characterizes so many prodigies. The critic of the *Boston Globe* further declared that "instead of playing as though he had been taught he plays as though teachers and methods do not exist. His technique is apparently his own; his interpretations are pretty certainly the result of his own spontaneous feeling."

During October of that year Vladimir de Pachmann agreed to hear the boy, though he had at first declared, "They are all alike, these prodigies. They never amount to anything. No I will not hear him." It was reported in the local newspapers on October 17, 1923, however, that when he had heard Shura the venerable old pianist quickly changed his thinking, stating, "Cherkassky had a real talent. No one—even at 45—could play the Nocturne of Chopin better." A week later, on October 22, the child prodigy made his orchestral debut with the Baltimore Symphony Orchestra inaugurating the symphony's tenth season, playing the Chopin F-minor Concerto, under Gustav Strube. It was also Strube, conducting the Baltimore Symphony Orchestra, who gave the first performance on February 16, 1924, of the orchestral version of the child prodigy's own composition, *Prélude Pathétique*, orchestrated by Gustav Klemm.

As the autumn of 1923 progressed, the child continued piano studies with his mother, gave scheduled concerts, and even squeezed in a few lessons in geography, arithmetic, history, and English as a fourth grader at the Park School in Baltimore. In his maturity Cherkassky confessed, "I was not interested in the subjects. I couldn't concentrate. I just wanted to play piano."

In the spring of 1924, Ignace Jan Paderewski declared an interest in hearing the boy prodigy perform and invited him to play at his home on Riverside Drive in New York City. On May 9 Shura and his manager Mr. Huber made a midnight trip by automobile from Winston-Salem (where Shura had finished playing a concert at 11:00 p.m.), to High Point, North Carolina. At High Point the two boarded a train for New York at 1:00 a.m. on May 10. Following the train's arrival in New York at 3:50 that afternoon, Shura went directly to Paderewski's studio where he played for the famed pianist and his wife. The program, selected by Paderewski, consisted of Handel's *Harmonious Blacksmith Variations*, Beethoven's Sonata in E Minor, Op. 90, a group by Bach, another by Chopin, and Moszkowski's Waltz in E Major. As reported in the newspapers of the time, Paderewski was delighted with the performances and stated that the little boy would take his place in the hall of fame among the great masters. "Genius and remarkable ability and personality, the boy possesses to an unusual degree. He must continue the course that has developed his talents." Paderewski then laid down general rules as follows: "Two concerts a month—no more. A sound, general and cultural education with special attention to languages. The rest will take care of itself, and his needs will be met as they arise."

Rachmaninoff had also heard the boy play at his own home at 33 Riverside Drive. Following a performance of the composer's own G-sharp Minor Prelude, Rachmaninoff declared the young boy the "most wonderful I have heard," but refused to teach him unless he withdrew from concertizing during his teen years. He also recommended that the child change his technique and that he study with Rosina Lhevinne, recommendations that puzzled Cherkassky to the end of his life. (Rachmaninoff's relationship to Josef and Rosina Lhevinne dated from their student days at the Moscow Conservatory where each won the school's Gold Medal in 1891, 1892, and 1898, respectively. But it was not until the 1950s that Rosina Lhevinne was to become one of the most respected and sought-after of teachers thanks to students like John Browning and Van Cliburn.) The arrangement suggested by Rachmaninoff was satisfactory neither to the child who adored public performances nor to his parents who thought Shura should perform more frequently. The family made the decision to ignore Rachmaninoff's advice, and an irreparable rift developed between Mr. Huber and Isaak and Lydia Cherkassky who had never been comfortable with the performance and financial plan laid down by Huber in the spring of 1923 for their son. The family subsequently left Baltimore for a new home in New York City, and on June 12, 1924, the *Baltimore Evening Sun* published a statement by Mr. Huber in which he said that the only question about the whole arrangement was whether two concerts a month might not be too many given the fact that Paderewski thought two the maximum, and Rachmaninoff opposed any concerts at all. For this reason he could not, in view of these opinions, think of allowing an increase in the number.

> The major issue between the Cherkasskys and myself, however, was the establishment of the educational fund. To this the boy's parents would not consent, and as it seemed to me and to others whom I consulted absolutely essential to the boy's cultural future that his education be assured in that way, I could [not] conscientiously continue. . . .
>
> The child is potentially a great artist, but what he will be depends on how he is handled in the next six or eight years. If he is "professionalized" in that period he may produce a good deal of money, but he never will be a master. I think all musicians agree on that.

How wrong they all proved to be! And how worthy of note it is that Mr. Huber recounted none of these sentiments in an interview given to the same newspaper some thirty-one years later.

Once settled in New York City, in an apartment at 501 West 111th Street on Manhattan's Upper West Side,[2] the boy prepared for his New York debut at Aeolian Hall on November 12, 1924. His performance of music by Handel, Rameau-Godowsky, Mendelssohn, Chopin, Mana-Zucca, Liszt, and his own *Prélude Pathétique* was a repeat of his Baltimore triumphs, and the New York press, normally grudging in its recognition of prodigies, acknowledged his astonishing artistry without reservation. Buoyed by her child's successes, Lydia Cherkassky made an appointment for her son to play for Josef Hofmann. Later in life Shura Cherkassky recalled, "Hofmann, Rachmaninoff, Godowsky, these were the names on my mother's lips." Hofmann believed that prodigies were born to music as fish were born to water, and urgently encouraged public performances for young musicians, citing his own forced seven-year withdrawal from the stage in his youth (not ten years as Huber had stated) as doing him great harm:

> In the first place, it would have been best for me to be out in public learning my business in the only way, eventually, that you learn it—by playing before audiences. Instead I was kept in my corner practicing my exercises and piling up repertory in which I had yet to prove myself. I should have been allowed to grow in my own environment.
>
> The second injury done by this enforced absence from the platform was hardly less regrettable than the first. My retirement as a young boy made it hard for me later on to escape the fate of the child wonder coming back. I should have gradually outgrown the child prodigy reputation.

Instead, I had to live down that reputation before the press and public in England, France, Germany, and America would take me seriously and give me recognition for what I proved I could do. In Russia, where I had not appeared as a prodigy but only after my studies with Rubinstein, I had great success from the start.

These things had [an] effect not only as regarded my audiences but my own reactions. I was spoken of as some sort of an animal who could once do graceful tricks. It was hard not to respond in kind.

There's a difference between proper experience and exploitation.[3]

World-wise artist Josef Hofmann and loving parents Isaak and Lydia Cherkassky were united in a single vision for the child prodigy, Shura Cherkassky, who entered the Curtis Institute as a student of Hofmann's in the autumn of 1925, the recipient of the Josef Hofmann Scholarship, a prize donated by the Braun family of Merion, Pennsylvania.

Notes

1. *Baltimore News American*, 18 August 1923.
2. During their years in New York City the Cherkassky family also resided at 305 West Ninety-eighth Street and 1864 Seventh Avenue.
3. *Sunday Call* (Newark, N.J.), 7 November 1937.

CHAPTER FOUR

Prodigies Compared: Shura and Jozio

> Towering genius disdains a beaten path. It seeks regions hitherto unexplored.
>
> —Abraham Lincoln

Shura Cherkassky and Josef Hofmann were child prodigies. So too were Mozart and a long list of others, some of whom survived the prodigy years, going on to pursue fruitful careers, while many more fell into oblivion. What then is the phenomenon that makes the true wonder child? As evident in the number of prodigies in history who have attracted attention in youth and then disappeared from public view, the phenomenon can never be explained by a prodigious facility or by a special capacity for imitation—aptitudes often exploited by ambitious and controlling parents. More often the true child prodigy is akin to the great phenomena of nature: each one is a unique event, each a manifestation of some unexplainable connection, each a survivor of exceptional circumstances.

Some things are abundantly clear about musical wonder children. They possess an innate process of analysis that allows them to solve problems for themselves with astounding rapidity and without the help of others. And while the genius of these children is theirs without effort, they work at that genius harder than the student without precocity who struggles, often fruitlessly, to achieve a fraction of the wonder child's accomplishments. There have, of course, been tear-stained prodigies, but their unhappiness has almost always been caused not by the development of their genius, but rather by unreasonable pressure from overreaching parents. Free from such pressure, the wonder child often finds work akin to play simply because they love their work so much it seems like play. While such children engage to an extent in the usual *divertissements* of childhood, their truest joy is in the study and the practice of that which interests them most. For them their art is a compelling fascination. And so it was with the child wonders Josef Hofmann and Shura Cherkassky.

Since Hofmann appears to have been the only significant musical influence in Cherkassky's life other than his mother, since Cherkassky prized his relationship with Hofmann for reasons and to a degree not generally known, and since the lives of these two prodigies were a curious mix of convergence and divergence, it is worth considering details of Hofmann's early childhood, his two years of study with Anton Rubinstein, and his subsequent teaching relationship with Cherkassky.

Born in Podgorze near Cracow, Poland, on January 20, 1876, Josef Hofmann learned the rudiments of music from his father who was a composer and opera conductor. Later in life Hofmann recounted how he was able to remember all sorts of melodies as early as age three and described how he would play them at the piano with the accompaniment always in the same key, whether or not it matched the right hand. At the same age Shura Cherkassky was running to the piano to match pitches and play tunes he had heard, and just as did Josef Hofmann, Cherkassky started composing shortly thereafter. Hofmann's early piano studies, following a brief period of lessons with his sister and aunt, took place with his father. Cherkassky's were with his mother.

Jozio, as the young Josef Hofmann was affectionately called by his parents, enjoyed a relatively comfortable home life, unlike Shura whose childhood was marked by severe deprivation. Also unlike the Cherkassky child, Hofmann had wide-ranging interests outside music, was equally gifted in mathematics, science, and mechanics, and had over sixty patents issued during his lifetime for inventions that ranged from automobile shock absorbers to improved piano actions. He made his public debut at the age of five playing works of Chopin, which were followed by two of his own compositions. It is said that the highlight of the debut was a performance of Schumann's Theme and Variations in B-flat Major for two pianos, in which the five-year-old was joined on the second piano by renowned Polish pianist Alexander Michalowski who made mistakes when repeating one of the variations the child had just played perfectly. Later in life Josef Hofmann said to one of his pupils, William Harms, that difficulties only exist if one is conscious of them. The Michalowski anecdote, if true, might prove his point. Would Michalowski, a seasoned professional and experienced teacher, have erred in this passage if a five-year-old boy who had played it so flawlessly had not intimidated him?

(When this alleged encounter with Michalowski was described to Anton Hofmann, Josef Hofmann's son, he said that while it was a charming story, he had never heard of it happening.)

Subsequently the child prodigy Josef Hofmann toured Europe as a pianist and composer, and at the age of eleven he made his American debut in the grandeur of the New York Metropolitan Opera House on November 29, 1887, playing orchestral and solo works.[1] While Shura Cherkassky had only his uncle-in-law to initially champion his cause, Josef Hofmann was presented by Henry E. Abbey, a noted American impresario. The debut caused an unprecedented public furor, with William Henderson of the *New York Times* reporting, "When he had concluded the Beethoven Concerto, a thunder of applause swept through the Opera House and pianists of repute were moved to tears. The child had astonished the assembly; he was a marvel." A beguiling child in a Lord Fauntleroy suit, Hofmann amazed audiences not only by his tremendous technical facility, uncanny interpretive flair, and complete lack of self-consciousness but also by the depth of thought that characterized his playing, the same quality ascribed to the prodigy Shura Cherkassky at the time of his American debut.

Both child prodigies experienced health problems, near starvation the cause in Cherkassky's case, overwork cited in the case of Hofmann. During the 1887–1888 season, eighty concerts were scheduled for Josef Hofmann, of which he played fifty-two before the Society for the Prevention of Cruelty to Children protested, insisting that the strain of concert appearances was damaging the child's health. On February 23, 1888, a medical court of inquiry was conducted by four physicians in New York, and the court concluded that Jozio did not show any evidence of physical disorder or of organic disease of the nervous system. The doctors stated that during performance he was in a state of more or less nervous exaltation, which might account for the elevated temperature and slightly irregular pulse he experienced. However, the medical court could not determine if this was abnormal for the child or a necessary condition of his particular system. Nonetheless, the philanthropist Alfred Corning Clark anonymously offered fifty thousand dollars to Hofmann's parents on the condition that their child retire from the stage and study until he was eighteen. Clark's generosity, which was not revealed until much later on, was accepted by Hofmann's parents, and the family subsequently went to Germany where the child pursued further study, not resuming his American career until 1894. (Henry Abbey sued Josef's father for breach of contract, in the amount of $57,000.) The philanthropic counterpart in Cherkassky's life to Alfred Corning Clark in Hofmann's would come in the person of Mary Louise Curtis Bok, who did not remain anonymous in her generosity, however.

Upon the move to Berlin, Jozio's father decided his son was getting entirely too independent in his piano studies, "banging the piano mercilessly," and refusing to heed the advice of the father who until that time had been his main teacher. When the family cook announced that she could no longer stand the child prodigy's handling of the piano and therefore would leave her position with the family, Jozio's father decided that a master teacher must be found immediately. At that time the well-known composer and pianist Moritz Moszkowski lived in Berlin, and the child prodigy was brought to him for an evaluation. As an adult of thirty-two, Hofmann recounted his encounter with Moszkowski, whom he described as smiling, kind, and obliging. When father and son arrived at Moszkowski's studio on the appointed day at five o'clock sharp, Moszkowski pointed to the piano chair and said,

> "Sit down and play."
> "Play what?" I asked.
> "Anything you like," he answered.
> I started. I fail to remember now what I played. Suddenly Moszkowski exclaimed: "I cannot teach this young man how to play the piano! He knows more than I do."[2]

In spite of the outcome of that audition, the young prodigy studied with Moszkowski for the remainder of the winter, following which Josef Hofmann became the only private pupil of Anton Rubinstein, who was residing in Dresden at the time. (This was thanks to a game of whist in St. Petersburg with Grand Duchess Xenia, during which Rubinstein made statements about her lack of prowess in the game and hurt her feelings. Subsequently the police arrived at Rubinstein's door in Peterhof and asked him to leave St. Petersburg within twenty-four hours, Russia in forty-eight. Once in Dresden he took up residence at the Hotel de l'Europe where the composer Christian Sinding was also a guest.) Over a period of two years, Hofmann took forty lessons with Rubinstein, one a week in winter and two in summer, each lasting two hours. The musical ideals of Rubinstein deeply influenced Hofmann, who once stated that their relationship was the most important event of his life. For Cherkassky too, the teaching of one giant, Hofmann, was the most powerful influence for most of his life. Unlike Hofmann with his mentor, however, Cherkassky had the good fortune to be able to renew and benefit from Hofmann's guidance for well over twenty years.

When the initial approach had been made to Rubinstein regarding lessons for Josef, the immediate answer was a flat refusal, with Rubinstein saying he was not interested in "music made by children," just as de Pachmann initially had said he had no interest in hearing the child pianist, Shura Cherkassky. Through the persistence of Mr. Hofmann, however, and the gracious hospitality of Mrs. Herman Wolff, wife of a highly influential Berlin concert manager, Josef and his father were invited to a dinner party at which Rubinstein was present. The hostess suggested that it would be "nice" to have some music after dinner and turned to Josef's father, saying, "Won't your son play for us?" Later in life Josef Hofmann reported he sat down with "fingers of ice and a big lump in my throat and poured out my soul in despair through my own music. I hammered away at the Theme, Variations and Fugue, Opus 14 in F Major, which I had written when I was fourteen years old."[3] After Josef had played these immense virtuoso variations ending with a nineteenth-century fugue, Rubinstein came to the piano and said, "You may not be a pianist yet, but you *are* a musician."[4]

Hofmann began his studies with Rubinstein when he was sixteen, left him at eighteen, and subsequently studied only by himself, convinced no match existed for the teaching of his former mentor. Cherkassky began his studies with Hofmann at sixteen, remained devoted to his mentor throughout his life, and sought his opinion well into the time when he had a full-fledged career. A prime objective of Rubinstein was to preserve the individuality and develop the thinking power of his students, for the purpose of making them independent artistically. For that reason he rarely played for his students at lessons, instead choosing to speak his musical meanings, which the student then had to translate into pianistic results. "In fine weather play it as you did, but when it rains play it differently,"[5] he would say when the same phrase in succession was performed the same way. The message was clear: play any repeat differently and be sure to follow one's mood when interpreting the contents of a piece. For Anton Rubinstein, art had to be sincere, and he often quoted Tolstoy: "What are the three most important factors in art? Sincerity, sincerity, sincerity."[6] Rubinstein told Hofmann that to be able to be sincere when one performed one had to express himself the way he felt at the moment of creation or reproduction. If not, the result would be artificial and not artistic. Many years later Josef Hofmann once remarked that if he played Beethoven's *Appassionata* on a sultry day the passion would be milder than if it had been played when the temperature was bracing. Thus changeability and unpredictability, which some critics found so unnerving in Cherkassky's playing, was for Rubinstein and Hofmann a matter of established policy.

Conception and interpretation could vary markedly for any one piece, and consequently the student was allowed to bring a composition to any lesson only once. Rubinstein told Hofmann that two exposures on the same photographic plate would result in a blurred picture, the *plate* being, of course, the mind. Nor was the pupil permitted to bring one of Rubinstein's own compositions to these lessons, which took place on a continuously out-of-tune Bechstein piano in front of a group of elderly Russian ladies and various other assembled guests. Rubinstein insisted on observing the printed notes to the letter, and when respectfully asked by Hofmann why he insisted on being so literal when he himself took such liberties, the master replied, "When you are as old as I am now you may do as I do—if you can."[7]

One afternoon, when Hofmann was playing a Liszt rhapsody, the dissatisfaction of the master expressed itself in a scene described by Hofmann, which clearly demonstrates the direction of Rubinstein's teaching.

> Once I played a Liszt Rhapsody pretty badly. After a few moments he said: "The way you played this piece would be all right for auntie or mamma." Then rising and coming toward me he would say, "Now let us see how we play such things." Then I would begin all over again, but hardly had I played a few measures when he would interrupt and say: "Did you start? I thought I hadn't heard it right—"
>
> "Yes, master, I certainly did," I would reply.
>
> "Oh," he would say vaguely. "I didn't notice. I mean this: Before your fingers touch the keys you must begin the piece mentally—that is, you must have settled in your mind the *tempo*, the manner of touch, and, above all, the attack of the first notes, before your actual playing begins. And bye-the-bye what is the character of this piece? Is it dramatic, tragic, lyric, romantic, humorous, heroic, sublime, mystic,—what? Well, why don't you speak?"[8]

When asked how to achieve this or that effect or what fingering to use, the classic reply was, "Play it with your nose if you like, if your fingers do not suffice, but make it sound well, and above all say something, suggest something. Do not play notes only."[9] Rubinstein's aim was for the performer to deliver an artistic message, and ultimately to find all his solutions in the imagination, with sound being of paramount consideration. The means to that end was none of Rubinstein's affair, and succeeding by one's own prowess generated an indispensable self-reliance. Conceptions should be one's own since they endured and were not the passing impressions created by another's idea. Hofmann also recalled Rubinstein saying to him, "Do you know why piano-playing is so difficult? Because it is prone to be either affected or else afflicted with mannerisms; and when these two pitfalls are luckily avoided then it is liable to be—dry! The truth lies between those three mischiefs!"[10]

On March 14, 1894, Hofmann made his Hamburg debut playing the Rubinstein D-minor Concerto on two days' notice under the baton of his master, never having studied or rehearsed the piece with him. The debut was a huge success, following which Hofmann learned he was never again to study with Rubinstein, who told him, "My dear boy, I have told you all I know about legitimate piano-playing and music-making and if you don't know it *yet*, why, go to the devil!"[11] On November 19, 1894, the day of Josef Hofmann's debut in England, Rubinstein died at his villa at Peterhof outside St. Petersburg, leaving Hofmann desperate for the master he worshipped not only as an artist but also as a man. The following day at a concert in Cheltenham, as Hofmann played the funeral march movement of Chopin's B-flat Minor Sonata, the audience rose to a man, one by one, in tribute to Anton Rubinstein.

How did this relationship with Rubinstein translate itself into Hofmann's playing and teaching? Chiefly in a brilliant, powerful, singing sound; in the notion of forming one's own conception and of using one's imagination to find the way to solutions; and in observing an absolute fidelity to the text before departing from it. Technique was not the basis on which an artist was judged, but rather the artist's use of that technique. It was the delineation of details that led the listener to the summit of art. While fidelity to the printed note was an absolute requirement, once the text was mastered the performer was allowed to "improvise the interpretation" by seeing in the score more than a literal blueprint to be realized. If the performer had done full justice to the score and then felt like adding or changing something, "Why do so," was Rubinstein's instruction. One of the most dramatic results of this particular style of mentoring was Hofmann's laying on of strand after strand of color, illuminating inner voices to create tension, and turning into polyphony what on paper appeared to be no more than straightforward harmony. Added to these dynamic differentiations were agogic accents and rhythmic alterations peculiar to Hofmann's, and subsequently, Shura Cherkassky's playing.

Most people who heard Josef Hofmann play as a child thought of it as the experience of a lifetime. However, newspaper accounts in 1923 give every indication that the musical history of the child-pianist Josef Hofmann replicated itself in the child-pianist Shura Cherkassky who, like Hofmann, was described as a wonder child. More often than not these two wunderkinder inspired awe and delight in their performances because of a tremendous spontaneity, which sprang from some unconscious spirit that directed their playing. Both child prodigies possessed this characteristic in abundance. Further, the same stirring qualities that marked the performances of Josef Hofmann in his youth were strikingly evident in the performances of the young Shura Cherkassky. From their very first hearing of Shura in Mr. Randolph's rooms at the Peabody Institute, people described his tone as full, rich, and vigorous; his sense of rhythm as incomparable; and his dynamics as unexpected as they were uncanny. There was, moreover, a great deal of humor, variety, and brilliance in his playing, qualities that remained until the very end of his days. What stood out most, however, was Shura Cherkassky's maturity, not because his playing was so clean-cut and his attack so sure, but because he so strongly indicated the sentiment and mood of the various and very different pieces he was interpreting. There were those who even believed that Cherkassky the child prodigy surpassed Hofmann, those such as Harold Randolph, who stated, "Shura Cherkassky is the most extraordinary instance of precocious musical talent I have ever come across—that is, since Josef Hofmann, and it is doubtful if even he at eleven years of age excelled him in technical facility or quite equaled him in general expressiveness and musical taste."

Just as Hofmann developed a close and deeply meaningful relationship with his teacher, Anton Rubinstein, so too did Shura Cherkassky bond with his teacher Josef Hofmann. When asked by interviewers around the world what lessons with the great Hofmann were like, and what it meant to be with him as a person, Cherkassky consistently replied in the same way:

> I can't quite say what Hofmann taught me. Pedaling, dynamics, general vibration. He didn't exactly teach me. He would say, "This is not right. You should use more pedal." It is very difficult to talk about his "method" because if I have to be quite honest Hofmann didn't teach in the traditional understanding of the word. A lot was not said and that's the best way. If one says too much that is not good. At his lessons the student played the piece, the master was sitting at the next piano and was playing the same piece but perfectly. The student was supposed to listen and make some practical conclusions from the playing of the master as he played along with the student. He was a great outstanding artist who didn't care too much about pedagogical details, and he taught only those students who had technical mastery of the instrument. He didn't intervene in their interpretations; he didn't suggest how to play certain pieces. He paid big attention to the beauty of the sound, to exemplary finger technique and especially to the way of the pedal, but nevertheless

> he didn't show how to reach a certain result. I think the most important thing in his "lessons" was the fact of direct interaction with this most unusual individual. It was an inspiration to be with him and studying with him will always live in my memory. We fitted very well together for we felt the same about interpretation. When I started with him I already had not [only] ideas, but intuitive interpretation.[12]

Having studied with William Harms, a protégé of Hofmann and a contemporary of Cherkassky at the Curtis Institute, I can attest to the accuracy of this description. A second piano was present in the teaching studio and Harms played simultaneously with the student. Tempo, color, mood, phrasing, and many details were set immediately in place. If a technical problem arose, the only advice given was, "Practice it with the other hand." Indeed, Josef Hofmann made it clear that he did not believe there was such a thing as a method, referring to the same as "a shoe to fit all kinds and sizes of feet and a strait-jacket for individual talent." He believed piano playing was not much more than good finger action, a good touch, and tone production, which were achieved by training fingers, hands, and arms to do their work naturally. Everything else came under the heading of music making, as distinct from piano playing, for which there was no method either. "Methods are for mediocrities," he proclaimed.

Obviously Hofmann did not emulate Rubinstein's articulate manner of guiding students, but more interestingly from a psychological point of view, he chose to communicate with his students by playing for them and with them. Listening was the primary teaching tool used by Josef Hofmann, and on February 9, 1929, in his capacity as director of the Curtis Institute, Hofmann wrote to Mary Louise Curtis Bok, president of the board, recommending the purchase of "a Duo-Art Steinway Up-right which costs $1985—less 30% granted me which is $1389.50. An instrument of that sort will be of great help to students in learning new piano pieces because before depicting them they may become acquainted with them tonally. When your rather dilapidated financial condition permits a Duo-Art would be a nice and welcome gift to the Institute."[13]

How did Hofmann's teaching translate into Cherkassky performances? Commentators and critics over the years have automatically concluded that the Cherkassky sound, color, and point of view came directly from Hofmann. Yet one must ask if this was the case when every critique of the child prodigy Shura Cherkassky, *prior* to his studies with Josef Hofmann, cited as already complete every aspect of his piano playing, from color and bigness and beauty of sound to pedaling, imagination, and interpretation—all characteristics that later were ascribed to his studies with Hofmann. Cherkassky himself stated that he couldn't quite say what Hofmann taught him, and that he learned his performing style from himself and not from Hofmann, but he did admit to being under the Hofmann influence for a very long time in one particular area: "I was trying to bring out too many inner voices. It's no good to copy anyone else."

The repertoire of the two child prodigies was ultimately enormous, but Cherkassky far outdistanced Hofmann in the sheer quantity of compositions he had mastered and performed by the time he reached his teenage years. At the age of eighteen, Cherkassky told a reporter for *Etude* magazine, in an article published in May of 1927, "In my repertoire I already have four to five hundred pieces and I play two hundred of them from memory. . . . Sometimes I find a composition that I did not know I knew; that is, I have heard the composition so much that I can go to the piano and play it without having seen the notes." The two prodigies also differed in their taste for composing, with Hofmann prolific and enthusiastic and Cherkassky producing only his *Prélude Pathétique*, the sophisticated composition raved over by critics, which was thought up one day by the child as he was out walking. The emotional quality as well as the technical comprehension evident in this piece was eerie for a youngster of his age. He was asked to make a recording of it for the Victor Talking Machine Company (Blue Seal), and subsequently did so. Late in his concert-playing life he also frequently programmed the *Prélude Pathétique* as an encore. On the subject of composition Cherkassky once said, "Between the ages of five and eight I composed all sorts of nonsense," and that following publication of the *Prélude Pathétique* many musicians told him he had a great future as a composer and that he should return to composing when time permitted. He told them he never would, and he never did.

After his prodigy years, Hofmann lost his pianistic prowess at a comparatively young age, due in no small part to problems in his personal life. In a 1999 article in *Piano and Keyboard*, music critic Harold Schonberg described being on leave from the service in 1943 and going to hear a Hofmann concert, which started a half hour late after Hofmann, who seemed to Schonberg to have been drinking, was assisted to the stage. After floundering around at the keyboard, the pianist ended the concert twenty minutes into his performance. In February of 1945, when Hofmann failed to appear at a rehearsal with the New York Philharmonic, Alexander Greiner from Steinway and Sons, rushed to Hofmann's hotel where he found Hofmann wearing only his underclothes and refusing to rehearse. That afternoon, Greiner persuaded Hofmann to go to the apartment of the conductor, Artur Rodzinski, where he played, according to Greiner, "as though he were in a trance. . . . A pupil without any talent whatever played infinitely better! All the notes were there, but it was without any expression, without any dynamics, completely lifeless!"[14] In February of the next year Hofmann gave a recital at Philadelphia's Academy of Music and some members of the audience demanded refunds. His last public performance was on January 13, 1947, on the Bell Telephone Hour ten years before his death. In contrast, Cherkassky persevered and thrived. He fulfilled the palmist's predictions of a hale and hearty old age, playing the most difficult works in the repertoire with consummate technical command and musical artistry, and following a punishing schedule (that would have defeated most pianists a quarter of his age) right up until six weeks before his death at the age of eighty-six.

Just as the two prodigies went opposite ways in regard to composing, so too did they diverge in regard to teaching. Anton Rubinstein taught Josef Hofmann and Josef Hofmann taught Shura Cherkassky, but Shura Cherkassky taught no one, notwithstanding occasional claims to the contrary. Cherkassky, in fact, was adamant on the subject.

> Teach? Never! Not for a million dollars. I don't know. I don't want to. I just don't want to. Perhaps I'm a bit selfish but I would be a terrible teacher, because while I can teach myself, if I would try to teach the same things to another person it could be rather harmful to them because it probably wouldn't suit their personality. In fact I believe to copy somebody actually does harm. Anyway, how can I tell someone how to do it when I don't know myself how I do it?

Hofmann thought otherwise. He believed it was the obligation of every musician who inherited a living tradition to pass it on to the next generation: "It is one of the few ways in which those traditions can be perpetuated. It is a duty." And he said, in an interview in 1926 given at "Swasticka," the Pennsylvania home of Mr. and Mrs. Edward Bok: "It will not hurt any young student to imitate so long as the thing he imitates is good. A true artist has the gift of distinction. He will select and reject in a manner that ultimately helps his own individuality."[15] Hofmann also thought the concert artist should welcome teaching because it enriched his life, and since art and life were synonymous, it followed that far from being impeded, one's art would benefit from this enrichment. Furthermore, he believed that many concert artists dreaded teaching because they "considered it a colorless occupation that clipped their wings and stultified performance."[16] "Go stale teaching?" Hofmann queried. "Never! It has been one of the most inspiring experiences of my life!"

Most pianists cannot acquire in a lifetime the singing sound, technical fluency, and breadth of color, rhythmic understanding, sensitivity, and brilliance that characterized the musical gifts of the child Shura and the child Jozio from their first performances. One reporter of the day offered the idea of transmigration of the soul as a probable explanation for a child with such gifts. He posited that Cherkassky had acquired all of his talent in some previous existence and, reincarnated, had brought it into his new life. While hardly provable, such a theory at least offers an imaginative explanation for Shura Cherkassky's genius. It was prescient of this reporter in 1923 to write so tellingly of Shura Cherkassky who, as an adult, told many of his friends that he firmly believed in reincarnation.

Notes

1. The child's program consisted of Beethoven's First Concerto, in which he included the Moscheles cadenza, and a *polacca* of Weber arranged by Liszt; a set of variations by Rameau; a waltz of his own composition; and a waltz and nocturne of Chopin.
2. Josef Hofmann, *Ladies' Home Journal*, October 1919.
3. David Ewen, *Men and Women Who Make Music* (New York: Merlin Press, 1940), 122.
4. Ewen, *Men and Women Who Make Music*.
5. Josef Hofmann, *Piano Playing and Questions Answered* (Philadelphia: Theodore Presser, 1920), 58.
6. Hofmann, *Piano Playing and Questions Answered*, 60.
7. Hofmann, *Piano Playing and Questions Answered*, 60–61.
8. Hofmann, *Piano Playing and Questions Answered*, 63.
9. Hofmann, *Piano Playing and Questions Answered*, 65.
10. Hofmann, *Piano Playing and Questions Answered*, 67.
11. J. Kanski, "Jak uczyl Hofmann?" *Ruch Muzyezny* 28, no. 1 (September 1984): 11.
12. Curtis Institute of Music, archives, MSS 18.
13. Curtis Institute of Music, archives, MSS 18.
14. D. W. Fostle, *The Steinway Saga* (New York: Scribner's, 1995), 482.
15. Curtis Institute of Music, archives, MSS 18.
16. *Houston Chronicle*, 9 October 1938.

C H A P T E R   F I V E

The Hofmann Years, 1925–1935

Very, very many have said I am like Hofmann. But they said that when I was a child prodigy, even before I went to study with him, that I resembled him, so afterward they said it all the more.

—S. C.

When the Curtis Institute of Music opened in Philadelphia in October of 1924 it had the enthusiastic support of Mary Louise Curtis Bok, daughter of Louisa Knapp Curtis and Cyrus Curtis, founder and head of the Curtis Publishing Company. Mary had come into a fortune when her mother died in 1910. Her mother had willed her estate to her husband but he, having no need for additional funds, passed it on to Mary, an only child, and suggested she become involved in arts-related philanthropy in Philadelphia. One of Mary's first acts of generosity was the donation of $150,000 for a building to house the Settlement School of Philadelphia. On January 28, 1917, the building was dedicated to her mother's memory, and at the celebration ceremony Josef Hofmann, who had met Mary's parents soon after arriving in Philadelphia for his second American tour in 1898, played a recital for a distinguished audience of some of Philadelphia's leading families along with two hundred neighborhood children representing many different nationalities. Contemporary newspaper accounts reported, "Music is taught at the Settlement, paying particular attention to children of immigrants as a means of Americanization and the development of the highest type of citizenship." Pupils who enrolled at the new school, which consisted of a library, classrooms, a three-hundred-seat auditorium, and basement community rooms and showers, paid tuition that amounted to one-quarter of the real cost of lessons in music, English, history, theories of American liberty, civics, and other subjects. Pleased by the subsequent development of the Settlement School (currently the largest community music school in America), Mary Bok turned her attention to the founding of a conservatory of music that would attract the crème de la crème of national and international music students. In the archives of the Curtis Institute can be found a copy of a news release sent to the *Musical Courier*, and published March 29, 1928, which explained Mary Bok's motivation for founding what became known as the Curtis Institute of Music, a name chosen to honor her father:

> Music was taught to increasing numbers at the foreign settlement, and the progress of young minds towards the adoption of American ideals went on apace. . . . Yet to the watchful eye of Mrs. Bok, the work in the best sense appeared incomplete. Students who showed every sign of high talent, even genius, were compelled to drop out because of a lack of time or money to prepare them fully. Into the workshops and warerooms they went, leaving behind all possibility of achievement in their art. It was obvious that this condition must prevail throughout the country. Everywhere there must be young people full of throbbing zeal for expression in music, but unable to take advantage of their gifts because of the compelling hand of necessity. Then there came to Mrs. Bok the idea of a national school of music, one in which the best instructors in the world would be available, and where the only qualification would be merit.

With her goals clearly in mind, Mary Bok purchased three elegant mansions to serve as the school's home in an exclusive quarter of Philadelphia known as Rittenhouse Square. She then settled a $500,000 endowment on the institution, chose John Grolle, a violinist with the Philadelphia Orchestra who had been headmaster of the Settlement School, to be the first director, and named Josef Hofmann head of the Piano Department, following a very persuasive letter that her husband, Edward Bok, had written to Hofmann in the summer of 1924, suggesting that Hofmann take over the Piano Department of the new school.

> I am very serious about your thinking over the idea of writing a book—You have a story to tell and can tell it—I don't like to think of you in Pullman's for the rest of your life, or touring Russia or anything else but making yourself very desirable by playing only a few times, and then filling in your time with composing, writing this book, and at the head of a great piano conservatory. You must begin to order your life better and stop this promiscuous playing before the public says goodbye to you. Let Levitzki or Godowsky or men of that sort do that. Keep yourself desirable. The time has come to think of this. You are now the master of them all and must remain so.[1]

Hofmann accepted the directorship of the Piano Department of the new conservatory, and it was from him and from Leopold Stokowski, conductor of the Philadelphia Orchestra, that Mary Bok, as president of the board of trustees, sought counsel in matters related to school policy and the hiring of faculty. Among the distinguished artists of the day who joined the Curtis Institute faculty during its first few years were David Saperton, Marcella Sembrich, Carlos Salzedo, Isabelle Vengerova, Carl Flesch, Leopold Stokowski, Wilhelm Backhaus, Wanda Landowska, Benno Moiseiwitsch, and Moriz Rosenthal. In 1927 when Hofmann was named to the position of director of the Curtis Institute, Mary Bok gave an additional endowment of $12 million to the school in the form of Curtis Publishing Company stock. In 1927 $12 million would be the equivalent of $130 million in 2005 dollars, making it one of the largest gifts ever to an institution by a living individual. Yet while this was an extraordinary sum, given the fact that it came from a single donor, precedents for such a gift had been established a few years earlier by George Eastman who founded a school of music in Rochester to which he gave $20 million between 1918 and 1932, and by the estate of Augustus Juilliard, which established the Juilliard Graduate School (and which merged with the Institute of Musical Art in 1926 to form what we now know as the Juilliard School of Music). The gift from the Juilliard estate is variously estimated at $10 to $12 million.

Once Hofmann was installed as the director of the Curtis, he made the goal of the institute the perpetuation of the great traditions of the past through the teaching of the greatest artist-teachers of the day. Only the most gifted students—the musically elite—were welcomed by Hofmann to the Curtis. If accepted, each student received every consideration and support, from free tuition to paid living expenses in the case of the truly needy. When a piano was needed, a Steinway was loaned to the student at no cost; when students wanted to continue study with their teachers who went abroad or to some other location in the United States, financial assistance was provided; graduates also received monetary support to launch their careers. Faculty members were treated just as magnanimously. Josef Hofmann's salary was quoted to the *New York Herald Tribune* in April of 1927 by Dagmar Godowsky, daughter of Leopold Godowsky, as being $100,000—the equivalent of over $1 million in 2005 dollars—a level reached by practically no one in the educational world today except for the most successful football or basketball coaches. The quoted sum was probably an exaggeration, however, with $75,000 being a more realistic estimate. But the economics of such generosity eventually caused the school financial problems, which Josef Hofmann decided to solve by cutting enrollment and reducing his salary. Then when the full effects of the Depression took hold, it was evident more restructuring would be needed, and in 1938 the board of trustees in conjunction with the institute's president, Mary Bok, instituted far-reaching changes that included, among other measures, the closing of departments, salary cuts for the faculty and staff, and a new policy that provided either minimal scholarship assistance for students or none at all. Hofmann was not in agreement with these changes, thinking they would destroy the philosophy behind the Curtis Institute, and he tendered his resignation in September of 1938. Attempts to dissuade him were all unsuccessful, and he left Philadelphia, moving to California in 1939. On February 14, 1939, at the Biltmore Hotel in Los Angeles, Hofmann gave an interview to the *Los Angeles Daily News* in which he spoke directly of his resignation:

> It proved to be just a little too strenuous to be director of the Curtis Institute of Music in Philadelphia, as well as to concertize and to teach. So I gave up the directorship. I spent too many hours and too many days at a desk reading letters and reports and composing more reports and more letters instead of composing music and reading new compositions.

Whether his departure from the Curtis was truly voluntary, and the outcome of financial considerations, philosophical differences, and overwork, or whether it was actually the result of a palace revolt hastened by Hofmann's alleged womanizing and drinking, or some combination of the foregoing, remains a source of speculation. As early as March 9, 1901, the Philadelphia press was publishing comments from the young Hofmann regarding his taste in women: "Your hotels and your girls are the greatest in the world—especially your girls. My they are quick—quick and pretty and splendid dressers. They can show off a dress too—much better than the women of Paris and 100% better than German girls."

Whatever the circumstances of his departure, Hofmann and Mary Bok maintained apparently friendly contact, at least in the early years of his move to California, during which time he continued to champion Shura Cherkassky's cause at every available opportunity. Hofmann had been Cherkassky's advocate since the time the sixteen-year-old pianist had received a scholarship for study at the Curtis Institute in 1925. Cherkassky's father, in May of that year, wrote a thank-you note to Josef Hofmann, which included a description of the financial arrangements to which the family had agreed (see fig. 5.1).[2] Thus started a long but eventually discouraging and humiliating

Mrs. Mary Louise Curtise Bok
The Curtis Institute Of MUSIc
RittenhoseSquare,Phila.,Pa.

501 W.111 St.
New York-City
May 17,1925

Dear Madame,
Mr. Sapertpn informed me,that my son Shura Cherkassky has been accepted at the Curtis Institute with a schopar ship in the class of Joseph Hoffman and olso of your kimd offer to us $300 a month for meintenance.

Please kindly accept our heartiest gratitude from Mrs. Cherkassky,Shura and myself. Now we are assured of the future of our boy.But more thanks will render you humanity for making it possible to bring aut such talents,which otherwise would have perished.

It is understood, that all the money.that you advance now for us as soon as Shura will be in a position to return it, we shallbe very happy to do it with the greatest gratitude.

Yours very respectfully

Isaak Cherkassky

Figure 5.1 Letter, May 17, 1925.

dependence on the generosity of Mary Louise Curtis Bok, whose bighearted-ness was consistently endorsed by Josef Hofmann.

When his piano studies commenced in the autumn of 1925, Shura Cherkassky entered into an enduring and highly meaningful relationship with Hofmann, in spite of the fact that the association was punctuated by long periods of Cherkassky's concertizing abroad. On tour for years at a time, Cherkassky attended lessons with Hofmann far fewer times than newspaper accounts would have the reader believe. His most intense period of study with Hofmann took place between 1925 and 1928 during which time Cherkassky's public appearances were strongly encouraged by Hofmann who clearly understood the problems of a child prodigy.

> How difficult it is to be a prodigy, and then to come back later and hope to be accepted as a mature artist. So many times I would hear this comment: "We heard him when he was nine. Wonderful boy then. But he hasn't lived up to his promise."
>
> It's rather like being the son of a famous father, except in this case it is your own self they are comparing you with, to your disadvantage. You are in the shadow of your early power, and it is a heart-breaking business to climb out of it into your own light. I went to England; I came to America, many times; I played on the

> continent, and I was in despair. I was not twice as good, but only half. Prodigies gain by their youth; lose by their gain in maturity, I would meditate bitterly. I should never have stopped appearing in public. . . .
>
> Public appearance is a spur to ambition. If a child is obviously going to be a professional musician, he will be a better one for encountering professional appraisal, at least in homeopathic doses, and with use of discretion about his health. It is like taking arsenic in small doses, beneficial in certain cases. It is like the stimulation of meeting a deadline in newspaper work—an absolute necessity with some natures. Exploitation for money is, of course, another matter.
>
> Public appearance is the test, the yardstick by which a musician can know if he is advancing. Do they put a fine automobile out on the road directly after its assembly from blueprints? No, they give it rigid tests. If there is anything wrong it can go back for correction. Just so can a young musician "go back to the laboratory" and make corrections on himself if he can come out in the world first and discover what's wrong. It is all very well for him to be sheltered and relieved to some extent from the tribulations of everyday life, but he should not be relieved of the responsibilities of an artist.[3]

During the first year of Shura Cherkassky's study with Hofmann, his most significant appearances took place in Boston's Symphony Hall, New York's Town Hall, and on broadcasts from the Curtis Institute. No matter where or what he played, the critics were unanimous that his was a "supernatural" talent, concurring with Hofmann's initial assessment of his student as written in his evaluation book of 1925 (see fig. 5.2).[4] For Cherkassky's part, in letters to friends the young student expressed his fervent admiration for his teacher. As the years passed this esteem escalated to veneration.

Just one month into his studies with Josef Hofmann, the pianist's October 25, 1925, performance in Boston's Symphony Hall was cited as not that of a nimble-fingered prodigy, but rather that of a sensitive and intelligent musician whose playing was characterized by individuality and distinction. Instead of the usual predictions by critics of crushed hopes and sordid parental ambitions, and of recommendations of more baseball and billiards and less Bach, this particular prodigy had forecast for him a brilliant future in which it was predicted he would take his place among the greatest of the great. This place would be guaranteed by his ability to scale the most difficult technical heights with ease and to convey in an uncanny way the emotional force of the works he was performing. Less than two months later on December 10, in New York's Town Hall, he once again enthralled an audience that quickly recognized they were in the presence of something transcendent that

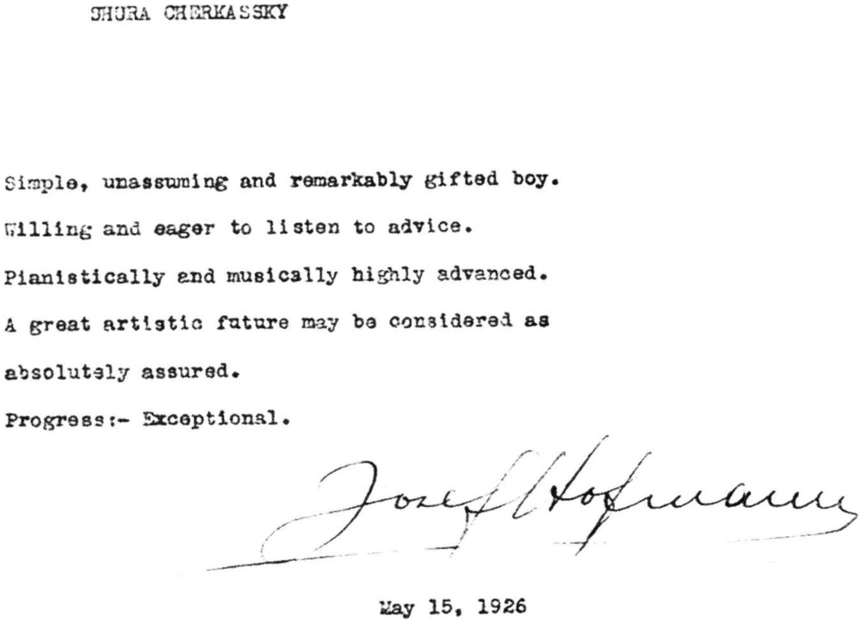

SHURA CHERKASSKY

Simple, unassuming and remarkably gifted boy.

Willing and eager to listen to advice.

Pianistically and musically highly advanced.

A great artistic future may be considered as absolutely assured.

Progress:- Exceptional.

Josef Hofmann

May 15, 1926

Figure 5.2 Evaluation, May 15, 1925–1927.

had absolutely nothing to do with mechanism. The critic of the evening offered up a prayer that to the end of his life Cherkassky might be the medium of such noble musical expression as given in that program, which opened with Bach's Prelude and Fugue in B-flat Major and continued with Schumann's *Symphonic* Etudes, then a Chopin group beginning with the Chopin B-flat Minor Sonata, and shorter pieces all "thrillingly played" and with no sense of "tax" since he seemed to be outside it all. On Sunday afternoon December 13 Cherkassky repeated his New York triumph in Lynn, Massachusetts, for the benefit of the Lynn Boys' Club.

Diligent study coupled with carefully scheduled performances continued throughout the winter months, and on April 25, 1926, Cherkassky appeared as soloist in the radio debut of the Curtis Student Orchestra performing the Rubinstein D-minor Concerto. Broadcast over radio station WIP in Philadelphia, the concert was also notable for the radio debut of Leopold Stokowski who conducted the student orchestra. At the end of the 1926 musical season, Josef Hofmann once again wrote an evaluation of his pupil (see fig. 5.3),[5] and

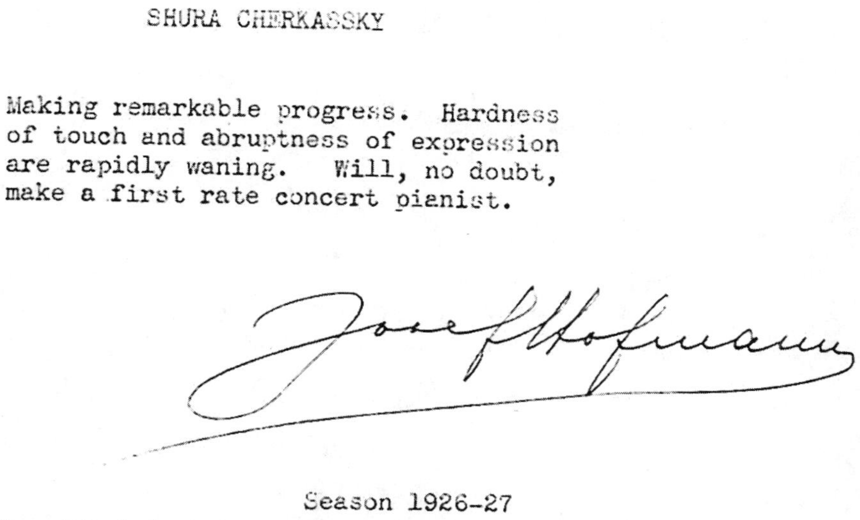

SHURA CHERKASSKY

Making remarkable progress. Hardness of touch and abruptness of expression are rapidly waning. Will, no doubt, make a first rate concert pianist.

Josef Hofmann

Season 1926-27

Figure 5.3 Evaluation, season 1926–1927.

the evaluation was accompanied by a list of compositions studied that year by his prize pupil (see fig. 5.4).[6]

Other evaluations of students in Hofmann's 1925–1926 class were not nearly so encouraging, with the exception of those of Olga Barabini, Jeanne Behrend, and Angelica Morales, for whom he had genuine words of praise. None however reached the level of his comments about Cherkassky. Hofmann's appraisals of his other male students fell far short of laudatory.

When the 1926 school year came to an end, six of the young Curtis students in violin and piano were invited to appear as soloists at the Orchestral Concerts of the Stanley Music Club the following winter. Conducted by Artur Rodzinski, the orchestra was composed of one hundred members of the Philadelphia Orchestra with the students the only soloists to be featured during the season. The November 28 concert presented Cherkassky in the Tchaikovsky B-flat Minor Concerto. His performance was cited as doing credit to any pianist on the concert stage, but for a boy of his years, it was said to be simply amazing. He made so profound an impression that the audience did not want to give up its effort to compel him to play an encore until it became evident no encores were permitted. Cherkassky was followed by Curtis students Iso Briselli, violinist, Jeanne Behrend, pianist, Lois zu Putlitz

SHURA CHERKASSKY

Compositions Studied During School Year 1926-27

Albeniz -	Seguidilla
Albeniz-Godowsky -	Tango
Bach-Liszt -	Fantasy and Fugue in G minor
Bach-Tausig -	Toccata and Fugue in D minor
Balakirev -	Islamey
Brahms -	Waltz in A flat major
Chasins -	Rush Hour in Hong Kong
Chopin -	Ballade in A flat major, Opus 47 Etudes: E major, Opus 10, No. 3 C minor, Opus 25, No. 12 Impromptu in F sharp major, Opus 36 Nocturne in G major, Opus 37, No. 2 Scherzo in B minor, Opus 31 Valses: A flat major, Opus 34, No. 1 A minor, Opus 34, No. 2
Daquin -	Le Coucou
Debussy -	Arabesque
Dvorsky -	L'Orient et L'Occident
Handel-Brahms -	Variations in B flat major
Hofmann -	Kaleidoscope
Liszt -	Concerto in E flat major Funérailles Sonata in B minor Venezia e Napoli
Mana-Zucca -	Etude Hommage Sketch
Medtner -	Fairy Tale in E minor
Mendelssohn -	Scherzo

Figure 5.4 List of Compositions, May 1926–1927.

and Jascha Savitt, violinists, and Lucy Stern, pianist. Of the six performers, four were from Russia and two were American: Lois zu Putlitz and Jeanne Behrend. Among these young performers Shura Cherkassky particularly admired Lucy Stern's talent and throughout his life found her suicide at a young age disturbing and incomprehensible. In 1926, Josef Hofmann wrote of Lucy Stern, in his evaluation book, that "she must be freed from influences that [are telling her] she is now already above criticism."

One nonmusical result of Cherkassky's master performance was the presentation of a wristwatch inscribed with his name made on behalf of Jules Mastbaum, founder of the Stanley Company of North America. Mastbaum had attended the Stanley Music Club concert at which Cherkassky was soloist and was so impressed with the boy's virtuosity that he bought him a watch, delaying the presentation so that similar gifts might be given to the other young artists at the end of the concert season.

During the summer of 1927, on July 2, Cherkassky sailed for Europe aboard the *Ile de France*, the newest and most fashionable of the great Atlantic liners, for a two-month visit. As a member of the Young Peoples Educator Tours of France, a group sponsored by the French government under the honorary direction of Maréchals Foch and Joffre, the young pianist visited England, France, Switzerland, Morocco, and Spain, whetting his appetite for travel, which would become a lifelong passion. Of this trip he recalled that when he saw Paris he couldn't believe it was on the same continent as the Soviet Union.

Upon his return to the United States intense preparation began for the 1927 fall season of concerts, the highlight of which was Cherkassky's Carnegie Hall appearance on December 7. Hailed by all as Shura Cherkassky's passage to artistic manhood, the concert elicited rave reviews citing his mastery of tone, tone color, and technique, his maturity of interpretation, depth of expression, unerring sense of proportion, nicety of detail, delicacy of shading, grace of phrasing, and an emotional power that put many older pianists to shame. Described as a born musician who got under the surface of things and stayed there as long as necessary, he opened with the Bach-Liszt Organ Fantasia and Fugue in G Minor, and he continued with Schumann's *Carnaval*; works by Chopin including the *Barcarolle*, two etudes, and the F-minor Ballade; Hofmann's *Kaleidoscope*; and Chasins's *Rush Hour in Hong Kong*. The concert ended with Strauss-Schulz-Evler's *Arabesque on the Blue Danube Waltz*. In *New York World* on December 8, 1927, Samuel Chotzinoff, a pianist who accompanied Heifetz and Zimbalist and who served as a critic for the *New York Post*, brilliantly summed up the whole experience:

> It may be said at once that in this boy is lodged a talent for playing the piano hardly equaled by any but one or two virtuosi now before the public. Notwithstanding his tender age, Cherkassky communicates first and foremost a sense of unstinted power, an unlimited reservoir of strength. This strength, however, is never noise, but always the pressure of a tone with the equality of a silver trumpet. Clear, solid, brilliant, this tone is the same from the top to the bottom of the keyboard. In chords, cantilena, in the swift flights of scales and passages, the tone is beautifully equalized. As for the mechanics of the pianist's art, the boy's mastery of his instrument is prodigious even in these days of super-technic. He is a youthful artist glorying in musical health, reveling in the sheer beauty of sound and sporting with thunderbolts like some infant Jove.

Less well known than his association with Hofmann was Shura Cherkassky's pianistic relationship with David Saperton, who was the assistant director and executive secretary of the Curtis Institute and also a teaching assistant to Josef Hofmann when Hofmann was the institute's director. As a member of the faculty at Curtis, which he joined in 1924 when the school was founded, Saperton taught many of the twentieth century's most prominent pianists including Jorge Bolet, Abbey Simon, Sidney Foster, and William Masselos. Born David Saperstein in Pittsburgh, Pennsylvania, in 1889, he studied piano with Arthur Shattuck and Leopold Godowsky, whose daughter Vanita he married in 1921. After a successful debut in Pittsburgh at the age of ten and a New York debut in 1905 at one of the Metropolitan Opera House Sunday concerts, Saperton appeared in a highly successful joint recital with Geraldine Farrar in Berlin in 1908 and subsequently toured Europe to critical acclaim. At that time he was closely identified with performances of Busoni transcriptions. He presented a cycle of greatly acclaimed recitals in New York in 1914 and 1915, and several years later performed in a series of memorable radio broadcasts. Saperton also became an outstanding exponent of Leopold Godowsky's music, and he went on to play and record many of Godowsky's compositions and transcriptions.

During his early years at the Curtis Institute, Cherkassky spent one summer studying with Saperton on Coney Island in New York and often recalled how he could do "anything" at the piano after those lessons with him. Saperton insisted that his student learn the exercises of Rafael Joseffy, which Cherkassky considered to be extremely important in his technical training. He described Saperton as a marvelous teacher who knew how to train a pianist's hand and who left nothing to chance. In his lessons Saperton demanded that the student respect the written text, and at the same time Saperton saw it as his responsibility to equip his students with the right tools to deal with the great works of the piano literature. Saperton's son told me that his father stressed weight and fingering as the basis of those tools, a stress that followed the teachings of Matthay and Leschetizky. In a letter to David Saperton written from Nice, France, on September 5, 1958, Cherkassky declared:

> I say quite sincerely that it is to you that I owe the development of my technic. . . . And always in the back of my mind (and I've told this to many people) I feel that it is your doings that I have this command of technic, and the pianistic method of playing. So I am proud that you have been responsible and played a strong part in my career.[7]

His opinion and sentiments were echoed by Jorge Bolet:

> New York, January 30, 1958
>
> Having studied with him exclusively from the age of 12, until my graduation from the Curtis Institute of Music in 1934, I feel I am eminently qualified to express my unreserved admiration and appreciation for his invaluable teaching during those eight important years of my musical career.
>
> Mr. Saperton holds a unique position in his ability to form a student's habits in all phases of piano playing. His grasp and understanding of the mechanism of the art of the piano in all the literature are unsurpassed by any other. His ability to develop and nurture talent to its fullness makes him quite unique.[8]

And by Abbey Simon:

> *Geneva, Switzerland, April 26, 1958*
>
> On this, your Jubilee Year of teaching activity, permit me as one of your most loyal and grateful pupils to say how much I appreciate the wonderful work you have done for me and all of the other talented people who have had the good fortune to be able to study with you.
>
> I know of no one who has been able to impart to his students the keyboard mastery and the musical understanding that you have. I am sure that the eminent list of people who have studied with you makes my personal tribute a very modest one.[9]

While still a student at the Curtis Institute, Cherkassky embarked on his first world tour in 1928, triumphing sensationally in 120 concerts that included appearances in England, France, New Zealand, Australia, South Africa, and the British Isles. The decision for him to go abroad was made by Josef Hofmann and Mary Louise Curtis Bok, who thought this would be the best way for Cherkassky to establish an international reputation and thus give impetus to his American career. Because of his falsified birth date, Cherkassky was considered a minor, and he traveled on his father's passport, which had been issued May 17, 1928.[10] In March of 1930 the pianist then received his own passport, which along with subsequent ones became a cornucopia of travel visas from around the globe.

When interviewed by the press prior to departing on the RMS *Niagara* for Australia, Shura Cherkassky was asked if he would be returning to Russia. In response he made a rare comment to the press concerning the bullet that drove him and his family from Russia in 1922: "There are nine bullets in the wall of the house where we lived and several people died there of disease. No we will not go back to Russia."

The trip started by boat from New York City to Montreal, continued from Montreal on the Canadian Pacific Railway to Vancouver where Cherkassky embarked on an ocean voyage to Australia that took nineteen days. The first two months of the world tour were spent in Australia and New Zealand as the result of an invitation from E. J. Gravestock, a local impresario and artist manager who handled some of the finest virtuosi in the world, including Backhaus and Levitzki. Throughout the Australian tour, concerts in Adelaide, Perth, Sydney, and Melbourne were played to full houses provoking scenes of enthusiasm previously unheard of on that continent. Six recitals were played in Adelaide alone, where Cherkassky was described as being able to do what the giants of the piano had been striving to do all their lives. In Christchurch, New Zealand, he played nine recitals on alternate days to mesmerized audiences. In Auckland and Wellington he was described as a master of the keyboard in the same sense as Paderewski, Hofmann, and Rachmaninoff. Of the Australian tour Cherkassky recalled, "Melbourne was a nightmare. The stage sloped towards the front and the piano and the stool had to be propped up on one side. It was very uncomfortable." He also remembered that his father who accompanied him greatly embarrassed the young pianist by his insistence on making a speech in hesitant English at each of his son's concerts.

On an extramusical note, the tour was also notable as being one of the two times in his life that Shura Cherkassky ever endorsed a product. The first endorsement followed an impromptu recital in Steinway Hall in New York on March 31, 1923, when the tiny Russian child declared, "I think the Steinway a very nice piano"—a quotation that was subsequently used in advertisements for his appearance at the Lyric Theatre in Baltimore on Sunday April 8, 1923. The second endorsement came during the 1928 Australian tour on which Cherkassky endorsed *Heenzo*, a syrup billed as a famous and money-saving family remedy for coughs, colds, bronchitis, and influenza. "Since my arrival in Australia I have occasions to use *Heenzo*, and I am more than delighted with the speedy way it banished the cold I contracted through climatic changes experienced whilst traveling. I shall certainly carry a supply of *Heenzo* throughout my world tour," declared the young artist. Or was it actually his representative? Following the Australian tour, Cherkassky and his family spent a good deal of time in Europe where he played concerts in France, and they settled in Paris where Cherkassky studied French music and the French language.

On February 9, 1929, Josef Hofmann wrote Mary Bok, addressing her as "My dear Mrs. President," and told her,

> [I] received a long letter yesterday from his [Shura's] father, written in Russian. . . . As much as I can gather after having looked it over casually Pappa Cherkassky is more desirous for his son to go on playing in public and us to help him to do so than for Shura to continue his studies at the Institute. However, when I get the exact translation I will be in a better position how to proceed and how to decide.[11]

As events unfolded it was clear that Hofmann's decision was to allow his student to perform publicly as much as possible.

In the spring of 1929 the soon-to-be twenty-year-old pianist proceeded to Switzerland, joining Josef Hofmann at his home in Vevey. Hofmann and his first wife, Marie Eustis, daughter of a United States senator and granddaughter of W. W. Corcoran, after whom the Washington, D.C., art gallery was named, had been charmed by the village of Vevey on their visit in 1908 to the Paderewskis, who lived in nearby Morgues. Flowers in blazing colors blanketed Mount Pelerin as it sloped toward the blue waters of Lake Geneva, and it was on this mountainside that the Paderewskis had their home. Other famous artists owned properties nearby where they sought the soothing salve of privacy after months of touring performances. One day while picnicking on the mountainside the Hofmanns went walking and stumbled upon a farmhouse nestled snugly into the mountainside with a For Sale sign on it. Their search for a home was over, and within a few days Hofmann bought the house, situated 1,600 feet above the lake, and engaged an architect for its renovation. Interior walls were removed and beautiful large spaces with elegant paneling were created. No expense was spared to fulfill the wishes of Hofmann's wife, and every room took advantage of the gorgeous view. Hofmann, the inventor, meanwhile indulged his fantasies and designed an electric and water plant for their exclusive use. Finally, a red-tile roof and

L-shaped patio were added to complete their dream home, which the couple named *Beaumaroche*. It was to this idyllic setting that Shura Cherkassky came to resume his studies with Josef Hofmann in the spring of 1929 in preparation for an upcoming South African tour.

Cherkassky's recital appearances in South Africa in May of 1929 produced remarkable results. Three thousand people crowded the Johannesburg city hall, the biggest and most distinguished audience Johannesburg had seen in many years. By all accounts Cherkassky held his audience enthralled for more than two hours, moving it to repeatedly call him back to the platform for an encore. A critic in the *Rand Daily* observed that "Cherkassky's pianism was so complete, so remarkable, so easy in its workings as to make the audience, after the unbelieving first gasp, unaware of the colossal nature of what [Cherkassky] was doing." This critic, writing under the colorful pseudonym "Treble Violl," also observed that perhaps some critics who were still bound to earth by academic readings would shake their heads at this performance. Certainly it is true that after his prodigy years Cherkassky's work was disturbing to some critics and to those listeners who were more comfortable with "correct" performances, which to the ears of others often sounded bland and uncommitted. Throughout Cherkassky's long career the purists among his critics would groan and say, this is not Bach, or this is not Beethoven, or this is not Chopin; but for those who listened with an open mind he was able to persuade and convince them, not by his virtuosity, but through the high intelligence behind his imagination, which produced the exquisite tone, the distinctive pedaling, the great marvels of fortissimo and pianissimo, and the emotion that the vast majority of critics repeatedly cited as the hallmarks of his playing.

Following the success of the South African tour, Cherkassky participated in an extensive orchestral tour, the International Celebrity Tour, with Albert Coates, conductor, from October of 1929 to March of 1930, performing in London's Queen's Hall and Royal Albert Hall as well as in twenty-five provinces all over the British Isles. The Royal Albert Hall performance created a sensation, and he received from Dame Nellie Melba a diamond and platinum tiepin in tribute to his playing. As the soloist in Tchaikovsky's B-flat Minor Concerto he was described as magnificent, using the piano like an orchestra. Indeed, during the early years of his career, the Tchaikovsky was for Cherkassky, as for many pianists, a warhorse. Throughout the International Celebrity Tour his playing of the work was referred to as the most remarkable feature of each concert, with the soloist in essence owning the concerto.

> The 16-year-old Cherkassky played the solo part, and may without exaggeration be said to have created a sensation. The music, to begin with, is abnormally difficult, and when this youth plunged with all the assurance in the world into those massive opening chords, going on to thunder to Heaven, positively in the grand manner, one almost doubted the evidence of one's ears and eyes.
>
> This boy has a colossal technique and an astounding vigorous style. His finger work was dazzling and incredibly clean. His octave passages and his scale passages—but particularly his octave passages—were the last word in brilliance, and his tone remains musical in the most strenuous moments.
>
> He managed throughout easily to hold his own with the orchestra, which in itself was a considerable feat. His marvelously facile playing of the cadenza in the first movement, his beautiful delicacy of touch when embroidering the fleeting waltz theme in the second, and the third were only some of the notable things about a performance which as a whole was quite astonishing.[12]

(The reviewer's arithmetic is in error when he describes Cherkassky as a "16-year-old." The pianist was actually twenty in 1929 but should have been reported as eighteen since the true date of his birth was not revealed until 1994.)

Numerous engagements and reengagements filled the next two years, and in February of 1931 Cherkassky revisited the scene of his previous triumphs in South Africa where he played twenty-five concerts. Following three years abroad, during which his career had enjoyed unprecedented success, he returned to America and in August of 1931 spent the summer studying with Hofmann at Hofmann's Rockport, Maine, home in preparation for an American tour. Also in residence at Rockport that summer were pianists Nadia Reisenberg, Joseph Levine, and William Harms, a student from Kansas with whom Cherkassky developed a keen friendship. In autumn Cherkassky opened his American tour, returning to the site of his debut at the Lyric Theater in Baltimore where this time he was described as a pianist of proportions to inspire any audience. The following month, on November 28, in an appearance at Carnegie Hall he drew rave reviews from most critics, although one critic from the *New York Sun* questioned his use of speed, described his pointing of inner voices as a mannerism, and labeled as an error his concentration on externals, all of which however this critic attributed to youth and to a phase that would pass at the onset of the pianist's greater maturity. In sharp contrast to this, the *Musical Courier* reporter viewed the performance as "one of splendidly realized expectations and compelling attainments marked by a feeling that was always refined and a sound that was always large and noble."

As the months passed more and more concerts were added to Cherkassky's schedule, and 1932 saw him play in a wide range of venues, starting in January when he performed for the Schubert Club of Hartford, Connecticut (the publicity photo sent to the local papers shows Cherkassky in full matador dress!) then hallowed Carnegie Hall on February 2, and the Ivanhoe School Auditorium in Kansas City, Missouri, where he gave a series of five recitals to school children, a setting in which he had difficulty adjusting to the youth of his audience. On this first trip west he also played in Tulsa, Oklahoma, before returning in March to perform the Liszt E-flat Concerto with the Brooklyn Symphony Orchestra in a benefit concert for Jordan Hospital. He continued the season playing in Quebec; Miami, Florida; Newark, New Jersey; Joplin, Missouri; Baltimore, Maryland; and Bronxville, New York, before leaving for Germany where he triumphed in a series of Berlin recitals.

On May 14, 1932, the twenty-three-year-old pianist sailed for Europe on board the SS *General Von Steuben* (torpedoed during World War II by a Russian submarine with the loss of three thousand lives) for recitals in Berlin and a summer at Lake Como, Italy. Berlin at this time was the center of the music world. The city was a mecca for musicians, writers, and actors with its four opera houses, music conservatories, symphony orchestras, and more than one hundred newspapers. Home to some of the most eminent pianists of the era, Berlin welcomed French, Slavic, and Hungarian viewpoints in concert, as well as German. Gieseking, Backhaus, and Schnabel, among others, lived in Berlin. Cortot, Moiseiwitsch, Sauer, Rosenthal, Friedman, Paderewski, Gabrilowitsch, and Erno von Dohnanyi made frequent appearances there. Arnold Schoenberg and Paul Hindemith lived and composed there. It was an exciting, vital, intensely energetic city where audiences devoured the culture brought by visiting artists, and it was a city that accorded the youthful Shura Cherkassky his share of fame. "By the side of these two great figures [Lamond and Gieseking] in the realm of art there may be placed the very promising young pianist, Shura Cherkassky—extremely musical, outstanding in technique, showing architectonic ability and temperament. The musician and virtuoso are united in him."[13] High praise indeed, given the fact Berlin critics were incorrigibly skeptical of all things American that had to do with art. In fact, not until Toscanini's European tour with the New York Philharmonic in May 1930 did the critics change their opinion, reporting in the *Zeitung Ammitag* that the best European orchestras could not compare with the New York Philharmonic in "tone, technique or symphonic cooperation."

Still, the crowning achievement of 1932 was the Carnegie Hall concert in which Cherkassky was hailed as a prodigy-made-artist whose performance that evening was described as unsurpassable. Pitts Sanborn in the *New York World Telegram* waxed eloquent:

> His command of tone color would grace Josef Hofmann himself, likewise his command of dynamics. He can summon from the piano the qualities and the timbres of orchestral instruments; he controls every nuance from a whispered *pianissimo* to a *fortissimo*, which for all its thunder is secure and musical. Further there is never the suggestion of him driving himself. He seems always to have unlimited strength in reserve.
>
> Last evening this extraordinary technical equipment seemed to be at the service of an authentically musical nature. He opened the concert with the now exceedingly familiar transcription by Busoni of the famous Bach *Chaconne* for violin.
>
> Only Busoni himself, one feels, could have played it better, and not much better at that. . . . It was remarkable not only for its color and shadings, but also for its breadth and its architectural strength and rightness.

Between 1932 and 1935 Cherkassky combined limited formal study with extended concert tours abroad on which he played to astounding critical acclaim. In spite of his pianistic success and the financial support he received from the Curtis, which was unwaveringly encouraged by Hofmann, he was never solvent and repeatedly turned to Mrs. Bok for help. There begins at this time a long and illuminating correspondence between Mary Bok (through her secretary, Elsie Hutt), Josef Hofmann, and Shura Cherkassky, whom Hofmann referred to as his "star pupil." In painfully explicit language, these letters clearly reveal the deep emotional suffering the young Cherkassky experienced at his inability to establish a career in America and the intense shame he felt at not being able to earn enough money to be independent. He claimed that his expenses exceeded his income; others named his inability to manage money as the culprit. Whatever the cause of his plight, Mrs. Bok's support was unstinting, but the effects of the Depression stressed her resources as well. When Shura wrote to her on April 4, 1933, asking her for $500 to subsidize a trip to Europe, complaining that his current stipend of $225 a month was not enough for three people to live on, and saying that he did not even have enough money to buy something as simple as a pair of badly needed shoes, then adding how terribly it hurt him to see how he and his family lived in such poverty, he received the following response, dated April 14, 1933:

> My dear Shura—
>
> The severely reduced income of the Curtis Institute which is making so many drastic changes at the Institute necessary at the present time has an exact parallel

in my own personal finances, inasmuch as the source of the two incomes is the same.

Because of this, I cannot possibly give you the money for going to Europe this summer that you ask. I cannot give away what I do not have.

I am sorry to pass on any discouragement to you who work so faithfully and well, but I cannot do otherwise.

With all good wishes, I am
Ever sincerely yours,
(signed Mary Louise Curtis Bok)[14]

In the deflationary days of the Depression (1933), $225 a month would be the equivalent of almost $39,000 a year in 2005 dollars—hardly poverty level for a family of three adults. Pleas for additional funds continued throughout 1933, and in August when the pianist was taken seriously ill and had to have a mastoid operation, it was Mrs. Bok who paid the medical expenses, for which Lydia Cherkassky thanked her profusely, stating that she had saved Shura's life. (Later in life Cherkassky referred to this sickness as "Stormy Malady," saying he did not understand what it was but that following the procedure he had much more energy.)

From this point on there are numerous lengthy letters to Mrs. Bok in which he grieves over the fact that he cannot make a living playing the piano, speaks of his complete discouragement, and wonders if there is any future for him in America. These letters eventually descend into increasingly more degrading appeals for more and more money. Interestingly, throughout these and subsequent years, at no time in any of the correspondence between Shura, Bok, or Josef Hofmann, is there even the slightest suggestion that Cherkassky should teach (as other Hofmann students were doing) or that he should find some other means to tide him over, not even later on in the early forties, when the war jump-started the economy and made jobs easy to find. His mother did some teaching in these years but told Mrs. Bok that whatever she earned she had to give to a sister who had no other means of support.

Behind the scenes both Bok and Hofmann worked to secure engagements for their favored student, and did their utmost to make him known to conductors. Through their influence Eugene Ormandy, then with the Minneapolis Symphony, agreed to engage him in March of 1934. As he prepared for the engagement Cherkassky instructed Mrs. Bok's secretary to "make sure [he] had lower berths on all trains." Later in March Mrs. Bok wrote to Eugene Ormandy, thanking him for giving their protégé an opportunity to play with the orchestra, to which Ormandy replied, "Shura Cherkassky came up to all our expectations and surpassed them. This young man should be heard and heard a lot." She also approached Otto Klemperer, cautioning Cherkassky not to have too much hope that an engagement would materialize and to be patient.

In the ensuing months conversations were held between Mary Bok and Josef Hofmann concerning the future of the twenty-four-year-old pianist. On July 6, 1934, Bok wrote Shura from Camden, Maine, with a suggestion that both surprised and pleased him (see fig. 5.5).[15]

His response to her suggestion was quick (see fig. 5.6).[16] During the autumn of 1934, Richard Copley, who was then manager of both Shura and Josef Hofmann, decided that it was necessary for Cherkassky to appear in New York in order to once again put his name before the American public since he had not played in America for three years. Cherkassky wrote to Mrs. Bok on October 5 requesting that she sponsor the recital (see fig. 5.7). Following receipt of this letter a budget was drawn up and approved by Mrs. Bok for a Town Hall recital to be given on February 9, 1935, with total expenses of $735.25 (see fig. 5.8).

During the month of November Mrs. Bok had the rare experience of receiving a happy letter from Shura, dated the twenty-sixth, telling her he had the "most marvelous news" in the form of a contract from the Soviet government for a concert tour between March 15 and 30, 1935, for which he would earn eight hundred rubles for each appearance, four thousand rubles guaranteed. He would be playing five concerts and would appear with the Moscow and Leningrad orchestras as the first foreign pianist to present the Shostakovich First Piano Concerto. The contract had been secured through the efforts of Josef Hofmann who had written to Bella Kashin, the Moscow correspondent of the *New York Times* for *Cinema News*. Kashin's contacts within the Soviet establishment, coupled with Josef Hofmann's letter, sealed the engagement. Following his "marvelous news" concerning the Russian contract, Mary Bok received another letter in which the pianist, lamenting his lack of earning power, said, "As you know I have nothing," and asked Mrs. Bok for funds for travel to London, which was not covered by his contract with the Soviet government. She replied on February 6, 1935, with a check for $300 to cover the projected expenses he had outlined to her in his letter: "roundtrip to London, $225; passport, $10; transit visas, $5; tips, $15–20; five days living in London, $35."

In January of 1935 sorrow entered the Cherkassky household with the unexpected death of Isaak Cherkassky on the twenty-sixth. A letter of condolence from Mrs. Bok to Mrs. Cherkassky produced a note from her saying

Camden, Maine
6 July 1934

My dear Shura :

When I saw Doctor Hofmann yesterday I told him of your letter to me, and we had a little talk about its contents.

I doubt very much if Stokowski would engage you as soloist next year, since he is to give only nine pairs of concerts, and has his programs made. Among the other conductors for the season is Ormandy. You need no introduction to him. Mr. Klemperer is another, and, while I do not know him personally, I will try to reach him by letter and tell him what I know of your work and that you are a Hofmann student. It may take some time before I even reach him, because I do not know whether he is in this country or abroad.

Your teacher seems to feel that you and your family could live to greater advantage abroad on the money the Institute is giving you, and that if you could play abroad for a year or so you would have a better chance with the American public upon your return. I pass this on to you for consideration.

Neither your teacher nor I doubt that we will yet be proud of you, and I hope very much you will fight discouragement. It is unproductive. Just work. And you need not doubt that your teacher and I will do what we can in opening up engagements for you. As you know, this is not easy, and it takes time.

With best wishes and kindest greetings, I am

Sincerely yours,

(Signed by Mrs. Bok)

Mr. Shura Cherkassky
305 West Ninety-eighth Street
New York City
New York

Figure 5.5 Letter, July 6, 1934.

305 West 98th Street
New York City
10th July 1934

Dear Mrs. Bok,

Thank you so much for your very kind letter. It encouraged me more than I can say. I am so happy to know yours and Dr. Hofmann's wonderful attitude towards my career.

Two years ago when I was in Berlin, I have heard about the new rule of the Institute that it can't give any money for promotion. Since then I felt that I was going backward, as my Carnegie Hall recital was canceled, N.B.C. stopped advertising me and I had no opportunity to appear with any orchestra in New York. Now, my new managers, Mr. Copley has no money even to print the circulars, and he tells me authoritatively: "you must play in New York; It is very

Figure 5.6 Letter, July 10, 1934.

necessary to get the fresh criticisms; the public is gradually forgetting you".

As regards to living abroad for a year or so, I find that it is a very good idea. I like Europe, but it would take a lot of money for the travelling expences, arranging concerts there, and the cost of living in Europe is almost twice as high as in America on account of depreciation

of the dollar. Besides that, I would not be able to study with Dr. Hofmann unless he would be there at that time.

I do hope I will be able to appear with the Philadelphia Symphony Orchestra, if not with Stokowski, then with Mr. Ormandy or Klemperer.

I fight discouragement and work very hard — in fact harder than ever

Figure 5.6 Continued.

before. I am doing everything to be better and better.
Again let me thank you from the bottom of my heart for everything.
With best regards,
Ever gratefully yours,
Shura Cherkassky

Figure 5.6 Continued.

her grief was inexpressible and that her son had "lost a rare father." On January 30 Shura wrote to Mrs. Bok, saying, "It has been my father's wish that I reach the heights. I shall do all in my power to carry out his wish."

In spite of his personal grief and his mother's shock, Cherkassky's plans for the Town Hall concert and Russian tour proceeded. Prior to leaving for Russia in March Cherkassky played a recital for the Rubinstein Club at the Starlight Roof Garden of the Waldorf Astoria Hotel on January 15; and he gave the Town Hall concert, which was highly acclaimed, on February 9. Performing works by Brahms, Chopin, Liszt, Ravel, Godowsky, and Shostakovich, the pianist thrilled audience and critics alike with his reading of the Liszt *Don Juan Fantasy* and his delivery of the *Brahms-Handel Variations and Fugue* which was specifically applauded by Olin Downes in the *New York Times*, February 10, 1935, for its "sense of form and architecture, feeling that was deep without ostentation, and a Master's grasp of his material." Downes also allowed that in his rendition of the Liszt, Cherkassky re-created the romanticism and virtuous passion with which the music was conceived.

Later in the month Eugene Ormandy responded to Alexander Greiner, Steinway artists representative, who had inquired if there were a possibility of Cherkassky appearing with the Minneapolis Symphony. Greiner received the reply shown in figure 5.9.

During February of 1935 Cherkassky also had the honor of playing at an elaborate sixty-fifth birthday celebration for Leopold Godowsky. Over four hundred people, among them Arturo Toscanini, gathered at the Astor Hotel

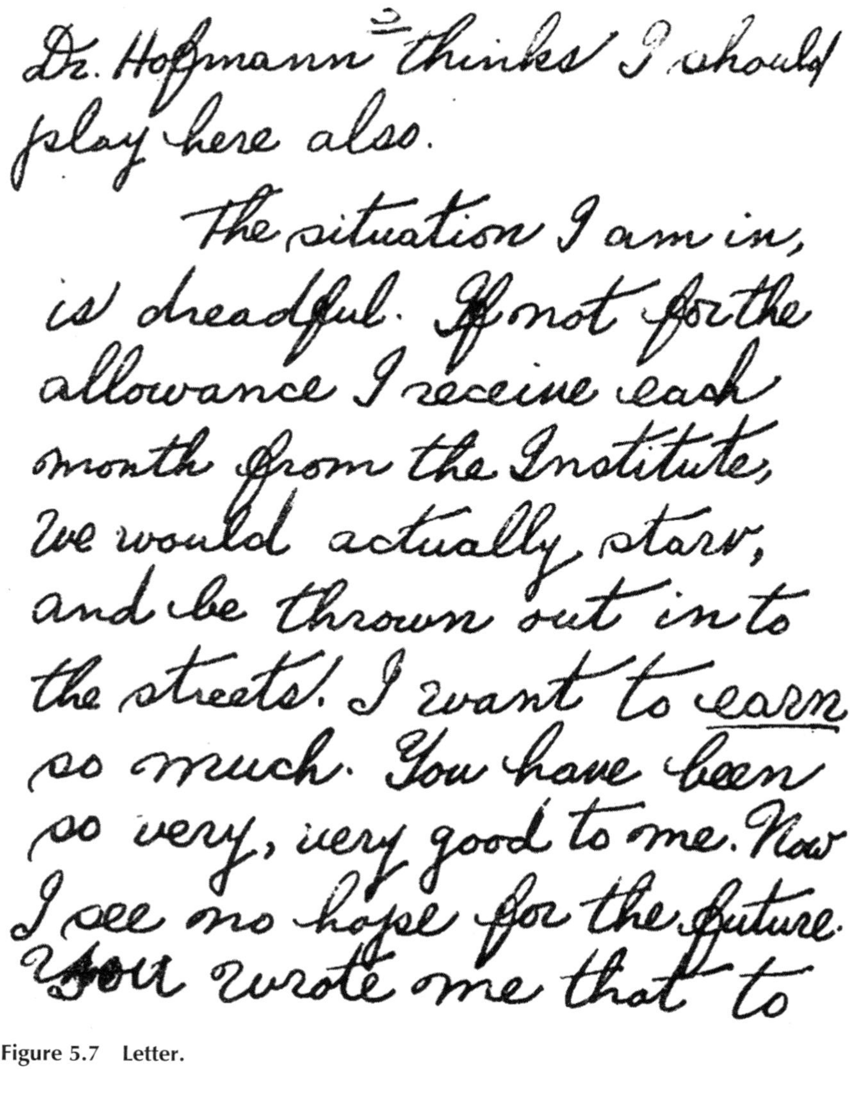

Dr. Hoffmann thinks I should play here also.

The situation I am in, is dreadful. If not for the allowance I receive each month from the Institute, we would actually starve, and be thrown out in to the streets! I want to earn so much. You have been so very, very good to me. Now I see no hope for the future. You wrote me that to

Figure 5.7 Letter.

be discouraged is unproductive. That is perfectly true. But oh! how I fight against being discouraged when I see no light!

Is there no chance at all for me to play with the Philadelphia Orchestra? I know so many modern Concerto, and have just learned Schostakowitoch's (Soviet Composer).

Please forgive me for writing you. I know that you understand. With warmest greetings Ever gratefully yours, Shura Cherkassky

Figure 5.7 Continued.

RICHARD COPLEY

CABLE ADDRESS "RICHCOP" | STEINWAY BUILDING 113 WEST 57TH STREET NEW YORK CITY | CIRCLE 7-0712

MEMORANDUM of contract for a concert to be given by

Shura Cherkassky on Saturday afternoon, February 9

in Town Hall under the management of RICHARD COPLEY, Steinway Building, 113 West 57th Street, New York City, and whereby it is understood and agreed that the following estimated expenses will be paid by the above named artist:

Expenses

Rental of Hall........................	$300.00
Set of Tickets........................	6.75
Ushers and Hall Attachees.............	
Box Office Charge.....................	
Printing Advance Programs.............	30.00
Window Cards..........................	
Posters...............................	3.50
Piano Cartage.........................	20.00
Half-tone Cut for Program.............	5.00
Special Tickets (Passes)...............	5.00
Special Cards.........................	
Special Announcements.................	
Word Books............................	
Accompanist's Fee.....................	
Page Turner...........................	
Stage Equipment and Labor.............	
Newspaper Advertising (English)........	150.00
Newspaper Advertising (Foreign) Jewish..	25.00
Advertising in Program Books	
Carnegie Hall..............	50.00
Town Hall..................	
Distributing Advance Programs..........	5.00
Distributing Three Sheet Posters.......	
Mailing Announcements and Passes.......	30.00
Mailing Special Cards or Notices.......	
Managerial Fee........................	100.00
Other Incidentals.....................	
" " .Addressing, Mailing..	5.00
" "	
Payments are to be made as follows:	$735.25

Artist

Manager

Figure 5.8 Copley budget.

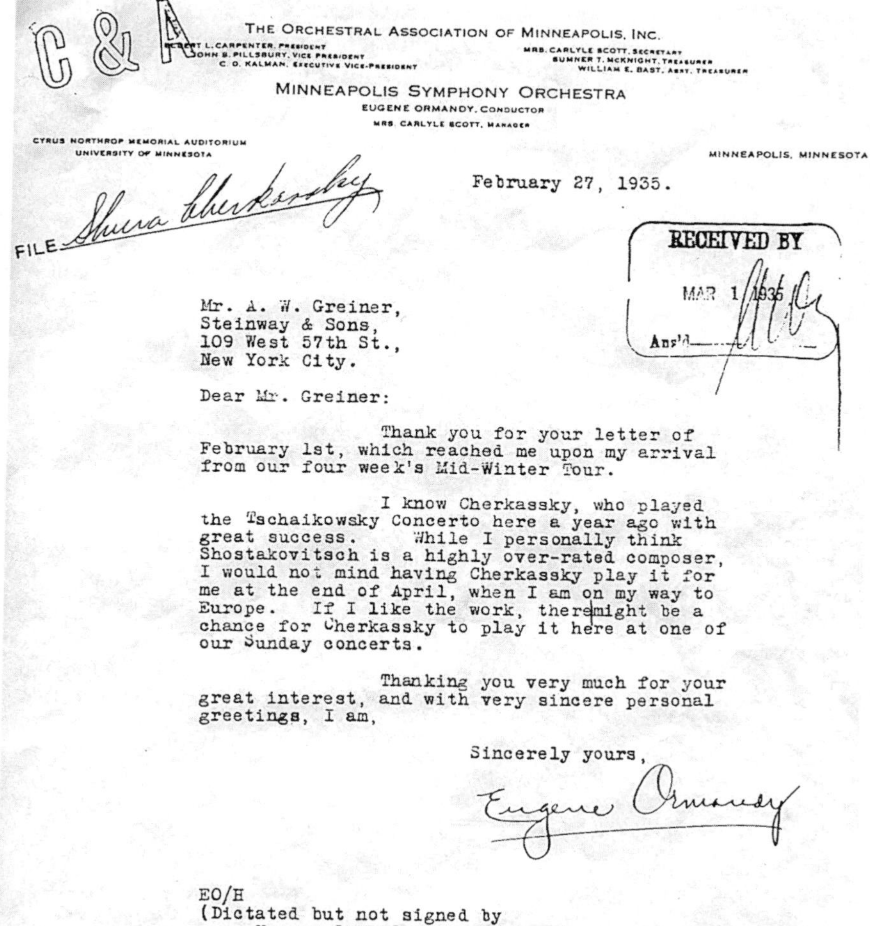

C & A

THE ORCHESTRAL ASSOCIATION OF MINNEAPOLIS, INC.

ROBERT L. CARPENTER, PRESIDENT
JOHN S. PILLSBURY, VICE PRESIDENT
C. O. KALMAN, EXECUTIVE VICE-PRESIDENT

MRS. CARLYLE SCOTT, SECRETARY
SUMNER T. MCKNIGHT, TREASURER
WILLIAM E. BAST, ASST. TREASURER

MINNEAPOLIS SYMPHONY ORCHESTRA
EUGENE ORMANDY, CONDUCTOR
MRS. CARLYLE SCOTT, MANAGER

CYRUS NORTHROP MEMORIAL AUDITORIUM
UNIVERSITY OF MINNESOTA

MINNEAPOLIS, MINNESOTA

FILE Shura Cherkassky

February 27, 1935.

RECEIVED BY
MAR 1 1935
Ans'd

Mr. A. W. Greiner,
Steinway & Sons,
109 West 57th St.,
New York City.

Dear Mr. Greiner:

Thank you for your letter of February 1st, which reached me upon my arrival from our four week's Mid-Winter Tour.

I know Cherkassky, who played the Tschaikowsky Concerto here a year ago with great success. While I personally think Shostakovitsch is a highly over-rated composer, I would not mind having Cherkassky play it for me at the end of April, when I am on my way to Europe. If I like the work, there might be a chance for Cherkassky to play it here at one of our Sunday concerts.

Thanking you very much for your great interest, and with very sincere personal greetings, I am,

Sincerely yours,

Eugene Ormandy

EO/H
(Dictated but not signed by
Eugene Ormandy

Figure 5.9 Letter, February 27, 1935.

on Times Square, then a favored stopping place for visiting artists. (It was at the Astor two years earlier that Toscanini had auditioned a young Vladimir Horowitz prior to their first collaboration, Beethoven's *Emperor* Concerto.) At this tribute to Godowsky, Josef Hofmann's star pupil played the pianist-composer's arrangements of Albéniz's *Tango* and Schubert's *Moment Musical* as well as Godowsky's two *Waltz Poems* for left hand alone which had been given their first performance at the Town Hall recital of February 9.

Now riding a sudden wave of phenomenal American success, and buoyant and self-confident in spite of his financial difficulties, Cherkassky, with his contract from the Russian government, departed from the United States in March of 1935 for a tour that would be remembered as one of the great adventures of his young life.

Notes

1. Gregor Benko and Terry McNeill, "Josef Hofmann and the first years of the Curtis Institute," liner notes, IPA 5007/8.
2. Curtis Institute of Music, archives, MSS 18.
3. *Musical America*, 25 November 1937.
4. Curtis Institute of Music, archives, RG 20.5 Cherkassky, Shura.
5. Curtis Institute of Music, archives, RG 20.5 Cherkassky, Shura.
6. Curtis Institute of Music, archives, RG 20.5 Cherkassky, Shura.
7. *Musical America*, 1967–1968.
8. *Musical America*, 1967–1968.
9. *Musical America*, 1967–1968.
10. Curtis Institute of Music, archives, MSS 18. The document is stamped for France, May 21, 1928; Sidney–New South Wales, June 23, 1928; Melbourne, date illegible; Italian visa issued in Melbourne, November 24, 1928; London, April 10, 1929; Table Bay, South Africa, May 8, 1929; Southampton, September 9, 1929; UK visa for father and son, July 31, 1929, good for one year; and a French visa on May 17, 1930.
11. Curtis Institute of Music, archives, MSS 18.
12. *Dundee Courier*, 28 November 1929.
13. *Verlag* (Berlin), 1932.
14. Curtis Institute of Music, archives, RG 20.5 Cherkassky, Shura.
15. Curtis Institute of Music, archives, RG 20.5 Cherkassky, Shura.
16. Curtis Institute of Music, archives, RG 20.5 Cherkassky, Shura.

CHAPTER SIX

Around the World, 1935–1939

Russia draws me as no other country.

—S. C.

Shura Cherkassky's attraction to Russia, the *Rodina*, his mother country, was with him from birth and never left him until the day he died, in spite of his brush with death as a child in Odessa. "The land where you were born seems to have an unfailing fascination," he explained in a 1935 interview.

> Last summer while I was in Finland, so near to Russia, it was all I could do to keep from dashing across, just for a moment, into Russia. But I had no visa. I patrolled the border so steadily one afternoon, that the Finnish guards at Rajajoki eyed me with suspicion and ordered me to move on. But I didn't—I crept down the bank of the narrow river that marked the boundary between Finland and Russia, and sat there for three hours, staring into the wonderful and mysterious country. Certainly I know now that everything I have and am I owe to America, including the great opportunity to study with Josef Hofmann—but even so, Russia draws me as no other country. I suppose it's because all the stories and associations of my childhood are bound up with it.[1]

When the twenty-five-year-old pianist left the United States in 1935 to fulfill his Russian engagements, he made the first of two important tours between March and December of that year, in which he circled the globe, giving concerts in Russia, Japan, and China, making three transatlantic trips, one transpacific voyage from San Francisco to Yokohama, and a long railroad journey through Siberia from the Chinese border and on to Paris. This rather unconventional route around the world saw him traveling in March to Russia, back to the United States for the month of July, and then across the American continent to the Pacific Coast, where he embarked for Japan. He went by boat to Shanghai and then, his Chinese and Manchurian itinerary completed, he took the Trans-Siberian Express back to Europe where he boarded a ship for America, arriving on December 3, 1935. Recitals during these two tours took place in Moscow, Leningrad, Kharkov, and Odessa in March, and in Tokyo, Osaka, Kyoto, Kobe, and Shanghai the following fall.

The crossing from New York to London, for the start of the Russian tour, made on the SS *Ile de France*, was so rough that his piano practice was reduced to two hours a day, a fact he lamented in a letter to Mary Bok. In spite of his reduced practice time, however, he enjoyed triumph after triumph in his beloved Russia where he was besieged by adoring fans. The following alleged quote from Cherkassky, which appeared in the March 27, 1935, edition of the *Moscow Daily News* (published in English) is worth noting for its propaganda slant:

> I am marvelously situated here [Leningrad] in a Hotel Europe suite of two tremendous rooms—bedchamber, drawing room, and bath, all decorated with French furniture in gold and oil paintings. I have never seen such an imposing hotel apartment anywhere else. . . . I am fascinated with life here; everything is so sincere, vital, forward looking. I spend much time alone but am never bored, for there is so much to see and to learn about this practically new nation with its eager, progressive people, living in and for a great cause based on a profound ideal.
>
> In Moscow, at the Electrocombinat I was told I was playing to ordinary workers who had finished the day shift, but actually, a more cultured, a more warm and enthusiastic audience I have never had. . . . I played a Mendelssohn Scherzo, some Johann Strauss paraphrases and three Fantastic Dances by Shostakovich. . . . After the concert the workers crowded the stage to thank me. It was a most thrilling adventure.[2]

Subsequent to the Moscow appearance he gave a recital in Leningrad on March 29 and two days later played the Tchaikovsky B-flat Minor Concerto with the Leningrad Philharmonic Orchestra. Appearances followed in Kharkov, April 6, and Odessa, April 10, after which he returned to the United States. At this time his years as a formal Hofmann student were coming to an end, and in June of 1935 he received a diploma from the Curtis Institute even though he did not attend the school in the ordinary sense, but traveled from New York City to Philadelphia once a week for lessons during the early years of his study with Hofmann. Student and master then fitted in meetings wherever and whenever possible, something that Cherkassky very much desired, as is evident in his correspondence to Mrs. Bok, where he tells her repeatedly of his supreme admiration for Josef Hofmann and his wish to have the great master listen to his newly prepared programs as much as possible.

Notwithstanding Cherkassky's devotion to Hofmann and his great pride in his Curtis diploma, the Curtis students of Hofmann provide a cautionary tale on the uncertainty of a musical career, even for elite students blessed with influential backing, or the "cream of the cream," in Mary Bok's phrase. Although he had a thriving career in Europe, Shura Cherkassky made a precarious career in America that did not blossom fully until fifty years later. Abram Chasins, to take another of Hofmann's Curtis students, made a start as a pianist and a composer but his real impact was in classical music radio and as a respected and influential critic. Walter Susskind enjoyed a major career, but as a conductor. Erza Rachlin also enjoyed a meaningful career as a conductor rather than a pianist. Harry Kaufman was an admired teacher and accompanist at Curtis. Ellen Ballon, Hans Ebell, Isadore Freed, and Teresita Tagliapietra, the daughter of pianist Teresa Carreno, at least earned mention in *A Dictionary of Pianists*. So too did Angelica Morales who went on to study with Emil von Sauer whom she subsequently married. She played a sensational New York debut in the 1950s, made a very brief career, and then spent her last thirty years teaching in Kansas. Joseph Levine, who Hofmann predicted in 1926 would not have a career as a concert pianist, became the then youngest member to be engaged on the Curtis faculty, served as pianist for the Philadelphia orchestra, accompanist to Joseph Szigeti, director of the Chamber Orchestra and Chamber Opera of Philadelphia, and eventually conductor of the Omaha Symphony. William Harms, whose Gatsby good looks and social polish made him so different from his friend Shura Cherkassky, spent his adult life teaching at Manhattanville College in New York (after a successful debut, and teaching at the Curtis), giving an occasional concert, living reclusively, recording sparsely, and maintaining an air of mystery regarding his years of study with Hofmann. Hofmann's remaining students simply receded from public view, with the exception of Nadia Reisenberg, who played well-received concerts during the 1920s and 1930s before concentrating on teaching and chamber-music playing, starting in the 1940s. In all fairness it should be noted that these young talents started their careers in the depths of the Depression, and they also faced a double problem at that most vulnerable moment of passage from youth to maturity: they first lost much of their backing in 1938 when Hofmann left the Curtis Institute and everything associated with him lost much of its luster; and then there was the war, which even Cherkassky's career barely survived.

For whatever reason, it was the next wave of Curtis students who made significant careers. But Abbey Simon, Jorge Bolet, and Sidney Foster were students not of Hofmann but of David Saperton to whom Shura Cherkassky gave so much credit for his technical accomplishments. Right behind these came Gary Graffman, Eugene Istomin, and the most celebrated of all Curtis graduates, Leonard Bernstein, each of whom was terrorized but very well taught by Isabelle Vengerova. Of all Hofmann's supremely gifted students, Cherkassky alone forged a significant performing career as a pianist. This would hardly have been a surprise to Josef Hofmann who, in 1955 two years before his death, when asked by his son Anton if any one of his students stood out above all the others, replied, "Without a doubt, Shura Cherkassky."

On June 29 Cherkassky the 1935 Curtis graduate wrote Mrs. Bok from Vyborg, Finland, where he was with his mother visiting his aunts, an experience he described as very dull. He told her how he prized his diploma and carried it with him everywhere. Looking ahead with great anticipation to his first tour of Japan, he wrote, "How I wish I could play all my programs and concertos for Dr. Hofmann. I would love to work with him before leaving for the East." At the time he was busy preparing eight concertos and four different programs for the tour and repeatedly exclaimed, "Oh, it is a wonderful feeling to work." His wish to study with Hofmann again came true when Mrs. Bok extended an invitation to him and his mother to join her in Rockport, Maine, the site of the Bok's summer residence, and stay in the barn studio where there was a bedroom for Mrs. Cherkassky, a large music room with a couch where Shura could sleep, and a bath and kitchen. Since meals would be provided, it was decided Cherkassky's monthly stipend would be slightly reduced. After a productive summer with Hofmann, he sailed in September aboard the *Chichibu Maru* and on September 6 wrote to Mrs. Bok, describing his happiness (see fig. 6.1).

The Japan tour, which had been sponsored by Mrs. Bok at a cost of $875.29, was yet another triumph in which newspaper accounts spoke of him as fulfilling the hopes and expectations of audiences composed of the most discriminating music lovers. Nine concerts in Japan won him ovations in every city where he played, and his programs were hailed for their substance and variety. In Tokyo he played four completely different recital programs in Hibiya Hall during one eight-day span. Among the thirty-seven works on the programs were the Bach-Liszt Organ Fantasy and Fugue in G Minor; the Bach-Busoni *Chaconne*; Beethoven's *Appassionata*; the *Brahms-Handel Variations*; Chopin's *Fantasy in F Minor*, B-flat Minor Sonata, a scherzo, ballade,

ON BOARD

Chichibu MARU

September 6 1935

Dear Mrs. Bok,

I have been on this boat eight days and have still five more days before reaching Yokohama. It is terribly exiting to be on a Japanese boat, I am glad of it because I can get used to the ways of the Japanese before reaching Japan.

I have a great admiration for the Japanese. They are a clean races very intelligent, extremely polite

Figure 6.1 Letter, September 6, 1935.

and always willing to learn
That's why they play such
an important part now
in this world.
Mr. Greiner of the
Steinways has arranged
through his San Francisco
agents to put an upright
piano in my cabin, so
I practise regularly and
doing my very best to
grasp everything Dr.
Hofmann told me in
Maine .. it is marvelous!
I hope you are
enjoying your European
trip.
I am so thrilled
about my coming tour.

Figure 6.1 Continued.

My first apperance is
on the twenty-third of
this month in Tokyo.
With very best
greetings, I am,
Ever devotely yours,
Shura.

c/o A. Strok
5, Enokizaka
Okasaka-Ku
Tokyo, Japan

It is so funny—today is Friday
the 6th, tomorrow is Sunday
the 8th. We lose a day.

Figure 6.1 Continued.

and various etudes; Liszt's Sonata in B Minor and *Don Juan Fantasy*; Schumann's *Carnaval*; Balakirev's *Islamey*; and various smaller works. Reviews recount him as surmounting every difficulty, technical and artistic, with the greatest ease, and further describe him as a thorough musician and a poised and brilliant pianist who possessed a phenomenal technique that was at all times under perfect control. Following a performance in Tokyo he was visited by the usual throngs of avid fans, among them Prince Kumi, who politely asked him for an autograph.

Continuing from Japan to Shanghai, Cherkassky performed a recital that resulted in the following account in the *Shanghai Times* of October 22, 1935:

> Known to New York as "The Little Hofmann," Mr. Shura Cherkassky, who made his first appearance before the Shanghai public last evening at the Lyceum Theater, is indisputably one of the finest pianists it has been our pleasure to entertain for many years. With his hands running across the keyboard like lightning, and with his heart in his fingertips, he kept his audience last evening spellbound for 2 1/2 hours. His rendering of the Liszt B Minor Sonata, with all its splendor and fire, was exceedingly brilliant, while his performance of Chopin proved his ability to play with exquisite delicacy of touch and beautiful fluency.

Regarding his Russia and Asia tours, Cherkassky gave this colorful description, which was published in the *Musical Courier* of January 18, 1936:

> The entire period of the tour—or rather, two tours—has been of the most absorbing interest. I had the valuable and gratifying experience of playing before numerous audiences in a far-flung itinerary, and also enjoyed the excitement of travel.
>
> I left New York on March 2 to go to Russia. There I gave a concert with orchestra in Leningrad, playing the Tchaikovsky Concerto. I cannot tell you how happy the reception of the audience made me. There were so many recalls that finally they had to carry the piano off the stage so that the program could go on. I gave two recitals in Moscow, and played at an electric factory there, making a joint appearance with Mme. Barsova, a fine coloratura soprano.
>
> *Impressions of Moscow:* Moscow is a marvelous city, an impressive example of Soviet accomplishment. The subway is like a marble palace, and of course this is only one of the outstanding civic achievements. I attended concerts, dramas, ballets and other entertainments while I was there, and the artistic standard is of the highest. When I re-visited Moscow for a few hours following my Oriental tour I was amazed to observe how much it had improved and to notice the new buildings gone up in only a few months' time.
>
> Kharkov also was on my list, and I presented two recitals in Odessa. The latter is my native city, where I lived until I was eleven years old. I saw again many places

that I remembered, and I was surrounded with old friends. My concert was so crowded that the city ordered police stationed outside the auditorium.

When I had finished my concerts in Russia, I found that I had earned quite a nice collection of rubles, and as I could not take it out of the country, I thought that a very rewarding way of spending it would be in traveling over the Soviet Union, so I visited Crimea and the principal parts of European Russia. I was in Finland when I received a cable saying that I was engaged for a tour of China and Japan.

Coming back to America, I spent July in Maine. I came to America especially to play over my repertoire with my teacher, Josef Hofmann, whom I worship as a musical Olympian.

Sails for Flowery Empire: In August, I took the train for San Francisco, and from there a Japanese boat to Yokohama via Honolulu. Arrived in Japan, one of the most beautiful and fascinating countries in the world, I gave four concerts in Tokyo, and before leaving there broadcast a program that was heard throughout Japan and Manchuria. Other concerts were in Osaka, Kyoto and Kobe, and I took some side-trips, for the opportunities for sightseeing would tempt any traveler. Nikko for instance, one simply must not miss—this city of Old Japan, full of temples and set in mountains. I felt an earthquake in Tokyo, which they tell me you must experience in order to feel really at home there. Also, as shown in the picture which accompanies this interview I was "taken for a ride" by a bevy of Geisha girls. I heard several of them sing. Almost all of their songs are minor in melody, quaint and strange to the western ear.

Visitors to Japan find that the Japanese are intensely interested in occidental music, and are trying to match the accomplishments of Europe in this direction.

In China and Manchuria: I went to Shanghai by water, through Nagasaki. In Shanghai I played several times for audiences which consisted mostly of Russians, this city having a large population of White Russians. I went on through Tsingtao to Dairen—the roughest trip on the Yellow Sea, which I shall never forget and then to Harbing. In this last city, I happened to look for my position on a globe and discovered that I was directly opposite New York. I reasoned that since I was half way around the world from the point I wished to return to, I might as well take the journey back across Siberia, Europe and the Atlantic as in the other direction.

Accordingly, I was soon on the train, going through Manchuria on the way north. We had one serious bandit scare, which impressed on me the fact that this is one of the most lawless, and dangerous places in the world just now. We had positive word that bandits intended to derail the train, but our officials were warned in time. However, as we passengers sat in the dining car, some of the trainmen came through in charge of a far-from-handsome stranger who, we learned, was one of those who had plotted against us.

It took eleven days to travel from Harbing to Paris, changing twice. Scenically, Siberia is rather dreary, but I enjoyed the journey because I was seeing a new part

> of the world. Also, there were interesting people making the trip on the same train, among them Kathleen Norris, the American novelist, and her cat, quite an important member of the party.
>
> Finally, we came to Paris, and while I was there I encountered Mr. Hofmann again, and was fortunate enough to hear him play. I thought his performance surpassing anything I had ever heard.
>
> *Experiences with a Dummy Keyboard:* On the trans-Siberian express I practiced constantly on my dummy piano of four octaves. This is a useful little contrivance, not only musically but also socially. Let the lonely traveler, if he wished to become the cynosure of all eyes, just take a soundless keyboard from his suitcase and begin to give a pantomime performance. Probably at first the spectators think he is crazy, and they may be rather disappointed at finding him an ordinary, rational individual when they talk to him. A fellow passenger saw me practicing on the train, and was amazed when I began to talk, for he thought I was deaf and dumb. However, all in all, the dummy piano will make its owner a lot of friends on the journey. At least, that has been my experience.[3]

Shura Cherkassky's fascination with travel stayed with him throughout his life, taking him to virtually every corner of the globe. He agreed wholeheartedly with Augustine of Hippo (AD 354–430) who wrote, "The world is a book, and those who do not travel read only a page." Although his concert tours led him repeatedly to every continent, his vacations were meticulously planned to include those places of interest, such as Siberia, Madagascar, Phuket, and the North Pole, that his professional travels had missed.

Following his Asian tour, Cherkassky returned to America where Mary Bok and Richard Copley decided the best way to capitalize on the pianist's success abroad would be to schedule a Town Hall recital for February 9, 1936. On November 1, 1935, Mrs. Bok approved expenses for the recital in the amount of $716.39, telling Mr. Copley that she hoped and expected there would be a smaller deficit than the one for $540.00 following the concert at the same hall the previous February. Copley and Bok conferred frequently concerning possibilities for Cherkassky's career and his endless financial difficulties. Correspondence between the two, in November of 1935, has the following figures penciled in with the title "Student Aid": August, $875.29 and $465.60; October, $360.15; and November, $100.00, for a total of $1801.04. The monies cited were in addition to the usual monthly stipend.

Other than travel expenses, there is no indication just how the generosity that Cherkassky and his parents experienced, thanks to Mary Louise Curtis Bok, was expended. No matter how much she provided it was never enough, and at the beginning of January of 1936 Lydia Cherkassky applied for a loan from the Morris Plan Industrial Bank of New York at 33 West Forty-second Street and received a letter, dated January 13, stating that the credit committee did not view her application with favor. The denial resulted in a letter from Shura to Mrs. Bok on January 14, 1936, erroneously dated 1935.

> It is with a very heavy heart that I write to you this. *Please* forgive me for worrying you. After I came back from my tour last month I found out that I have no engagements at all until February, so at once I asked Mr. Copley to try his best to get me some kind of engagements quickly and he was unsuccessful in getting them. I tried every way possible to earn but couldn't find anything, so mother and I applied to the Morris Plan Industrial Bank. It is a special bank that makes loans, and we have just received this letter I am enclosing to you with a refusal. Tomorrow we have to pay the rent and we have exactly nine dollars to our name. I am just desperate and don't know *what* to do. Last year I had few engagements and now until February, nothing at all. I hate to ask you to help us, but *what* can I do? Dear Mrs. Bok, you have done so much and it will be my greatest happiness when some day I will be in a position to repay you. So I am asking with a very heavy heart to help us. I cannot approach any of my friends here in New York. I am so worried and upset and my mother is desperate. Please, please forgive me, but there is nothing at all that I can do at present but turn to you.
>
> With gratefulness always and ever devoted, Shura
>
> When I see Dr. Hofmann I will ask him to give me some kind of a steady way of earning.[4]

While few in number, there were various engagements on Cherkassky's agenda for the first nine months of 1936. On the evening of January 27, 1936, the pianist appeared as soloist with the National Orchestral Association under Leon Barzin in Carnegie Hall, and the following week on February 9 he gave the scheduled recital in New York City's Town Hall. Later in the season he played for the Music Club of St. Paul, Minnesota, for a fee of $250, and also performed in Granville, Ohio; Baltimore, Maryland; Red Bank, New Jersey; Miami, Florida; and Brooklyn, New York. On April 28 he appeared as guest artist with Mildred Dilling, harpist, at the embassy of the USSR in Washington, D.C., going on to summer in Rockport, Maine, before leaving in September for what was supposed to be a three-month concert tour of Europe, where he opened in London and continued with appearances in Manchester, Amsterdam, Paris, Vienna, Warsaw, Stockholm, and other major European cities. It was subsequently reported that Cherkassky's stay on the continent had lengthened indefinitely as he added engagements and reengagements. His European manager at the time, thanks to Hofmann's intercession, was the highly regarded Wilfred Van Wyck, Hofmann's European manager. While sailing to Europe on board the SS *Washington* for this tour, Shura wrote Mary Bok, saying,

> I suppose you know about the financial arrangements made for me before I left. It is very hard to travel counting every penny, especially when one cannot foresee different expenses on route. I have already spent more than was on the list not through my *mismanagement* [underlined in the original] but all kinds of things come up like tips and lots of unexpected things. I wish I could just put my mind on the work and not worry about pennies![5]

From Warsaw, Poland, on January 2, 1937, the pianist sent his patron a letter telling her of his great happiness at his success, his humiliation at his financial situation, and his curiosity as to what Josef Hofmann will think of his playing, which had now developed a certain freedom through the experience of playing for so many different audiences (see fig. 6.2).[6]

The winter months of 1937 continued with numerous engagements. Scheduled for the post-coronation season, Cherkassky's planned June 22, 1937, performance with the London Symphony Orchestra in Queens Hall under the direction of Artur Rodzinski was cancelled due to labor troubles, but all his other appearances went as planned. The puzzle of Shura Cherkassky's financial life deepens at the time of these highly successful years in Europe when he was playing numerous dates to critical acclaim. Copious correspondence between the pianist and Mrs. Bok continued during his years abroad, and the message was always the same: while he is having great success, he has no money and due to expenses he needs her help. On a letter of Cherkassky's from Paris dated July 26, 1937, Bok's secretary Elsie Hutt noted, "always the same story, no money." But occasionally there was positive news, as in December of 1937 while Cherkassky was living in Paris at 19 Rue Faraday, when he wrote of his joy at having a small concert to play on January 6, 1938, in honor of Hofmann's jubilee. By June of 1938, however, his patron was having her own financial problems, and in response to requests for more money she wrote, "We have in past years shared our good fortune with you and I am sorry that we must now ask you to share our present difficulties." She referred here and later to the danger that the Curtis Institute might have to close and told him his $100 per month stipend might end. He replied, "My situation is desperate. *Please* keep up the $100 a month."

When he learned in February of 1939 that his subsidy would definitely

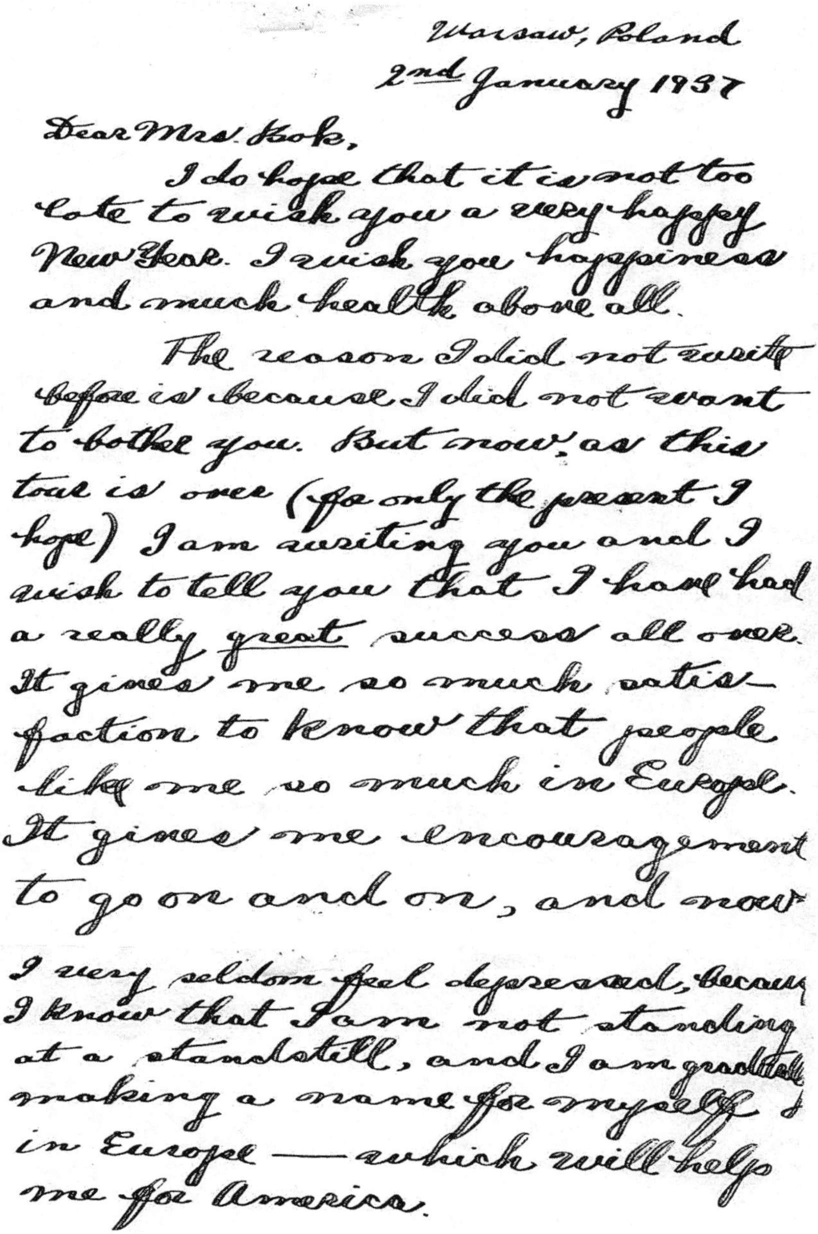

Warsaw, Poland
2nd January 1937

Dear Mrs. Kok,

I do hope that it is not too late to wish you a very happy New Year. I wish you happiness and much health above all.

The reason I did not write before is because I did not want to bother you. But now, as this tour is over (for only the present I hope) I am writing you and I wish to tell you that I have had a really <u>great</u> success all over. It gives me so much satisfaction to know that people like me so much in Europe. It gives me encouragement to go on and on, and now I very seldom feel depressed, because I know that I am not standing at a standstill, and I am gradually making a name for myself in Europe — which will help me for America.

Figure 6.2 Letter, January 2, 1937.

I hope that when I come back next season, I will have a tour, of course the most important thing is to find the right, energetic manager. It would be awful to come back to America and do nothing.

It has been extremely difficult to travel on the money I have had. I am sure that you know the conditions, so I will not bother you. It was quite humiliating to arrive in a strange city without a penny in

my pocket and wait until the local managers provide me with some money. Sometimes they are not even aware of it, as the letter from Mr. Van Wyck came too late.

My last concert now is taking place on the 5th in Kraków, and I shall leave afterwards for London. I am

Figure 6.2 Continued.

afraid that on \$150 a month it would be difficult to live in London, unless I make something besides. In Paris, mother and I could live far better on this amount due to the recent devaluation of the franc. I have written to Dr. Hoffmann explaining that Paris would be cheaper to live in. Of course, if I would have <u>work</u> to do in England—it's different, but otherwise Paris would be cheaper, and if I am staying away from America, I might just as well get the benefit of learning French.

I am enclosing here some critisisms. As you will see, they are wonderful, and they would be marvellous to advertise.

Mother is in Finland now, and will join me in London shortly. I haven't seen her almost three months.

Figure 6.2 Continued.

Europe is fascinating, and I am sure that the plan of staying away from America for awhile would be very beneficial. I am most anxious to know what Dr. Hoffmann will think of my playing now. I think that I have developed a certain freedom in my playing having played so often for different audiences – it's a wonderful experience! I can not tell you how grateful I am to have this chance. I know that I am lucky. Yes, and I want to get further and further.

I believe I have written enough and will not take any more of your time.

I forgot to say that I have had sensational success last Sunday here playing with the

Figure 6.2 Continued.

Warsaw Philharmonic Tschaikowsky
and Shostakovich Concertos.
Again wishing you the
very best of everything for 1937!
Most affectionately
Shura.

When I will see you I will tell you
some terribly funny experiences
I have had while travelling. I
know you will be amused!

c/o Wilfrid Van Wyck, Esq.
170, Piccadilly
London, W. 1, England

Please forgive this mess!

Figure 6.2 Continued.

end in May, Cherkassky wrote to Mrs. Bok from Helsinki, "I am *terrified* of actual *starvation*." (The words *terrified* and *starvation* are double underlined in the original.) He added that he was playing in Scandinavia, "almost every town," and he also named Denmark, Holland, Belgium, and Switzerland, but went on to say that because of "political and racial issues," other countries are closed to him. From Paris on April 11, 1939, he wrote that he had no work at all until the end of October in Norway and no money as well. Further, he could "save practically nothing after paying terrific travel expenses and managers' fees." Bok then decided to extend his subsidy through the summer, and he informed her he had moved in with a Russian family, renting two rooms "one of them very dark," at a cheaper rate than his old place on the Rue Faraday. He cited his new rooms as being at a "very good address," Rue Kléber near the Etoile, and hinted that he needed more money to rent a piano, which she refused to send in a letter dated May 10, 1939. On August 7 he mentioned to Mrs. Bok a small lot on Long Island that his father had bought in 1923 or 1924 for one or two thousand dollars and asked her to sell it for him so that he could pay his debts. He also referred to the fact that he could "now play eighteen concertos on a few weeks notice." Following this letter, Mary Bok engaged the services of an agent who investigated the possible sale of the land in question and who subsequently reported that it was worth only four hundred dollars, perhaps less. On August 23 Josef Hofmann interceded on his student's behalf, urging Mary Bok to help Shura, and Shura wrote Bok on August 30 telling her he was vacationing at a pension in Beaulieu at the cost of $1.05 a day, including full board, and he complained he had only seven concerts in Scandinavia. Two days following this letter, the world situation exploded.

Notes

1. *NBC News Service*, 1935.
2. *Moscow Daily News*, 27 March 1935.
3. "Colorful experiences in the Far East marked pianist's concert itinerary" from *Musical Courier*, January 18, 1936. Copyright 1936 Summy-Birchard Music, a division of Summy Birchard, Inc. All rights reserved. Used by Permission of Warner Brothers Publications U.S. Inc.
4. Curtis Institute of Music, archives, RG 20.5 Cherkassky, Shura.
5. Curtis Institute of Music, archives, RG 20.5 Cherkassky, Shura.
6. Curtis Institute of Music, archives, RG 20.5 Cherkassky, Shura.

CHAPTER SEVEN

~

Shattered, 1940–1945

> In its dazzling perfection, its purifying seriousness, and its intellectual richness, the playing of this young man is not a performance of the keyboard, but a sermon in tones.
>
> —*Nya Dagligt Allehanda*, November 23, 1939

The euphoria that had marked Shura Cherkassky's pianistic success in Europe from 1935 forward ended when the Nazis invaded Poland on September 1, 1939, while he was vacationing in southern France. Just the week before Josef Hofmann had written to Mrs. Bok expressing his deep concern for Shura and his mother (see fig. 7.1).[1]

In response to Hofmann's plea, on September 2 Mrs. Bok cabled the Cherkasskys one thousand dollars for their passage back to America and on September 19 wrote Josef Hofmann saying she had heard nothing further from Shura since sending the money. In an effort to quell any fear she added that in a previous letter he had told her immediate passage was not possible and that they would sail as soon as they could, so she presumed "he will soon turn up." She also informed Hofmann that a bit earlier Shura had sent a raft of papers regarding the property in Long Island, which he hoped Mrs. Bok would purchase. Finally, she received a reply from Shura, written on September 27, 1939, from Stockholm, apologizing for his delay in responding. After telling her he would have "absolutely been without a cent" had she not cabled the one thousand dollars, which was not received until September 18, he explained that the consul in Nice had advised him to go to Bordeaux. His mother had then joined him in Bordeaux, where many thousands of Americans from all over Europe were also waiting for transportation home, and they registered with a steamship company for passage to America. In Bor-

October is nearing and I wonder
what is going to happen to Shura!
It is entirely out of the question that
– in spite of his artistic success – he
will be able to support his Mother
and himself without some help from
you or the Institute. I have written
to Coppicus of the Metrop. Mus. Bureau
a month ago but the answer was that
it was too late to plan anything for
the coming season. They promised,
however, to consider my request for
1940–41. What shall happen to
Shura and his Mother in between?
I am worried! Would it not be
possible to let him have say $50.00
a month which, in addition to what-
-ever he may earn abroad, – if there
is no war – would save them from

Figure 7.1 Handwritten letter, August 23, 1939.

deaux the American consul wired Sweden to find out whether the engagements that had been booked in Scandinavia would take place, and to Cherkassky's surprise, he was told the engagements had not been cancelled and that he must fulfill them. The Swedish consul in Bordeaux therefore issued them false visas for travel to Stockholm, for which mother and son paid forty francs each. They then traveled to Stockholm via Paris, changing five times en route for Amsterdam, from which they took a Swedish plane for Malmö, where upon their arrival they came close to being deported back to Amsterdam by the Swedish authorities for traveling with false documents. They were informed that the consul in Bordeaux would be punished for

starvation? It would be a shame if
such a great pianistic talent should
deteriorate and all that you and
your Institute has done for him, in the past, (3
come to naught. If he could obtain the help for
say a year amounting to $600.00 in all, I feel
that sufficient time would be gained to arrange
for an American tour with the Metrop. Mus. Bureau
Please let me know at your earliest convenience
if there is hope to help the poor fellow. —
Here all's well. Edward is doing finely. Peter
talks incessantly. A very amusing little chap.
Mrs. Short gained 5 lbs. I lost six. Weather
is perfect, cool in spite of daily sunshine.
Have started to practice. Have a brand
new A Style piano with J. H. action. It is
a peach. Voila tout. Kindest greetings
and best wishes from
faithfully yours, Josef

Figure 7.1 Continued.

accepting money for his charitable work, but Cherkassky would be allowed to stay for the duration of his concert tour thanks to the intervention of the Swedish concert manager, Mr. Enwall of Konsertbologet. Cherkassky described the amount of money spent to reach Sweden as "colossal," amounting to over three hundred dollars, due to the fact all transportation had gone up 20 percent, the plane fare from Amsterdam to Malmö had increased 50 percent because of a war tax, and their excess baggage cost nearly as much as the plane ticket. In spite of all these difficulties, he and his mother settled in relative peace in a pension in Stockholm where Steinway gave him a parlor grand on which to practice at no charge, and he promised Mrs. Bok he would pay for all their expenses from the money he was earning in Sweden. In his letter he also asked for reassurance that he had done the right thing in honoring his Scandinavian engagements instead of returning to America where he would "just sit doing nothing. It would be terrible to come back and not play. Dr. Hofmann wrote that he is trying to arrange a tour for me. . . . Please see what could be done!"

On October 17 Shura sent another letter giving his reasons for not wanting to return to America, in spite of the conditions in Europe:

"I have hardly any engagements at all. I cannot be so humiliated anymore and suffer seeing that many mediocre artists have so much work." The postscript to this letter reads: "I love America and am proud to be an American, but why can't I have real work in my own country?"

In response, Mrs. Bok wrote she could see no reason why he should not have gone there to keep his engagements. "Almost everything is a gamble now, and no one can be wise. One can only do the best one can." She also informed him that Dr. Hofmann had been ill, had to cancel all his concerts up to January of 1940, and was currently recuperating on Balboa Island off the California coast. She assured Shura of Hofmann's continuing interest in his career, stated that he had moved to the Metropolitan Music Bureau, and that he had spoken to his new managers about taking on Shura. In fact, Hofmann had written a lengthy letter to Mr. Schang of the Metropolitan Music Bureau (see fig. 7.2).[2]

Mr. Coppicus, Schang's partner, responded on November 30 to Hofmann's plea, saying he "would take special pains to investigate what could be done for this artist next season," and adding that the most practical means of finding out if Cherkassky would be able to duplicate his European successes in America would be for him to give a New York recital the following January or February. Hofmann then telegrammed Shura in Stockholm and informed him that it was impossible to arrange concerts for the current season but that he was "trying hard to influence Metropolitan Music Bureau to engage you for season forty-forty one." Communications between Shura and Mrs. Bok continued throughout November, always with requests for money, and on December 11, 1939, Bok wrote to Hofmann, "I am more or less besieged with letters like this from Shura." In return, Hofmann wrote Mary Bok on December 13 that he had been trying to help Shura since the end of June, and he asked, "Do you think the C.I. [Curtis Institute] could 'swing' a New York recital for Shura?"

While Hofmann and Bok worked on his behalf in America, the now thirty-year-old pianist, in spite of the difficulties of traveling in wartime Europe, honored his engagements in Scandinavia. And the staggering criti-

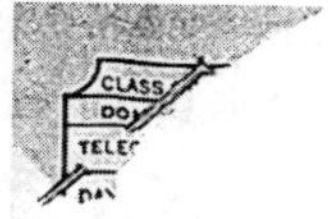

COPY FOR MRS. BOK

Asbury Apartment Hotel
2505 West 6th Street
Los Angeles, California

November 18th, 1939

F. C. Schang
c/o Metropolitan Musical Bureau
113 West 57th Street
New York City, New York

My dear Mr. Schang:

First of all let me thank you most heartily for your willingness and efficient help in rearranging my concert tour which was necessitated by my illness. I am glad to inform you that I feel very much better, and that by the end of this rather unlucky year I hope to be quite fit to resume my artistic duties.

Now another matter. From the enclosed data you will gather that Cherkassky has been doing extremely well abroad. If he is in demand over there, why should he not succeed over here? All he requires is a good start, and a manager who has faith in his future. Your organization is a powerful one and if you and Mr. Coppicus would find it possible in helping Shura to get a start, even on a very modest scale to begin with, I am convinced that he would make good.

I haven't my files in Los Angeles with me but I recall having written to Mr. Coppicus about Schura when you were on your vacation in the summer; an in his gracious reply, Mr. Coppicus requested a list of Schura's European engagements expecially his appearances with orchestras, but by the time I secured this information, I was in the hospital.

1 of June (1939)

I have at Newport Beach quite extraordinary criticisms of Shura's (in various languages) but I think the enclosed list of his engagements and re-engagements will speak for itself.

I think it quite extraordinary that in these precarious times in Europe that Shura was recalled to Scandinavia for concerts.

I might add that he has, without exception, the largest repertoire of <u>any</u> pianist - he actually <u>eats</u> up music - and remembers it infallibly.

Please be so good as to let me know if there is a chance. Kindest greetings to you and Mr. Coppicus.

Most sincerely yours,

Josef Hofmann

Encls:

Figure 7.2 Letter, November 18, 1939.

cal acclaim of the four-year European tour begun in 1935 continued in spite of the blitzkrieg. Numerous orchestral and recital appearances took place in Norway, Sweden, and Denmark where he gave as many as four concerts a week with overwhelming success. Rameau, Scarlatti, Bach, Beethoven, Mendelssohn, Chopin, Liszt, Schumann, Scriabin, and Shostakovitch were the favored composers on Cherkassky's 1939 programs. Ovations greeted both his virtuosity and the new insights into the piano repertoire he gave his audiences. Cold routine did not figure in his performances, inspiring critics to write he left his audiences wanting for nothing. Reviews from this era of Cherkassky's career are so consistent in their admiration that they dispel any thought that what was printed in the press kits was the figment of a publicist's imagination or the manipulation of a skilled marketing director. Indeed, contemporary critical sources show a singular similarity of opinion in regard to Cherkassky's playing. Twelve criticisms of considerable length and detail, written between October 29 and November 29, 1939, by twelve critics for twelve newspapers in Norway, Sweden, and Denmark, three countries on the verge of war, were consistent raves. Consider just one from the Oslo *Morgenbladet–Stener Kolstad* of November 1, 1939.

> When an artist like Shura Cherkassky sits at the piano, all one's old conceptions of piano playing are turned upside down. Without doubt, he stands today in an exceptional position among the great pianists of the present, both when technical mastery of the instrument and spiritual grasp of the music he interprets are considered. There is a sincerity in his playing which breaks all conventional barriers and ties. He lives his music so intensely, sets it forth so richly, that it is no longer piano technique in the usual sense we are faced with but prophecy, poetry, instantaneous improvisations of all human feeling and passion. As marvelously subjective as Cherkassky is, he never encroaches on the honor of the composer; he is respectful to and presents cleanly the music he interprets, but with his flaming temperament and enormous knowledge of the possibilities of the pianoforte he makes the work greater and deeper and more glorious than we have known them to be before. With Cherkassky, virtuosity is driven up to its highest border; no difficulties exist for him. His technical mastery serves the most artistic intention. Bach's Passacaglia, which opened the program, resounded as from outside the large room, eternal and mighty, and rose like a column, borne by the beautiful theme which sings through the work in a constantly new illumination. And Cherkassky made Liszt's B minor sonata—other pianists' parade number—an event; it became a play of life and death, where demons raged and gleams of genius lit up the dark like flashes of lightning. It was the outstanding adventure of the evening and possibly the one which showed best the span of Cherkassky's mastery. The Aula was sold out to the last seat and the enthusiasm was great.

Of this period in his life Cherkassky recounted, "I even gave two recitals in Riga in December of 1939 but my last concerts were in Oslo on April 2 and 5 of 1940, and I know now that had the ship been scheduled to sail one day later I should have been stuck in Scandinavia."[3] Cherkassky sailed on the Norwegian-American liner *Bergensfjord* on April 6, just ahead of the Nazi invasion (and received a vote of thanks from the passengers and ship's officers for the concert he played on board for the benefit of the war orphans in Scandinavia). In fact, a German task force weighed anchor on April 7 while the British were preparing to mine the entrance to Narvik harbor. Scattered naval encounters then took place on April 8 indicating a major German operation, but reconnaissance by the British was hindered by bad weather. Early on April 9, German war ships put small army units ashore at Oslo, Kristiansand, Bergen, Trondheim, and Narvik, and airborne troops seized Sola airport and Stavanger. Meanwhile, Denmark was swiftly overrun, to give the *Luftwaffe* advance bases to support the Norwegian operation. Cherkassky described his European career as "shattered" by the events of 1939 and 1940, which forced him to return to the United States where he would have to wait until October 16, 1940, before setting foot onstage again. In spite of the enthusiastic reviews that crossed the Atlantic with him, the bleakest years in the life and career of Shura Cherkassky were about to begin. The only bright light in his life at this time was Josef Hofmann. Although Hofmann had left the Curtis Institute in 1938, he maintained communications with Mary Bok and remained a much concerned supporter of Shura Cherkassky, whom he advocated tirelessly over the years. In April of 1940 Hofmann wrote to extol the genius of the young artist to numerous conductors, one of whom was John Barbirolli, then conductor of the New York Philharmonic–Symphony Orchestra (see fig. 7.3).[4]

The same month, Mary Bok contacted Mr. Coppicus of the Metropolitan Music Bureau (one of the five artist-management organizations that merged in 1930 to form Columbia Concerts), concerning a recital in Town Hall, which at Hofmann's urging had been moved to Carnegie Hall. Bok asked Coppicus to "save the date [Town Hall] for another brilliant young Curtis pianist, Jorge Bolet."

In April of 1940 Shura and his mother moved to Los Angeles, and the ensuing summer Mrs. Bok wrote a friend, Mrs. Hatfield of Rockport, Maine, telling her of new details in Hofmann's continuing efforts both to launch Cherkassky's career in America and to find a means to cut his student's expenses. Dr. Hofmann, as Mary Bok referred to him, after giving a recital in Philadelphia as a benefit for Polish relief, stopped off in Cincinnati to

J H

New York, April 2, 1940

Dear Mr. Barbirolli:

May I kindly request your considering an extraordinary American pianist of the younger generation as one of next season's soloists? Since 1936 he has been in Europe touring with very outstanding success. Because of uncertain conditions abroad, he has been advised to return to this country without delay, although even in these precarious times he has been kept busy with recitals and orchestral appearances in the Scandinavian countries.

He is SHURA CHERKASSKY - my prize pupil. I dare say that this young man's repertoire, which includes moderns, is perhaps the largest of any artist now before the public. And should you desire his performing a composition unknown to him he could learn it in short notice as he literally eats music.

True, it is rather late for next season's bookings, but the Metropolitan Musical Bureau and I hope that an appropriate tour may still be arranged for him, considering the wonderful criticisms regarding his recitals and his appearances and reappearances with leading orchestras abroad.

Because your orchestra's budget is probably exhausted by now, Cherkassky would play for you next season at a nominal fee.

Assuring you that your kind consideration and an early reply will be greatly appreciated, I remain, with best greetings,

Most sincerely yours,

Josef Hofmann

Mr. John Barbirolli,
New York Philharmonic-Symphony Orchestra,
113 West 57th Street,
New York City.

Figure 7.3 Letter, April 2, 1940.

interview the president of the Baldwin Piano Company, having Shura Cherkassky in mind. Mrs. Bok then quoted Hofmann's description of the subsequent visit by the Baldwin president to Hofmann's home in California.

> I found that Mr. Wulsin and his wife were coming to California on a visit. They accepted my invitation here to hear Shura play. Shura, who was, (and still is) unaware of Mr. and Mrs. Wulsin's identity, played beautifully and Mr. Wulsin was very impressed.[5]

The Baldwin president then wrote Hofmann on June 21, saying,

> I want to confirm what I said to you at your house after hearing the young man play. The Baldwin Piano Company will be very happy to welcome Cherkassky to the Baldwin family, and supply him with pianos for his concert appearances and a piano for him to work on, etc.

According to Hofmann, all that then remained was

> [to] try to convince Shura that Cherkassky can make a success on the Baldwin. After all, Iturbi and others have done so. I will try to explain this to Shura when I see him in Los Angeles next Monday. Also I will try to make him realize the expense for you, and the expense for himself later if there are huge bills to pay for the use of pianos in concerts, at hotels, and at home. When I learned that Steinway could not make an exception in Cherkassky's case and furnish him with pianos free of charge, the matter worried me. I hope for your and Shura's sake the Baldwin offer will be the solution.

Cherkassky, however desperate he might be for money, was unwilling to compromise his art by playing a piano he considered inferior to the Steinway. Unfortunately, the Steinway firm was in grave financial difficulties at this time and had terminated virtually all its free services to artists as part of a draconian cost-cutting program designed to help it survive the Depression. Baldwin, which depended on the sale of smaller spinets rather than expensive grand pianos, was in a much stronger financial position and could have saved Cherkassky a significant amount of money during the dark days of the forties, but this was not a trade-off he was willing to make. He did not switch to Baldwin, informing Mrs. Bok, "I would go without food to have a Steinway."

In Mrs. Bok's letter to Mrs. Hatfield, she also made the observation that Hofmann was a little dubious as to whether Shura would be willing to consider not using Steinways, and she found it interesting, she said, "that Hofmann is thus open-minded." As the summer progressed, Coppicus wrote that Cherkassky "should not expect a single engagement this season," following which the now destitute pianist wrote Mrs. Bok, "I have absolutely no money." At this point he personally tried to sell the property in Long Island, only to learn in July that the property had already been sold, possibly for back taxes. Throughout the summer of 1940, as he prepared for the Carnegie Hall recital, there were numerous letters to Bok, in one of which he appears to be reaching a breaking point. On August 31 he wrote, "I need not tell you how desperate I am. I am going mad. It is no pleasure for me to beg constantly. It is my fault I am penniless as I have no way of making a living."

These letters also spell out in detail how he loves to play for Hofmann. Cherkassky declares on September 30 that "Dr. Hofmann has been especially marvelous and warm towards me. . . . I adore him!" This warmth and interest was amply demonstrated when on October 3 Hofmann wrote to Bok telling her he had sent Shura to New York on the Mercury airplane instead of the train.

> He can't miss four and a half days of practice shortly before his two important appearances: Casimir and Carnegie Hall. The difference in cost is but very slight if food and tips on the train and a few days extra of N.Y. Hotel bills (for practice in preparation for his appearances) are taken into consideration, whereas the total saving in time and effort is very great. Hope this arrangement meets your approval, if not I am, of course, only too glad to put up the difference. . . . May I quote here: "It is the woman who pays and pays!"[6]

Hofmann also ordered a larger ad for the Carnegie recital, and though he asked Bok to pay for it he once again offered to make up the difference. Two weeks before the New York appearance Cherkassky's feelings of failure were raging, and he wrote his patron "I am ashamed that at my age I am not yet independent."

October 16, 1940, the day of Cherkassky's Carnegie recital, was also the date set for the draft registration of 1,107,000 men in New York City. Selective Service headquarters at 331 Madison Avenue had for its principal worry the answering of questions that were being phoned in at a rate of 1,500 an hour. One man in particular called to say he had to give a concert at Carnegie Hall that night and could not exhaust himself standing in line to register. He insisted on permission to register the next day. Permission was not granted and he was told to register that day—which is exactly what Shura Cherkassky did.

The sea change that greeted Cherkassky at his return concert to Carnegie Hall on October 16, 1940, and following five years of worldwide triumph starting with the Town Hall recital of 1935, was bewildering. He was attacked for his alleged lack of attainment in musical interpretation, belittled for affecting a "grand manner," accused of resorting to effects, and some reviewers even dismissed his performance that evening as empty pianism. Critics such as Irving Kolodin and Jerome Bohm thought the pianist had lost his unique musical voice, a victim of his own prodigious gifts, citing his astounding virtuosity as not enough in itself to satisfy the most discriminating listener. Only Howard Taubman of the *New York Times* heard the recital differently:

> Cherkassky has returned with even a finer command of the piano than before he left. . . . He can make the instrument do almost anything. He has speed, dexterity, power, finesse, a dazzlingly varied palette, and a tone of wide range and subtlety. If ever a musician had the equipment to dominate as a pianist Cherkassky is the man.

Unfortunately, Taubman's perception of the recital did nothing to lessen the damage done to what had begun as one of the most stellar careers of the twentieth century. In spite of the outcome of the Carnegie Hall concert, Mary Bok agreed to Hofmann's requests on behalf of Shura, and on October 21 from Newport Beach he telegrammed her, "Splendid your helping Shura in all ways. Feel you won't be disappointed." However, she did not advance any money at this time, and two years later she would receive a somewhat troubled letter from Hofmann for a promise he felt she had made and not kept.

The damage from the October 16 recital was compounded in January of 1941 by another Carnegie Hall performance, of which Olin Downes wrote, describing Cherkassky's performance of the Chopin B-flat Minor Sonata:

> There was the sensation of a musician who had long since mastered a task of which he had perhaps tired, seeking for some fresh effects to vary routine in performance. . . . There was constant over-emphasis. It was all black shadows and blazing lights; with a restless search for the uncommon, as in the emphasis of inner parts of the harmony which are not really important; in capricious treatment of tempi and exaggerated pauses, nuances arbitrarily designed, one would say, for the sake of novelty and escape from the beaten track of interpretation. . . . We heard virtuoso interpretation as well as technique, and one would not necessarily call this sensationalism insincere. Neither could it be called a justly proportioned or undistorted reading.[7]

Following the concert, Coppicus wrote to Mrs. Bok saying he agreed with the review but thought that nervousness was the cause of the disconnect between Shura's abilities and this most recent performance.

Few engagements followed the 1941 recital, and on February 20 Shura Cherkassky's frustration is palpable when he writes Bok, "How terribly anxious I am to stand on my own and stop being a financial burden." During the next three months he played sporadic engagements for fees ranging from $150–$250, lamenting the 20 percent commission paid to the manager.

While the fact that he was no longer a child prodigy and no longer *new* contributed to the changed reaction to his performances, this negative press is more readily understood when one considers that an emerging generation of music critics came on the scene in the early 1940s. As pianist Gyorgy Sandor pointed out, it wasn't Cherkassky who had changed but the critics: the academic had become the standard, and the New York critics who espoused this new standard, headed by composer Virgil Thomson who wrote for the *Herald Tribune*, greatly influenced not only the New York musical scene but that of other major musical centers around the United States. Romanticism, and an attendant individuality that had commanded respect for nearly half a century, fell into disfavor and were replaced by a resurgence of classical composers, and of interpretations that were applauded for their academic and intellectual correctness. Freedom, individuality, and the use of imagination were now often characterized as vulgar pianism. By virtue of chronology, previous critics had been born to and trained in the tradition of nineteenth-century Romanticism. The new breed of critic instead focused on literalism, structure, and an intellectual performing style; virtuosity at the keyboard became suspect. While Cherkassky was relegated to obsolescence, Rudolph Serkin played hero to the intellectuals, Robert Casadesus championed French precision and objectivity, Arthur Rubinstein represented a new and restrained Romanticism, and all flourished, receiving critical acclaim for performances that many audience members found emotionally constricted. The other towering pianist-stars of the era, José Iturbi and Alexander Brailowsky, both rode the wave of a Chopin craze inspired by the movie *Song to Remember*. These two pianists were sneered at by the intellectual community, which Virgil Thomson called "the college and university trade," for although he had no patience with Romantic virtuosi and vivid personalities, Thomson, who favored French elegance and objectivity, was really no friend of the intellectual population either, who dismissed certain of his compositions as lightweight and superficial. Of course, Horowitz was still King of the Hill, personally depressed but professionally unaffected by Virgil Thomson's

"Master of Distortion" label. Fortunately for Horowitz, he was too well established and had too much extramusical momentum to be stopped by smart-aleck reviews.

Other factors were at work as well. Cherkassky himself spoke of feeling overshadowed by Horowitz and Rubinstein and drinking began to color the picture in a serious way. Managers, even though they liked him personally and thought of him as most reliable, were frustrated by his lack of political savvy in playing the games necessary to propel a career forward. No one denied the fact that he was at heart a very modest man to whom self-promotion was unknown, but at the same time it was extremely difficult for managers to deal with his business naïveté. Perhaps most damaging of all was the reputation he had earned by the 1940s with some conductors who could not cope with his spontaneity in performance, and who strongly resisted reengaging or recommending him. His aversion to making studio recordings, while not as extreme as Hofmann's, was yet another ingredient that adversely affected the development of his career in the United States. With all these factors at work, the six years following his return to the American concert stage in 1940 were bleak professionally and personally, dotted with few engagements, and filled with major emotional and financial problems. Yet while Cherkassky struggled, other artists thrived. Claudio Arrau had 197 American engagements in 1944, of which 32 were with orchestras: 11 with the Philadelphia Orchestra, 9 with the Chicago Symphony Orchestra, 6 with the Boston Symphony Orchestra, and 6 with the New York Philharmonic. A fine achievement, to be sure, but still not the equal of Anton Rubinstein, who from 1872 to 1873 played 215 concerts in 239 days.

For Cherkassky, and other younger or less well-established pianists, this change in the critical climate was devastating. It was as though a sign that read Only Intellectuals Need Apply had been hung on the stage door at Carnegie Hall. The varied program with its lush romantic favorites and collection of bonbons was gradually being replaced with blocks of granite programming that included only what Arthur Schnabel described as "music which is better than it can be played." Unfortunately, the audience had not voted on this change in critical attitude. They still liked Romanticism and its distinctive personalities, and they reacted to the change by staying away from concerts in increasing numbers, a trend that has persisted to the present and contributes to the continuously decreasing number of piano recitals presented across America each season.

With the outbreak of World War II and the bad press from his Carnegie Hall concerts of 1940 and 1941, Shura Cherkassky's career began a long decline. For close to a decade he lived in Los Angeles, in virtual obscurity. Cherkassky and his mother settled at 1418 1/2 North Sierra Bonita Avenue. Surrounded by lush California vegetation, the two-story stucco apartment building was conveniently located at the end of the Red trolley line in a residential neighborhood just one block from Sunset Boulevard and seven blocks from Hofmann's home. Small apartment buildings peppered the angled streets leading from the trolley stop to the foot of the Hollywood Hills. Discouraged and still in debt, overshadowed by Horowitz and Rubinstein, and his concert engagements minimal, Cherkassky played in people's living rooms to earn rent money. In January of 1941 Mary Bok sent him an extra twenty dollars a month for piano rental, and after Steinway stopped charging him she allowed him to keep the extra money. Later in life he told others, "Mother and I didn't know where our next meal was coming from." Things became so desperate that an application was made to the Musicians' Union for financial aid. Cherkassky told me, while we were dining at the National Hotel in Moscow in 1987, that things were so bad then he didn't even have the money to go to the dentist when a visit was very much needed, adding it was Hofmann who had provided the means to do so. The only avenues of employment open to him related to the piano were Hollywood and teaching, neither of which whetted his appetite. However, he did provide the music and hand doubling for Francis Lederer in *Voice in the Wind* in 1944 as well as the hand doubling for the 1945 Sidney Buchman production of Chopin's life story, *A Song to Remember*. The music in the latter film was provided by José Iturbi, who could not take screen credit for his work because he was under contract to rival studio MGM. Cherkassky did however record the music for the sound track of the film *Deception*, starring Bette Davis, in 1946. As for teaching, he continued to say he'd rather die than teach, and throughout his life he thought it was a great mistake for people to think that performers are good teachers.

During January of 1941 he came in contact with Mary Bran, an artist representative, whom he described to Mrs. Bok as the foremost woman manager in Europe, and whom he wanted to engage as publicist and personal manager, in addition to Mr. Coppicus. By May of 1941 he had only four dates for the coming season, and he asked Mrs. Bok if she thought Coppicus was really doing enough for him. Mrs. Bok surmised that Cherkassky wanted her to pay for Mary Bran and wrote him saying she had already paid for two Carnegie Hall recitals, was sending monthly checks, and was therefore unwilling to pay for Bran as well. Shura responded that he didn't mean for her to pay Bran, and he apologized for the confusion. At the same time, Hofmann wrote to Mary Bok on April 22, 1942, reminding her of her promise in 1940 to reimburse him for the expenses he had paid relating to Shura's October 1940 Carnegie Hall recital, and outlining the gifts he had made to Shura in the form of "badly needed" new concert clothes, a business suit, and the doctor's bills he had paid. In his letter Hofmann also lamented his own financial position, stating that he had not had "a very remunerative tour this season as people are uncertain as to the future and not willing to spend their savings on unessential matters such as music." When he received no reply, another letter was sent on April 30, this time including a meticulously detailed, two-page, single-spaced, typewritten list of expenses he had made on behalf of Shura, and once again he asked for reimbursement, informing her, "I am very short of cash." On May 4 Mary Bok sent a terse reply to Hofmann stating that she could not meet his request and saying, "I had already written Shura, on April 27th, that I can no longer help him financially." Undeterred, Hofmann pursued the matter, and on May 16 he composed a lengthy letter in which he explained that the money she owed him and her decision to no longer support Shura "were in no way inter-related—whatsoever." He wrote he was simply taking the liberty of reminding her of "a promise given me over a year and a half ago," and he appended statements of bills, vouchers, and charges amounting to $792.11. He added that the submitted figure did not tell the whole story:

> The fact is that in order to make it possible for Shura to start and cultivate his American career I have—aside from the already mentioned $792.11—advanced him an additional $738.87, as per the attached statement. . . . These expenditures covered the period from October 7th 1940 to September 29th, 1941 and only the absolutely essential items and factors have been taken into account and due to my standing and efforts the expenses involved reduced to a minimum.[8]

From the list submitted by Hofmann we learn that in addition to the usual living and travel expenses, Cherkassky had substantial medical bills for house calls to treat the flu, problems with his eyes, and "pain in shoulder and arm which was of long standing and was so bad at times that his hand was nearly incapacitated." X-rays were taken in March of 1941 "to ascertain that there was no deformation of bones in Shura's spine, shoulder, arm, hand, etc., that might have been the cause of his severe shoulder pain." Frequent massages and trips to the beach were recommended as therapy. On April 23 Hofmann also gave thirty dollars to Shura to employ "a scrub woman for his old and sickly mother," and an additional ten dollars for "monthly help to starving relatives in Finland, whose plight had Shura's mother half crazy, and the mother, in turn, was making a nervous wreck out of Shura." (The relatives were Lydia Cherkassky's sisters.) Monthly checks from Hofmann to Shura continued through September 29 of 1941, and in a comment to Mary Bok Hofmann noted that Shura had cut down on the recommended massages and instead "bought his mother a few clothes as she was in rags."

Throughout this statement of expenses Hofmann called attention to the fact that he was a very good bargainer and managed to reduce many of the fees to a "VERY special price."

Mary Bok responded on May 21 with a four-sentence letter in which she stated she recalled some but not all of the expenses listed for Shura, but since she wanted to keep any promise made she was enclosing a check for $792.11. She added that she did not feel responsible for the other expenditures.

The few bookings that did take place in the Los Angeles years occurred in some of the city's principal concert venues: the Wilshire Ebell Theater and the Philharmonic Auditorium, as well as at the Huntington Hotel's California Artist Series. Presented by the Mary Bran International Artist Agency, tickets for the June 23, 1942, performance at the Wilshire Ebell Theater sold for $2.20, $1.65, $1.10, and $0.83. At the November 13 Philharmonic Auditorium concert of the same year, Cherkassky programmed Stravinsky's new *Circus Polka*, which in response to the audience's long applause was repeated. Noted in the B'nai B'rith *Messenger* report of the recital were the jealous grumblings at intermission of the well-known pianists and composers in attendance who insisted Cherkassky's stunning display of virtuosity only proved he was a "showoff." The critic of the evening strongly disagreed.

What little additional money came into the household in those years was the result of Lydia Cherkassky's piano teaching. One of her students in Los Angeles was Raymond Lewenthal, who would become a world famous champion of the music of Charles-Valentin Alkan, and who remained friends with Shura until Lewenthal's untimely death from heart disease in 1988. In addition to Lewenthal, one of the people whom Cherkassky befriended during his Hollywood days was another former prodigy who had become an even further-down-and-more-out pianist, Ervin Nyiregyhazi, who constantly urged his younger colleague to find him girlfriends. Five years older than Cherkassky, Nyiregyhazi, whose public career ended in the mid-1930s except for a brief resurrection in the 1970s, married at least nine and perhaps as many as twelve times, and so finding him girlfriends could have become a full-time career for the then needy pianist from Odessa.

Cherkassky's decision to move to California in April of 1940 had been influenced by his desire to get away from New York, by Hofmann's move to

Los Angeles in 1939, by his love of a warm climate, and by the fact that Lydia Cherkassky's brother lived in Los Angeles. But whatever the particular force behind the decision, Cherkassky was far from alone in making the move to the West Coast. Serkin headed for Vermont and Schnabel chose the mountains of New Mexico, but Rubinstein, Heifetz, Piatigorsky, Klemperer, Rachmaninoff, Stravinsky, Horowitz, Toscanini, and many others made Hollywood the summer capital of the classical music world. Even the serious-minded Joseph Szigeti and composer Arnold Schoenberg became Californians. For Shura and his mother an added impetus was the well-established, lively, and influential Russian community that had developed around the motion picture industry. Movie director Gregory Ratoff, longtime friend of Heifetz and Piatigorsky, was the unofficial leader of this group that included Dimitri Tiomkin and impresario Sol Hurok, who would become Cherkassky's American manager in 1960.

Although Cherkassky demonstrated lifelong reticence on matters of self-promotion, a rare exception occurred in 1944 when he contacted conductor Artur Rodzinski. In an effort to obtain an interview that would hopefully lead to an engagement he sent a letter to the maestro with whom he had first performed while still a student at the Curtis Institute (see fig. 7.4). On February 18 the conductor responded, saying he was sorry not to have gotten in touch sooner, and since he would be busy with rehearsals and concerts over the weekend Shura should come backstage to say hello. Encouraged by Rodzinski's response, Cherkassky contacted him again on February 29, including with his letter reviews from his February 13 performance of the Shostakovich Concerto No. 1, Op. 35 with the National Symphony Orchestra under the direction of Dr. Hans Kindler at DAR Constitution Hall in Washington, D.C.

In spite of the *Washington Star*'s positive review of the February 13, 1944, performance citing Cherkassky's powerful touch, brilliant technique, musical feeling, and fiery temperament, no engagement was forthcoming. Composed in 1933, Shostakovich's Concerto No. 1 broke away from the conventional piano-bravura style of Rachmaninoff and Tchaikovsky and avoided the lyrical sentimentality associated with them, while incorporating enough Russian folk song to mark it as typically Slavic. It was a composition well suited to Cherkassky's talents because it demanded drastic and sudden contrasts of power along with a softness of tone that rose to thunderous climaxes, and called into play "every known variety of keyboard technique plus some new patterns which the composer had invented."[9] Cherkassky's performance of the concerto in Constitution Hall had been followed by an encore, the

1418½ North Sierra Bonita Avenue
Hollywood (46), California
February 5th 1944

My dear Dr. Rodzinski,
You will probably be surprised to hear from me, and I hope you will forgive me for writing this to you!

I am leaving tomorrow for several concerts in the East. Amongst them, I am a soloist with Dr. Hans Kindler in Washington, playing Shostakovich Concerto.
I will be in New York from 15th to 20th of this month, and would be ever so grateful if you

Figure 7.4 Letter, February 5, 1944.

Rachmaninoff *Elegie*, about which the critics wrote that had he played only that piece, "he still could have been identified with the small coterie of a chosen few."[10]

Later that year on November 20, 1944, Rodzinski received yet another letter from Cherkassky, who was then in New York and would be staying at the Great Northern Hotel on Fifty-seventh Street until November 29. Shura asked for a few minutes of the conductor's time and enclosed his recent Carnegie Hall criticisms (see fig. 7.5). Once again, no favorable result came from the communication.

Cherkassky would only speak in the vaguest terms of those years when there were few engagements, little money, and essentially no management. But at the very end of his life he admitted that, discouraged and depressed, he drank excessively in the California years; and he once told me while he was on tour in Prague, Czechoslovakia, "I sank so low I was in the gutter."

will kindly give me few moments of your time. Of course I know how busy you are, but please grant me this favour and give me an appointment. It is terribly important for me. Please! I will stop at Hotel Windsor (100 West 58th Street). I will not bother you again, unless I hear from you.

Hoping to hear from you.

In great admiration,
and thanking you in advance,
Very sincerely yours,
Shura Cherkassky

Figure 7.4 Continued.

Life, however, would shortly begin to change, and with those changes he moved in the late 1940s from the scene of his self-disgust in Los Angeles to Nice, France, where he remained until relocating to London in 1961.

Notes

1. Curtis Institute of Music, archives, RG 20.5 Cherkassky, Shura.
2. Curtis Institute of Music, archives, RG 20.5 Cherkassky, Shura.
3. *Herald Tribune* (New York), 16 April 1940.
4. Curtis Institute of Music, archives, RG 20.5 Cherkassky, Shura.
5. Curtis Institute of Music, archives, RG 20.5 Cherkassky, Shura.
6. Curtis Institute of Music, archives, MSS 18.
7. *New York Times*, 21 January 1941.
8. Curtis Institute of Music, archives, MSS 18.
9. *Times Herald* (Washington, D.C.), 13 February 1944.
10. *Washington Star*, 13 February 1944.

Jack Dempsey
Hotel Great Northern
118 WEST 57TH ST. NEW YORK 19, N.Y.
TELEPHONE CIRCLE 7-1900
OWNED AND OPERATED BY JACK DEMPSEY'S PUNCH BOWL, INC.

November 20th 1944

My dear Dr. Rodzinski,

Would it be possible to have few minutes of your time and see you? I would like so much to see you, and I am leaving New York for California on the 29th. Last time I missed you when I was in New York.

Would you be so kind as to let me know when and where I could see you? I know that you are very busy — but only for few minutes. I will be grateful.

I am enclosing an add with my recent Carnegie Hall critisisms.

With kindest regards,
и надеюсь до скораго.

Very sincerely yours,

Shura Cherkassky

PLAN TO VISIT
JACK DEMPSEY'S
BROADWAY RESTAURANT AND BAR
49TH STREET AND BROADWAY

Figure 7.5 Letter, November 20, 1944.

CHAPTER EIGHT

Oblivion to Triumph: The Postwar Years

I never thought of giving up. Why should I?

—S. C.

Things began to improve in 1946 when Cherkassky appeared at the Wilshire Ebell Theater in Los Angeles with the Santa Monica Symphony playing the Tchaikovsky G-major Concerto, followed by performances of the same work at the Hollywood Bowl under Stokowski, and at Grant Park in Chicago under Malko. During March of that year, in the beautiful oceanfront setting of Laguna Beach, he married a widow and concert manager, Eugenie Blanc, entering a union that would end in divorce two years later. Then in the autumn he undertook a six-week Scandinavian tour, playing thirty-two concerts in six weeks to critical acclaim throughout Finland, Sweden, Norway, and Denmark. Of this recital tour, Cherkassky remarked:

> Audiences were tremendously enthusiastic everywhere, but perhaps the biggest response came in Helsinki. And do you know, one of the numbers they liked best was Morton Gould's *Boogie-Woogie Etude*? I played it as an encore, with some trepidation, because who would expect a concert audience to like boogie-woogie? When I had finished I just sat there waiting for their reaction. It came, in applause and cheers and stamping of feet.
>
> On my tour I discovered that European audiences can't get enough of American music, and I'm afraid I don't have enough in my repertoire to satisfy them. I expect to remedy that this summer; I'm going to learn lots of American piano pieces to take back on my European tour next spring.[1]

Again commenting on this tour, he said he found Sweden to be in the best condition of all the Scandinavian countries, observing that there was no unemployment or illiteracy, and the people were charming, immaculate, and completely reliable. He also noted that the Norwegian people were very bitter about Kirsten Flagstad's conduct during the Nazi occupation, and that in Finland, despite the grim conditions and shortages of food and other necessities of life, people stood in line for hours to obtain tickets to his concerts. Scheduled to play four recitals there in eight days, he had to add an extra program to satisfy demand. On November 30, 1946, he left Stockholm aboard the Scandinavian airliner Monsun and returned to the United States where he proceeded to Worcester, Massachusetts, appearing there in concert on December 3.

After this extraordinary success in Scandinavia, the pendulum swung in the opposite direction when a Carnegie Hall recital played on January 17, 1947, did not receive glowing reviews. "For every outstanding feature there was something less praiseworthy to match, and in some respects the recital turned into a musical battle of Blenheim, with the victory going to the virtuoso."[2] Sporadic engagements dotted the next two years until the spring of 1949 when Parisian concert manager Nadine Buchonnet sent Cherkassky a one-way ticket to Scandinavia where he had been engaged for ten recitals. Later that season, under the sponsorship of impresario Irwin Parnes, he played a recital at the Wilshire Ebell Theater, which was pointed to by the few people in attendance as a milestone in Los Angeles concert history. This performance marked Cherkassky's final American appearance until 1960.

Although his career had gained favorable momentum from 1946 forward, the true turning point came in December of 1949 when he accepted, against the advice of all concerned, an invitation from the Goette Concert Agency to play an engagement in Hamburg, Germany, performing the *Rachmaninoff-Paganini Variations* with the Hamburg Radio Symphony under Hans Schmidt-Isserstedt. Later in life he recalled that he played the performance as though hypnotized. One critic of the performance wrote that not since Rachmaninoff and Horowitz had he heard such playing, and that Cherkassky "proved himself to be a superb musician who enthused his audience with a technique that bordered on the fantastic. . . . His all around musical quality is developed with equal perfection."[3] Forty-three years later, in 1992, the German newspaper *Die Welt* commented that Cherkassky's 1949 appearance in Hamburg "opened up for younger members of the audience musical and historical horizons hitherto kept in the dark and falsified to serve nationalistic needs." Following the Hamburg performance, Cherkassky's career exploded and he enjoyed enormous popularity all over Europe from Scandinavia to the Mediterranean. His playing caused a sensation in the European music world and among concert managers who eagerly sought him out for engagements, producing a dramatic change in his life and career that made his professional story in Europe, with the exception of France, totally different from his American experience. As concerns France, in 1927 he had performed to rave reviews at the Salle Gaveau in Paris, but although he lived in Nice from 1949 to 1961, he played infrequently in his onetime country of residence even in his busiest seasons until he was near the end of his life. Then, during the nine years preceding his death, he performed at several of the major French music festivals and in Paris at the celebrated Salle Pleyel and Theatre des Champs-Elysées. Two months before his death, in October of 1995, he played one of the last recitals of his life in Paris.

Following the Hamburg triumph he never looked back, saying in an interview with the *Los Angeles Times* in 1982,

> The past is gone. But especially those days—those were difficult times. But the struggle was good for one learns from such a struggle what one really values. Let's just say I went to Europe after having lived in Los Angeles and *immediately* I had success. I think I owe my whole career to the city of Hamburg because there they recognized me first.

Five years later after the Hamburg concert in 1954 Irwin Parnes, who had sponsored Cherkassky's last concert in America, ran into him at the Israel Philharmonic Orchestra House in Tel Aviv where Cherkassky told Parnes that he was booked for two hundred concerts during the 1953–1954 season. That evening in Jerusalem Cherkassky would be playing his seventeenth appearance with the Israel Philharmonic, following which he would fly to Turkey, Italy, the British Isles, and South America for more concerts. Interestingly, the fact that he had played in Germany in 1949 and reestablished his career there did not prevent him from being engaged and applauded in Israel only four years later. In this startling turnaround one could say Cherkassky truly experienced the American dream of "rags to riches," but at what cost no one ever knew since he spoke so rarely of his Los Angeles years. But while he refused to talk of those dire days, the Shura Cherkassky of 1954, expensively dressed and completely positive, recalled with a certain relish an engagement with the Symphony Orchestra of Barcelona, where the guest conductor was Alfred Wallenstein. Following the performance, Wallenstein took his soloist aside and was beside himself with praise for Cherkassky's virtuosity. With a smile Cherkassky recounted that Wallenstein, who was conductor of the Los Angeles Philharmonic from 1951 to 1962, then said, "And don't forget, you absolutely must play in Los Angeles."

During the postwar years the pianist commanded particular success in Germany, Austria, and the Netherlands, and appeared regularly at Europe's most prestigious music festivals, including those of London, Edinburgh, Salzburg, Bergen, Zagreb, Carinthia, and Vienna. He often noted that his biggest followings were in Germany and Holland, while his most demanding audiences were in London and New York. In addition to performing in Europe, Cherkassky toured throughout the Far East, traveling to Japan, China, Hong Kong, Singapore, and Thailand, with invitations also extended for appearances in Australia, New Zealand, South Africa, India, and South America. Once again he became part of the cinema, playing music by Mozart, Chopin, and Liszt in a 1952 film, *So Little Time*, a United Kingdom production starring Marius Goring and Maria Schell in a tale of a Nazi's enchantment with a Dutch girl during the Occupation. This required four days of shooting at Elstrip, outside of London, for which he received his first screen credit.

In London, Cherkassky's home base from 1961 onward, his frequent recitals were considered major events, with as many as eight in one season drawing sold-out houses. He had made his British debut with orchestra in 1929 at Queen's Hall and his recital debut on June 18, 1937, at Wigmore Hall where in 1975 he gave three recitals in the space of three weeks to celebrate his birthday, each played to a full house. In terms of his career, a particularly significant London recital took place under the sponsorship of the Quas-Cohen family of Cheshire on March 27, 1957, once again at Wigmore Hall. The recital received such an extraordinary reception that the long-established and powerful concert management firm of Ibbs and Tillett requested to oversee his career, an association that lasted thirty-three years until the company suspended operations in 1990, at which time Cherkassky transferred to Artist Management International. He told a friend in 1965 that "Emmie Tillett [cofounder of Ibbs and Tillett] is an angel, she is rare, I am lucky to have her, she believes in me very strongly, she sees things very clearly."

At this point America reappeared on Cherkassky's career compass, and on November 18, 1960, following an eleven-year absence from the American stage, he made a highly successful appearance at Carnegie Hall playing a program of works by Rameau, Schubert, Chopin, Stravinsky, and in honor of the centenary of Paderewski's birth, the composer's Variations and Fugue on an Original Theme, Op. 11. Of this Carnegie Hall recital Raymond Ericson of the *New York Times* wrote, "Mr. Cherkassky established himself as one of the most exciting pianists around . . . played a Petrouchka larger than life . . . has an unlimited command of the keyboard . . . can summon any color he wanted from the instrument."[4] An American pianist, Richard Casper, who was present at that concert recalled, "I still remember the *Petrouchka* which Cherkassky unleashed in Carnegie Hall in 1960, the first time I heard him live. Pianists and critics were stunned by the clarity, precision and uniqueness of his reading. Subsequent live encounters made much the same impression."

The autumn of 1961 saw Cherkassky make a round-the-world tour including India, Singapore, Hong Kong, and New Zealand followed by a highly acclaimed appearance at Carnegie Hall playing the Prokofiev Second Concerto under Josef Krips, which was described as a breathtaking triumph. The collaboration of the two artists was perceived to be a superlative understanding between two profound musicians who possessed eloquent communicative powers. In particular, the pianist was cited for his dynamic range in which "infinite gradations evolved like more and more unsuspected petals of a flower."[5] Why his concert at the Grace Rainey Rogers Auditorium in New York City the following year was not well received is a puzzle. It would be fourteen years before he appeared in the United States again.

With the continuing exception of America, between 1962 and 1976 Cherkassky enjoyed a thriving career around the globe in solo and orchestral appearances. His stamina was indeed legendary and one has only to look at his agenda for almost any year following 1949 for proof. As just one example, take 1971. In February of that year Cherkassky played the Rachmaninoff Second Concerto twice in Albert Hall followed by a concert in Sardinia on February 17, before appearing in Goteborg, Sweden on the twenty-fifth. In March he gave performances on the fifth, sixth, and seventh in Madrid before proceeding to Belfast in Northern Ireland and Bangor in Wales where he performed on March 13 and 14. The nineteenth of March found him in Belgrade, Yugoslavia. From the last week of March through April he played the major capitals of Europe, and on May 6 he performed Chopin's Concerto No. 2 in London's Festival Hall, before flying to South America on May 7 where he gave eleven concerts. In October he performed in Australia, Japan, Korea, Singapore, Kuala Lumpur, and Hong Kong, before finishing out the year in Chur, Switzerland.

In addition to his unflagging energy, his huge repertoire and readiness to perform also made him a favorite choice to cover last-minute cancellations. In February of 1966 the pianist found himself at a moment's notice in Israel, substituting for an indisposed Yehudi Menuhin, and playing twelve concerts: Chopin's E-minor Concerto seven times and Rachmaninoff's Third Concerto five times. The same year, on February 25, he left for a concert tour of Germany and returned to London for the March 13 television filming of a Rachmaninoff special, which was essentially the story of Rachmaninoff's life, with conductor Eugene Ormandy narrating. Performing with the New Philharmonia Orchestra under Walter Susskind, Cherkassky played excerpts from Rachmaninoff's First, Second, Third, and Fourth concerti; his *Paganini Rhapsody*; parts of the C-sharp Minor Prelude; the entire G-sharp Minor Prelude; parts of his *Corelli Variations* (coda); his *Polka de W.R.*; and the Prelude in B-flat Major. As an admirer of the composer from early childhood, Cherkassky felt greatly honored to have been chosen to participate in this television film of Rachmaninoff. It is a particularly important document since no other record has been discovered of Cherkassky playing even parts of Rachmaninoff's First and Fourth concertos. Interestingly then, when asked in 1985 to substitute for pianist Gitta Gradova in a performance of the First Concerto at Ravinia Park in Chicago, an invitation that he declined, Cherkassky wrote in a letter dated May 8, 1985, "I strongly feel and believe it is my duty to learn Rachmaninoff's First Concerto. I believe Gitta would have liked me to do it. I will play it in public later on when it is completely in my system."[6]

During the next year, on May 30, 1967, Cherkassky gave a recital in Prague, which he described as one of the greatest concerts of his life. When asked why he thought he did so outstandingly, he replied that he thought it was the result of working constantly, controlling his life, resisting fattening food, and sacrificing everything for the piano. At the end of the Prague concert people screamed, gave him a standing ovation, and after seven encores still refused to let him go. The piano had to be shut and the lights put out. He wrote to friends, describing his great happiness at the outcome, and continued to enjoy similar receptions wherever his engagements took him.

For the following ten years, Cherkassky's career in Europe and the Far East thrived, but he gave only the aforementioned performances in the United States in the early 1960s until he resumed regular appearances on the American concert stage in 1976, the same year he made his first return to Russia. Cherkassky's tours to his homeland had great emotional significance for him. They were also undisputed triumphs, the 1987 tour being a shining example. The Russian newspaper *Tass* on May 20, 1987, reported,

> Almost a week has passed since the concert given in Leningrad last week by Shura Cherkassky, a pianist, but newspapers continue to comment on his truly unquali-

> fied success. . . . Cherkassky displayed unfading technique, subtle musicality, frankness and artistry that are rooted in the beginnings of [the] Russian piano school.

Boris Berezovsky, a musicologist, wrote in the Leningrad newspaper *Smena*,

> The performer, with a pronounced romantic streak, made the audience recall the art of such pianists as Heinrich Neuhaus and Alfred Cortot and taught an instructive lesson for our young pianists who quite often profess an excessively rationalistic approach to rendering piano masterpieces.

It was also in 1976 that pianist Earl Wild, who had been with concert manager Sheldon Soffer, went to another management company, leaving Soffer with the need to add a "romantic" pianist to his roster of artists. On the recommendation of Elly Ameling, noted lieder artist and friend of Cherkassky, Soffer flew to London where he met Cherkassky and contractual matters were discussed and settled. Described by Soffer as a phenomenal artist without any political savvy whose mother dominated him, and who sometimes acted like a child, Cherkassky reignited his American career and began the slow ascent that would end in a blaze of recognition. It was under Soffer's management, on March 13, 1976, that Cherkassky returned to the American concert stage after an absence of fourteen years, playing a program of Beethoven, Schubert, Chopin, Scriabin, and Balakirev. While a legend to connoisseurs, he was virtually unknown to the American public because his last appearance had taken place in New York in 1962 in the ill-received recital at Grace Rainey Rogers Auditorium. For his return performance in 1976, fewer than one hundred people were present in the 2,200-seat auditorium in New York City's Hunter College. Still, the concert represented another major change in his career, as critics were rapturous, with the influential *New York Times* critic Harold Schonberg stating:

> He brought a vanished age of piano playing temporarily back to life. In his way he is unique. He plays as though nothing in the past fifty years has touched him, nothing at all. This is romanticism undiluted and the next time Mr. Cherkassky comes around, don't miss it.

Following this concert both his cult following and his American audience grew significantly, and Cherkassky's American career was propelled forcefully forward. Unfortunately, the auspicious beginning of the relationship with Soffer did not lead to an equally auspicious partnership, and just prior to the 1983–1984 season Cherkassky's general manager in London, Ibbs and

Tillett, requested Shaw Concerts to take over representation for him in the United States.

Harold Shaw, president of Shaw Concerts, was a widely experienced and sophisticated member of the musical establishment. Having managed Vladimir Horowitz for many years, Shaw knew a good thing when he heard it and was wise enough to know what to do and when and how to do it to advance Cherkassky's career. Soon the New York Philharmonic, the Chicago Symphony, Carnegie Hall, and Lincoln Center were engaging the pianist at fees double to what he had been receiving. His American career skyrocketed as he performed across the United States in the most prestigious halls and in the most important of venues. The autumn of 1989 saw the pianist play in Carnegie Hall and Avery Fisher Hall at Lincoln Center in the space of one month. The fact of these two engagements managed to impress even Cherkassky, who told a reporter for the *Fort Worth Star Telegram*,

> I'm doing something very unusual. I'm giving a recital at Carnegie on the 14th, and on December 10th, which is not even a month later, I'm giving another recital at Avery Fisher Hall at Lincoln Center. It's very unusual for someone to get two recitals at two major New York halls in less than a month's time. Very unusual.

At the same time he was relishing all the invitations to perform elsewhere, he refused several opportunities to appear at the renowned Tanglewood Music Festival simply because it would interfere with his precious summer holidays (see fig. 8.1). And he addressed the matter of the importance of vacation time in yet another letter written in 1992 (see fig. 8.2).

In 1991, on his eighty-second birthday (billed as his eightieth) he was given a lifetime invitation to play in New York's Carnegie Hall, Amsterdam's Concertgebouw, and Tokyo's Suntory Hall. His extraordinary success in Holland had begun in 1988 when he substituted, at the last moment, for Vladimir Ashkenazy. A representative of Interartists in Amsterdam, Charlie de la Cousine, described the event as "a revelation and from that memorable performance on, he was considered a living legend."

In spite of his great success the pianist needed constant reassurance that his career was going well. Harold Shaw tells of frequently meeting Shura at the Pierre Hotel for long lunches.

> As I greeted him, coming off the elevator of the Pierre Hotel, he always said, "Harold, I am so happy to see you. I have something important I must ask you." The important question was always the same and it was "Tell me, tell me. Do you think

Hôtel Bauer Grünwald
& Grand Hôtel

Venezia December 13, 1992

Dear Betty,
It feels wonderful to relax a bit. My next concert is only at the end of January. I had a call and fax from Harold Shaw, Tanglewood wants me for a Gala Concert, closing one at the end of August, but as I'm playing at the beginning of August for the Proms at Albert Hall, and then Germany, that would spoil at least 17 to 20 days (we figured that out) of my holiday, and my health is more important

Figure 8.1 Letter, December 13, 1992.

October 3, 1992

REGENTS PARK · LONDON NW1 3UP · TEL: 071-387 1200 · TELEX: 24111 · FACSIMILE: 071-388 0091

Dear Betty,

All I do now is practicing and practicing. This Summer was badly planned, as I really had only two weeks vacation (in St. Thomas) the rest even in St. Thomas I practiced, so altogether having had too close the last and first concert of different seasons there was not sufficient time to prepare and wotk properly on these programmes. However, in the long end it will be alright. I will never, never allow it again that I would not have enoguh time to holidays and preparing. I prefer to lose concerts, even important ones, if they would spoil those periods of time.

Shura.

Figure 8.2 Letter, October 3, 1992.

my career is going all right? What should I do about my career? What do I need to do? Now tell me . . . don't be afraid to say anything . . . just tell me."

Cherkassky here sounds very much like the child who approached Mr. Huber in Baltimore in 1923 following his recitals there and asked him in all earnestness if he had played well.

While Cherkassky was with Sheldon Soffer, oversight for his American career had fallen to Tom Parker, a member of Soffer's staff. When Cherkassky left Soffer to join Harold Shaw, Parker went along, not an uncommon occurrence in New York musical management circles. Then in 1990 when Parker left Shaw's office, responsibility for Cherkassky passed on to Richard Probst who had come to Shaw after working as artist's representative for Steinway and Sons. Probst was devoted to Cherkassky and kept the pianist's career in high gear, but his aggressive personality and tendency to overreach sometimes did as much harm as good. A case in point was Probst's insistence in 1991 that the pianist learn a new concerto by Schederin for performance at the Kennedy Center in Washington, D.C. Probst in fact asked me to encourage Shura to take on the project. My suggestion that Shura do so received the following response (see fig. 8.3), in which Shura speaks not only of his reasons for not accepting the Schederin proposal but also of his continuing unhappiness in spite of a career that was then in high gear.

Still, there is no doubt that during the twelve years he was under Harold Shaw's management, Cherkassky's American career thrived. It was also Shaw in 1986 who was responsible for signing Cherkassky with his Japanese management company, Kajimoto Concerts, by encouraging him to accept an initially smaller fee for playing in a two-hundred-seat hall, assuring him he was exactly right for a Japanese audience and that he was destined to have a huge career in Japan. Shaw's counsel was accepted and although Cherkassky had performed in Japan in 1935, 1971, 1976, 1981, and 1983, his trip there in 1988 was so successful that it stimulated an invitation for annual tours that continued into the last year of his life. Truly beloved by Japanese audiences, Shura Cherkassky was chosen to receive the Grand Award of International Music Awards 1993, a prize established in 1986 by the Asahi Broadcasting Corporation (ABC) to commemorate its thirty-fifth anniversary. In celebration of its thirtieth anniversary, ABC had already commissioned the building of Symphony Hall, Japan's first hall devoted exclusively to the performance of classical music, which upon completion in 1982 was ranked among the world's foremost concert venues by music connoisseurs. The Asahi Grand Award selects those artists who have given the most outstanding and moving musical performances at Symphony Hall during the previous year. Former winners included the Vienna Philharmonic, Alfred Brendel, and Jessye Norman. Maestro Cherkassky received five million yen (about forty thousand dollars at that time) as a reward for his efforts. His success in Japan continued undiminished, and in February of 1996 he was scheduled for a month-long tour. Following his death on December 27, 1995, instead of the scheduled

Flat 158

THE WHITE HOUSE

REGENTS PARK · LONDON NW1 3UP · TEL: 01-387 1200 · TELEX: 24111 · FACSIMILE: 01-388 0091
England

December 13, 1991

My dear Betty and Richard,

It is such a satisfaction to know that I am fully acclaimed i two principal cities of the World: London and New York. I thank God what has happened. However, this does not complete my personal life completely. Will it ever? I do not blame Mrs. Horowitz for saying she will leave all her money to the dogs. Probably no one was interested to make her personally happy. Nor do I blame the fabulous Martha Argerich who does not wish to play many concerts. What personal happiness does it give her? I never and never forget what Mischa Elman said to me: "The tragedy of an artist is that people like to entertain the artist the way they think the artist likes to be entertained".

I recall what you said about that Natioanl League in Washington, but I ca not possibly learn Schedrin Concerto in such a harry when I play constantly concerts, I have already told Richard Probst.If I was asked to play some Concertos that I already know, of course I would have done it!

I realize that that occasion could have brought my many possibilities, but not at the expense of worrying and losing part of my holiday. Now I am aswering all your letters including the one from October 3rd. About Scherdin again, I was right not to go through it, I really do not regret, should I? The music all of it was given to me ly now when I got to New York.

Shura

Figure 8.3 Letter, December 13, 1991.

Cherkassky concert in Tokyo's Suntory Hall on February 12, his manager Masa Kajimoto refunded to the audience of the sold-out house all ticket sales, and presented instead a memorial of great dignity for over two thousand of Cherkassky's devoted fans. The pianist's satisfaction with Japan was clearly expressed in many letters to me, in one of which in 1988 he describes his recitals there (see fig. 8.4).

As Cherkassky indicated from his earliest days with Hofmann, the importance of good management in developing and sustaining a concert career cannot be overestimated. In this arena Cherkassky's life shows a fractured history. Few careers can easily cross national boundaries, in no small part because there are few managers who have contacts and influence beyond their borders. As a prodigy pianist in America, Shura Cherkassky was first

158, The White House,
Regents Park,
London, N.W.1 3UP, England.
February 25, 1988

My dear Betty,

At last I am writing to you. I am sure I need not explain what is is to play 6 different Concertos in a month's time, different programmes, packing, unpacking - no time for anything else, and even if yhere are few moments one is not apt to writing! But you know well, you are always in my heart, and I hope you are getting along marvelously. Please let me know how you are progrgressing. JAPAN, it was definitely one of the greatest triumphs of my life.4 concerts completely sold out, endless ovations (more thcn Carnegie HaOO, five encores, could have play more. Result: I am engaged to Japan every year.

Figure 8.4 Letter, February 25, 1988.

managed by Frederick R. Huber, in Baltimore, Maryland. After Cherkassky's break with Huber in 1924 and his enrollment in the Curtis Institute in 1925, Josef Hofmann's firm belief in his student's gifts caused him to secure for Cherkassky a contract with New York–based Loudon Charlton Management, which represented Hofmann. During his 1929 tour of Great Britain, as a soloist with International Celebrity Concerts, Cherkassky was represented by British impresario Lionel Powell, and upon his return to the United States he signed with NBC Artists Management (George Engles was managing director). During the mid-1930s he changed management companies, once again thanks to his mentor, this time to Richard Copley Management, which also managed Hofmann from its offices in the Steinway Building at 113 West Fifty-seventh Street in New York City. Simultaneously, his European engagements were handled by Wilfred Van Wyck, Hofmann's European manager. Following Cherkassky's return to America in 1940, Hofmann's new American manager, F. C. Coppicus of the Metropolitan Music Bureau (which had become a division of Columbia Concerts), took over Cherkassky's American career on short notice and without meeting the pianist, even though there was little prospect of any immediate success for the then thirty-one-year-old Cherkassky. As the 1940s progressed Cherkassky again changed management several times and was represented in turn by Albert Morini, Mary L. Bran and Annie Friedberg, who managed Horowitz for eight seasons.

Following the Hamburg triumph in 1949 and his move to London, it was Ibbs and Tillett, considered by many to be the premier English artist-management firm in the 1950s and 1960s, that oversaw Cherkassky's flourishing European career until the death of its founders, at which time he switched to Artist Management International until he finished his career with Lies Askonas, a well-known second-tier London management company. In America, following World War II, Mary L. Bran International Management lined up a few concerts, primarily in California, but no first-rank management company expressed an interest in Cherkassky until Sol Hurok signed him in 1960.

This should have been a major breakthrough for Cherkassky because Hurok, then the best-known and most highly respected American artist-manager, was at the height of his fame and power. Hurok was a star maker. He had gambled on a shopworn, middle-aged Polish pianist and made Arthur Rubinstein into a household name. He also turned Marian Anderson's exclusion from Constitution Hall by the Daughters of the American Revolution into a major media event that launched a huge thirty-year career. He even took a stodgy, bespectacled Spaniard and soon made a guitar recital by Andrés Segovia into a must-see phenomenon. Hurok was also the principal architect of a cultural exchange with the Russians that began in 1955 with Gilels's arrival. Isaac Stern, a longtime fixture on the Hurok roster, when congratulating Cherkassky following a 1992 performance under Kurt Masur and the New York Philharmonic, succinctly summed up Hurok's management of the cultural exchange, saying, "It's simple. They send us their Jews from Odessa and we send them our Jews from Odessa." Surely Hurok could have capitalized on Cherkassky's Russian background and birth in Odessa as well as his thriving European career to reignite his long dormant American career. But he couldn't, or at the least, he didn't. The pianist did his part with a brilliantly successful Carnegie Hall recital, but almost nothing came of it. Perhaps Hurok was too busy preparing for Arthur Rubinstein's ten-concert Carnegie Hall marathon the following season, or supporting his newly acquired young superstar, Van Cliburn, then at the peak of his phenomenal career.

In fact, unlucky timing may have been the greatest obstacle of all in Cherkassky's path because he reached Carnegie Hall barely two weeks after Sviatoslav Richter had completed the five-concert series that marked his American debut. These five concerts, all recorded live and quickly released, and the enigmatic and exotic Russian who played them, were the talk of the musical world. Only the "historic return" to the New York concert stage by Vladimir Horowitz five years later in 1965 could have the same impact on a pianist's career and public visibility. Additionally, Richter, like Cliburn before him, was a political as well as a musical happening. One can understand why Hurok, overwhelmed by his front-page sensations, might give short shrift to the unassuming and little-known Cherkassky. Those who knew Hurok, among them American concert manager John Gingrich, who worked for the great impresario, stated that in his experience Hurok "clung to the success stories and jettisoned the others." It is also possible that the time was not yet right for such a stylish and individual artistry as Cherkassky's to succeed against the straightforward and sober piano playing that was still in fashion. Perhaps Harold Schonberg, critic for the *New York Times*, said it best when he wrote in July of 1986, "Every age makes music its own way and the 1960's was a period in which the printed note all but strangled the artist. . . . The concept of artist was all but abandoned." Whatever the reasons, the net result was the same: Cherkassky disappeared from the American concert scene until 1976.

In 1960 Cherkassky needed Sol Hurok, but Hurok had no need for him. When the pianist returned to America in 1976 under Sheldon Soffer's management, the equation was very different. Having just lost his most saleable pianist, Earl Wild, Soffer saw in Cherkassky a major opportunity. Simultaneously, a piece of good fortune entered Cherkassky's life in the form of Omus Hirshbein, manager of concerts at the 92nd Street Y in New York City. Hirshbein had been long captivated by Cherkassky's playing and for fifteen years the 92nd Street Y played a major role in reestablishing regular appearances for Cherkassky in New York City. Further, several appearances at Xavier University in Cincinnati, Ohio opened the door to the Cincinnati Symphony. When Cincinnati Symphony manager Judy Arron left Cincinnati to become executive director of Carnegie Hall in 1986, she brought along her enthusiasm for Cherkassky's playing and saw to it that he appeared at Carnegie Hall every other year until his death.

Just as effective management and bookings were of prime interest to Shura Cherkassky, so too was the negotiation of concert fees and ticket prices. Fees in Europe were low compared to what he was paid for his engagements in America and Asia, and in 1990 he wrote me to say he "had decided to accept fewer of the lower paying European engagements." As a child prodigy in the 1920s, Shura Cherkassky earned $1,000 per concert (more than $11,000 in 2005 dollars) a staggering sum in those days. From the late 1980s forward his fees averaged $11,000 to $16,000 in America, and $20,000 to $25,000 in Asia. Even at the pinnacle of his career, in spite of increased earnings, he needed reassurance that all was going well not only artistically but financially. His gross American bookings with Harold Shaw went from $179,000 in the 1991–1992 season to $264,000 in the 1992–1993 season, and had he been willing to accept a fee of $9,000 to $12,000 for bookings in halls with under 1,200 seats, the total would have increased significantly. Tokyo recitals in 1992 were booked at $20,000 per concert with appearances in Aomari and Nagoya paying $15,000. Only for his performance at the Ohara Museum in Kurashiki, famous for its collection of western paintings by Monet, Picasso, and Renoir, was his fee lowered to $10,000, and then because the small hall accommodated only two hundred people.

The price of concert tickets mattered to the pianist almost as much as the fee he was paid. Following his Carnegie Hall birthday celebration concert in 1991, when scalpers were out in force since the concert was sold out, Cherkassky commented that Hofmann had crusaded against the practice of marking up ticket prices for personal gain. In fact, when Hofmann learned that scalpers were at work in front of Carnegie Hall prior to one of his sold-out concerts in April of 1938, charging $7.70 for tickets that cost $2.75, he complained to New York Mayor LaGuardia in a protest that was published in the *New York Herald Tribune* and reprinted as an insertion in the program for the second Carnegie concert given by Hofmann later that month. The pianist pointed out that many of those who attended his recitals and other concerts were persons of modest means, many of them struggling students. He added that he had not raised the ticket prices for any of his concerts, out of consideration for this type of concert patron, and he implored the mayor to assign police to the concert hall in order to prevent scalping of tickets. Furthermore, "If speculators were to be stuck with tickets, it would discourage their handling them in the future for musical events, and thus permit all music lovers the benefit of hearing music at normal prices."[7] Subsequent to Hofmann's plea, Mayor LaGuardia ordered Police Commissioner Louis Valentine to station plainclothesmen and police officers around Carnegie Hall to see to it that tickets were sold only at the box office.

While managers could become frustrated with Cherkassky's quirky ways and business naïveté, they tended to like him just the same because he was absolutely reliable. Cancellations, other than those due to weather, did not figure in the career of Shura Cherkassky: "I never in my life cancelled concerts. Just never." Only once because of a "poisoned finger," as reported in the London *Evening Standard* in January of 1930, when he entered a nursing home for treatment, and again on the occasion of his beloved mother's death in 1961, when doctors urged him to cancel and feel his grief, did he rearrange several engagements, and then, he said, only with great discomfort. A near cancellation occurred in 1924 when the child prodigy was booked to play a concert in Philadelphia on January 26. Backstage before the concert began, the fourteen-year-old pianist told Mr. Huber he was sick and couldn't play.

Huber, speaking in English, tried to persuade him to go on, all to no avail; Cherkassky's Uncle Julius Bloom, speaking in Russian, attempted to do the same, again to no avail; then the audience started applauding when the hour for the concert to begin went by with no pianist onstage. At the sound of the applause the child prodigy forgot his illness, strode onstage, played brilliantly, and the next day went to bed where he stayed for a week with the measles. Otherwise that year he remained in good health, notwithstanding a trip to Sinai Hospital in Baltimore later in 1924 to take care of a severe cold that was cured in spite of the hospital's refusal to give in to his command to give him chocolate cake, his favorite food, and "Guggle-Muggle," a drink made of milk and honey, a pinch of whiskey, and nutmeg and egg. A nurse at the hospital called her friend Ruth Bloom, one of the child's older cousins, saying, "Get him out, he's too demanding!"

There was also one recording session in 1989 that was cancelled due to a contractual misunderstanding between Cherkassky and the Milwaukee Symphony Orchestra. Koss Classics intended to record the pianist following his performance of the two Chopin concertos with the Milwaukee Orchestra, Zdenek Macal, conducting. The pianist, however, had understood that the recordings would be made during the performances instead of in two additional sessions.

> The MSO asked me to record for a very small fee. But the fee doesn't matter, as long as it's during a concert so that there's no extra time involved. Now two extra sessions. That's a lot of time. If I am forced to do these recordings I am certainly not going to do them with my heart.[8]

David Snead, the orchestra's marketing and public relations director, said the symphony had a contract with the pianist's management to do the sessions. "But we have mutually agreed not to do the recordings at this time. If Cherkassky feels for various reasons the recordings wouldn't be a good idea, then we can go along with that."[9] The additional time required was the controlling factor here because Cherkassky had just finished a long tour of Japan and had to prepare two concertos for upcoming performances. His unwillingness to cancel was evident once again in 1990 following a cataract operation when he flew to Seattle to perform the Chopin F-minor Concerto in spite of feeling "lousy," as he put it, from the effects of the intravenous anesthesia that had been injected into a vein in his leg because he would not allow any foreign object to enter his hands or arms.

A mix-up caused by his management company regarding a date at the

Ambassador Auditorium in Pasadena, California, in 1984, resulted in a cancellation that created guilt feelings that were assuaged only when he was able to fulfill an engagement on the same Pasadena series three years later in 1987. It was rare to have a glitch in any Cherkassky itinerary, but because of a scheduling oversight, the Ambassador date was his only American concert appearance, and his manager told him he should be released from the commitment, as it did not make sense for him to go across the ocean and on to the west coast for just one engagement. The problem arose when his manager neglected until the last minute to inform the concert's sponsors in Pasadena that Cherkassky would not be performing. Cuban pianist Santiago Rodriguez substituted for him on very short notice and Cherkassky was certain he would never again be engaged to play in Pasadena. Instead, he was invited back, and in 1987 he gave a critically acclaimed recital there. He was quick to point out to the *Los Angeles Star News* that he no longer used the services of the management company that had never given adequate notice to the Pasadena sponsors.

In his ninth decade and still in full control of his powers, Shura Cherkassky showed no signs of slowing down. After more than seventy-five years of performing around the globe following his Odessa debut, he still relished carrying out an international concert schedule that would have defeated many pianists half his age. He said he never thought about age, but observed that the most difficult transition came between the ages of forty-five and sixty. "Either one went down or went up." He never gave any thought to stopping: "Why, should I? I'm not a singer or a dancer." His only concession was to enjoy longer holidays than he had earlier in life. The 1991–1992 concert season saw him celebrate his eightieth birthday (in reality his eighty-second) playing 78 engagements in 15 countries, requiring 64 flights (of which 12 were transatlantic, transpacific, or transasian), and stays in 59 hotels.

During the last decade of his life Cherkassky would reflect on a lifetime of performing, and he would say, when asked if he thought his playing had undergone any changes, that there was a change in the sense that he tried to be less unpredictable, reining himself in where dynamics and tempo were involved. He continued to be extremely self-critical, and following a 1993 recital at New York State University, Stonybrook, he sent me a critique of his performance (fig. 8.5). He also said,

> Music is everything in life for me. In former years I used to think I was missing out on the rest of life with all the practicing and devotion of time and energy. I envied the people who came backstage and wondered where they would go next, to a

* 158, The White House,
Regents Park,
London, N.W.1 3UP, England.

November 29, 1993

Dear Betty,

There is so much on my mind-not always so easy to put it all in writing. But still, we are keeping contact! Thanks for cassette safely recived. To my surprise there are quite a number of things in it I did not like: Rameau was probably one of the best. Haydn O.K. some very beautiful, not always steady. Hindemith fine, but not always many contrasts of dynamics. Chopin, Nocturne too hard. Mazurkas all of them too fast and hurried not relaxed. Scherzo some of it is wonderful, but also too fast too nervous, not controled. Berkeley O.K. but there again not too rythmical. Rhapsody very, very good. "October" is really wonderful, so is Schumann, Boogie Woogie not steady enough. This is a marvelous lesson for me.

Figure 8.5 Letter, November 29, 1993.

> nightclub or something and why they didn't invite me along. Now I finally realize that I'm not missing anything and I think that subconsciously projects itself into the music.[10]

Asked why he was gaining in popularity as he entered his eightieth year, (in fact, his eighty-second), he quipped, "Probably because all the others are dead."

Shura Cherkassky's career was distinguished by many factors, not the least of which was its unprecedented length, which one can argue was unmatched in its duration. This statement presupposes some agreement as to what constitutes a debut, what constitutes a career, and how one determines the end of a career. If one defines a career as involving a substantial number of annual recitals performed in principal concert venues of the world at realistic fees, the obvious candidate to challenge Cherkassky's nomination is Arthur Rubinstein. Both pianists in their old age satisfied the suggested criteria for a career, playing a generous number of annual recitals in the principal recital halls of the world at commanding fees. However, in terms of length the edge goes to Cherkassky. In the case of both artists the end dates of the careers are very clear: November 10, 1995, for Cherkassky and May 31, 1976, for Rubinstein. The latter considered his debut to be his concert in Berlin on December 1, 1900, which means his career lasted seventy-five years and six months. Cherkassky told me that his debut took place "in March in Odessa at the age of nine." The *Sunday Times Magazine* in March of 1995 quotes him as saying "I've been performing in public for over seventy-five years," which would indicate a date earlier than 1920. If this is so, and there appears to be no evidence to the contrary, Cherkassky's career actually started in 1918 at the age of nine and lasted seventy-seven years and seven months. If, for argument's sake, because his parents falsified his birth date as 1911, Cherkassky was actually eleven when he started playing in public, then his Odessa debut took place in March of 1920, making his career seventy-five years and seven months. Either way Cherkassky eclipses Rubinstein in terms of career length. Technically one might also offer up the name of Mieczyslaw Horszowski, who played his last recital at the age of ninety-nine, as a principal contender for the longest running career. But his career was a very special one, with relatively few major orchestral dates and very few solo appearances in the last thirty years of his life.

One can also state, arguably, that Cherkassky's old-age career had virtually no parallel in the history of great pianists. Other pianists who reached the "longevity" category might be named to challenge this statement, such as Earl Wild, whose career, even though he continues to occasionally play as he turns ninety, unfortunately trailed off as he reached his seventies, by which time his memory and power began to fail him. Jorge Bolet enjoyed a solid second-rank career until a rapturously reviewed Carnegie Hall concert in 1974 vaulted him into the top tier of pianists at the age of sixty, which can hardly be considered elderly. His death in 1990 at the age of seventy-six left him with fewer than half as many golden years as Cherkassky. Vlado Perlemuter enjoyed a limited but viable career until he was eighty-nine and recorded much of his repertoire for Nimbus starting at age seventy-five. These records brought his name to a larger public but did little to spark any upturn in his career. Francis Planté stopped touring at age sixty-one but gave occasional concerts until he was ninety-four. The last thirty-three years of his life hardly constitute a career by any definition, and the recordings he made at age eighty-eight of several Chopin etudes and other works cannot stand comparison to the playing of Cherkassky at age eighty-six. To suggest that these recordings rival Cherkassky's live performances requires the listener to totally ignore the emergency ritardandos and intermittent failures of power that mar these performances. Sergio Fiorentino, whose career regained momentum following his return to the concert stage in Italy in 1991, in Germany in 1992, and with a debut at the Newport Music Festival in 1996 at the age of sixty-eight, did not sustain that momentum in spite of excellent reviews following his Tully Hall performances in 1997 and 1998. In July of 1998, while appearing at the Newport Music Festival, Fiorentino told me there were only a few scattered dates on his future calendar. (He died in August of the same year.)

Standing in sharp contrast to all the forenamed pianists, during every season in the last decade of his life Cherkassky played a full schedule of concerts on three continents and offered a generous choice of concertos, including the supremely demanding Prokofiev Second and Rachmaninoff Third, along with two different virtuoso recital programs. His Festival Hall birthday recital in 1991, at the age of eighty-two, was described in the *Times* as revealing

> not a smudged note, not a stiff muscle. Here was neither the desiccation of age nor the degeneration into eccentricity, which can so often plague the veteran performer. No reservations or qualifications had to be made. This was Cherkassky from everlasting to everlasting.

The same was true when he was performing with an orchestra. In October of 1993, at age eighty-four he delivered Tchaikovsky's First Piano Concerto in Essen, "with stupendous self-confidence and power . . . nimble finesse . . . still holding in reserve furious energy for the finale." Six weeks before he died in 1995 at age eighty-six he played, during a four-day period in Prague, one solo recital and three performances of the Rachmaninoff Third Concerto with complete mechanical security and unfailing memory. While there could be occasional finger slips toward the very end of his life, they were of minor significance relative to the totality of the performance, and were noted as such by the majority of critics.

In the last year of his life, Shura Cherkassky was colorfully described by a Rome critic, "As though he were an 86-year-old Alberto Tomba tackling the slalom and not knocking over a single stake." At that age he was still happy to accept challenges, the more demanding the better. To the end of his days Shura Cherkassky purely and simply loved the instrument—its capacity for expressiveness and virtuosity, its colors and pedaling. He played in an immensely compelling and personal way, making few concessions to tradition. Everything was looked at anew with vision, vitality, wit, and poetry. His power with audiences came not only from the opulence of his playing but through the insights he delivered and the intensity of emotion he projected. His age was simply insignificant because the piano was his universe, and his joy in playing the instrument was equaled by nothing else in life.

As one looks back on the career of Shura Cherkassky, the words of *New York Daily News* reporter Terry Teachout come to mind. In 1993, as he watched Cherkassky take his bows on the stage of Carnegie Hall, Teachout thought of a line from Dickens: "Father Time is not always a hard parent, and, though he tarries for none, often lays his hand lightly on those who have used him well."

Shura Cherkassky used Father Time well indeed.

Notes

1. *Los Angeles Star News*, 10 January 1947.
2. *New York Times*, 18 January 1947.
3. *Hamburger Allgemeine Zeitung*, 28 December 1949.
4. *New York Times*, 19 November 1960.
5. *New York Post*, 26 November 1961.
6. Thomas J. Cottle, *When the Music Stopped* (Albany: State University of New York Press, 2004), 263.
7. *New York Times*, 10 April 1938.
8. *Milwaukee Sentinel*, 28 February 1981.
9. *Milwaukee Sentinel*, 28 February 1981.
10. Carol Montparker, "Shura Cherkassky, Sprightly Sage of the Piano," *Clavier* (November 1990): 13.

CHAPTER NINE

Shura and the Gramophone

> I don't have the patience to go into a recording studio and wait for a red light and a green light. I'm not very good at it.
>
> —S. C.

Paralleling Cherkassky's stage career was a recording career that extended over a period of seventy-two years, from his first Duo-Art recording in 1923 to his last sessions in May of 1995, making his the longest recording career in music history. As one of the few pianists in the industry to record in the acoustic, electrical, analog, and digital eras, he began recording when piano rolls were considered high-tech, continued through the electrical age with its endless retakes, and on into the digital stereo era when editing possibilities became virtually unlimited. When asked by me to comment on the current editing situation in the recording industry, record producer Thomas Frost replied:

> Splicing has gotten progressively worse since the early 1990s when some recordings averaged one edit [splice] every fifteen seconds. My estimate for some of the extreme cases now [2004] is an average of one edit every ten seconds. This is not limited to pianists but includes other soloists as well. Many of these extreme cases involve young musicians who have learned about the almost limitless capabilities of digital editing systems and are driven by an obsessive desire to produce the ideal performance that exists in their mind. Perhaps some feel they have to compete with their colleagues for perfection in recordings. In some cases the editing craze is producer-driven. It should also be pointed out that there are also many artists of all ages recording now who are much more concerned with the musical message than obsessive note-perfection.

Retakes and splicing figured little, when at all, in Cherkassky's recording output, making his work product even more remarkable. Most of his pieces took as long to record as it takes to listen to them. A case in point is his recording of the Tchaikovsky Concerto No. 2 in G Major made with the Cincinnati Symphony Orchestra in 1979, Walter Susskind conducting. Susskind commented with admiration on the recording session, calling attention to the ease with which the pianist had worked and to the lack of splicing that had taken place.

> Cherkassky and I don't believe in patching a tape together from hundreds of short bits and pieces. You know, in a concerto, it's difficult to expect the pianist to stop and start again in the middle of a phrase—just to patch one wrong note. . . . The first movement—except for the main cadenza which he recorded outside the recording time—I think will possibly consist of three bits of tape—which is very little. I've done recordings in years past . . . where a movement of a concerto might consist of 60 bits of tape.[1]

Susskind also explained there were time constraints in this recording because Cherkassky had a plane to catch. A four-hour session had been called but regulations demanded that for every hour of work there be a twenty-minute break, leaving two hours and forty minutes of actual working time, which worked out just fine.

> The orchestra is a very disciplined group; there is no time wasted. . . . And the pianist, in spite of his rather advanced years, did not tire or show any signs of what's called artistic temperament—no outbreaks, no scenes. . . . Actually, the time turned out just right. In fact, when we were through, we computed the actual time and found we came in two minutes under.

The conductor had tremendous respect for Cherkassky and had no difficulty in giving credit not only to his character but also to his pianism, remarking that his hands were very small, but one wouldn't think so when he started playing since he was able to cover a terrific amount of the keyboard with tremendous speed and power.

> He also uses a minimum of pedal, and it's entirely his own which, to my mind can only be compared to Horowitz. . . . To use little pedal is ideal for recording. Many a tape has been muddled by the pianist using the pedal heavily and profusely. That will not be the case with this recording. . . . And, you know an orchestra usually plays up to the quality of the soloist. If they're playing with an artist they admire

> and respect, they almost automatically reach a higher level than if they feel a little put upon by a lesser artist.[2]

Cherkassky, who had introduced the Tchaikovsky Second Concerto to Cincinnati at an appearance with the Cincinnati Symphony Orchestra, had his own comments to make concerning the recording session, reflecting that beauty of sound didn't concern pianists anymore, and that he feared the subtleties of tone color and inner voices for which he was so well known would be lost in recording. Susskind had no such worries, stating that he didn't think the inner voices in Cherkassky's playing would be lost, but instead that this aspect of his playing would be picked up more clearly by the microphones than by the human ear. Of the ultimate result Cherkassky was his usual taciturn self, explaining he did not study the work with Hofmann.

> But I do remember performing it at the Hollywood Bowl while Hofmann was in attendance. He had the most curious reaction to the piece. I recall he came up to me afterwards and remarked, "You know, that doesn't *sound* like Tchaikovsky." But of course it does.[3]

Susskind reacted further to their collaboration by saying that when a recording is published, one is too far away to remember it exactly, as the time lapse plays a very important role. When the moment came for him to listen to one of his new recordings he approached the task with trepidation, but in this case he remained satisfied with the outcome of the session.

Not surprisingly, considering the length of his career, Cherkassky recorded for a variety of labels (at least thirteen), not counting those that have reissued old recordings or produced unauthorized performances since his death. Over the course of his lifetime Cherkassky made recordings for HMV, DGG, Victor, Cupol, Columbia, L'Oiseau-Lyre, Eurodisc, Decca, ASV, Vox, Tudor, Ermitage, and Nimbus. His relationships with these diverse recording companies were driven by sales results, economic conditions, personal contacts, and sheer chance. At the other end of the spectrum, Sergei Rachmaninoff, who began recording in 1919, just four years earlier than Cherkassky, switched to Victor following an unsatisfactory one-year relationship with the Edison Company and never again recorded for anyone else in his twenty-two-year recording career. (Rachmaninoff's loyalty to Victor was never reciprocated. Victor ignored much of his repertoire as well as his own compositions and did not get around to recording his First and Third Concertos until 1939, both on the same day.) Arthur Rubinstein, who cut his first record in 1928 for HMV, recorded virtually his entire repertoire for this company, much of it several times, shifting to what had become its American affiliate, RCA Victor, at the start of World War II, then straying only once at the very end of his career to record the Brahms D-minor Concerto for Decca/London with Zubin Mehta and the Israel Philharmonic in 1976.

Cherkassky began recording in 1923 with six acoustic sides for Victor's Blue label, a less expensive brand than its Red label. These first releases, in which the child prodigy shows so many of the features of his mature playing, were well received and the four sides were rerecorded using a new electrical process in 1928. In spite of their popularity, the child pianist's recordings were still not expected to sell like Rachmaninoff's records, for which Victor guaranteed Rachmaninoff $15,000 annually for five years for just five sides per year. In 2005 dollars, Rachmaninoff was paid a total of over $700,000 for what amounts to less than two CDs' playing time.

Two years before Rachmaninoff's first Victor recording session, on March 26, 1918, Josef Hofmann had written his wife Marie concerning what he believed to be a coup in relation to a recording contract:

> I finished recording for Columbia, after many days of hard and enervating work of making and remaking ten records, and today I gave my consent to the Aeolian Company for an agreement of ten years and the total of 100 pieces for $100,000. They wanted twenty years and two hundred pieces, and so I got out of them double, anyhow—that is the utmost one can get. Adams and Godowsky thought this offer was phenomenal. Godowsky played for the Aeolian Company, twenty pieces for $5,000, and that is all they want him to do for them; so I think I can be pretty proud of my agreement with them.[4]

Later he again wrote his wife concerning this contract saying,

> The recording will be spread over fifteen years instead of ten. . . . The work for me will be extremely easy. Seven pieces a year for five years ($1,000.00 a piece = $35,000). Six pieces a year the next five years ($30,000) and seven pieces the last five years ($35,000). As these records can be corrected at will, this recording is not one-tenth as strenuous as for Columbia. It is a great contract and Adams, Steinway and Godowsky were simply amazed. We are now safe financially for the next fifteen years, if not entirely.[5]

For a more contemporary frame of reference, RCA guaranteed Arthur Rubinstein royalties of $110,000 annually in the 1960s, and during the first six months of 1980, his royalties were reported to have exceeded $196,000. But by the time Cherkassky's recording career was in high gear such sales and royalties were impossible. With virtually all the standard repertoire recorded and rerecorded many times by many artists, the market was so fragmented that the average release did well to sell 10,000 copies. Even Rubinstein saw sales of his 1971 recording of Rachmaninoff's Second Concerto drop to 20,000 from over 350,000 sold when he had recorded the same concerto in 1956.

The crash of 1929 and the Depression that followed devastated the record business. Victor Company was taken over by Radio Corporation of America in 1930 to become RCA Victor, and Cherkassky's Victor labels and a few piano rolls in 1925 and 1927 became his last solo recordings until after World War II almost twenty years later. He did undertake one project that was extraordinary in every way in 1934 for American Columbia: a recording of Rachmaninoff's Cello Sonata, with Marcel Hubert. That such a relatively long and obscure work should be recorded at all in such a bad economy, that Cherkassky (never identified before or after with chamber music) was chosen to do it, that he should have agreed to do it, and that it should be a performance of such excellence that Rachmaninoff praised it lavishly, is still a puzzle. A possible explanation is Cherkassky's financial need. As to why Rachmaninoff never recorded the work, there is no clear answer other than the neglect shown him by RCA Victor. From 1930 onward Rachmaninoff did not even have a recording contract until the unexpected success of his new "*Rhapsody on a Theme of Paganini*" in 1934 bestirred company officials to record the work on Christmas Eve of that year.

During the remaining years of Cherkassky's career, other than the acoustic sides made in 1923, and the 1934 Rachmaninoff Cello Sonata, he never again made an American recording except for a Tchaikovsky Second Concerto with the Santa Monica Symphony issued by Concert Hall Records in 1947. And although they were recorded in America, a 1979 Tchaikovsky Concerto No. 2 with the Cincinnati Symphony (conducted by his old Curtis-Hofmann classmate, Walter Susskind), and his eightieth birthday recital at Carnegie Hall in 1991, were both produced on European labels.

The revival of Cherkassky's career in the postwar decades was undoubtedly helped by his return to the European recording studio. First Vox in 1946 released four Liszt rhapsodies, the Brahms F-minor Sonata (Cherkassky's first recording of a major work except for the Rachmaninoff Cello Sonata), and some short pieces. The Santa Monica Tchaikovsky No. 2 followed in 1947, and the succeeding year Cupol, a Swedish company, issued six sides in Scandinavia where Cherkassky's career had already been reignited. The 1950s brought forth renewed interest in him by major companies and resulted in some of his most important recordings: Chopin and other works for HMV, and both Tchaikovsky concertos for Deutsche Grammophon. His first concerto recording released by HMV, made with the Philharmonia Orchestra in 1952, was Liszt's Concerto No. 1 in E-flat Major with Anatole Fistoulari conducting. In 1954–1955 he recorded the Prokofiev Second Concerto in G Minor under Herbert Menges, and Shostakovich's First Concerto with Harold Jackson, trumpeter. Also in 1954 DGG released his Tchaikovsky First Piano Concerto, which had been recorded in 1951 with the Berlin Philharmonic under Leopold Ludwig, followed four years later by an equally brilliant Tchaikovsky Second Concerto under Richard Kraus, again with the Berlin Philharmonic.

For those who identified Shura's musical appetite with the stream of encores he had given and musical bonbons he had recorded for twenty-five years, the Brahms F-minor Sonata that he recorded in the late 1940s must have been a shock, a powerful and rather chaste performance with only the occasional inner voice or bass line to remind us who is playing. Even more surprises were coming with the Shostakovich First Concerto, Stravinsky's *Petrouchka* (only the second recording ever made of what would become an ubiquitous tour de force), and a recording of the colossal Second Concerto of Prokofiev, then even more uncommon than *Petrouchka*. After this flurry of activity in the 1950s, the next two decades saw relatively few recordings, mostly emphasizing Chopin, including the complete preludes, scherzi, and polonaises to complement the complete etudes from the 1950s. However, mostly short virtuoso works were produced.

In 1981 Nimbus recognized the need to seize the moment and document Cherkassky's vast repertoire. They made a bold try, recording over nine hours of solos, but sadly neglected many of his most significant works, such as the Brahms F-minor Sonata, the Schubert Sonata in A Major D. 959, the late Beethoven sonatas, and the Schumann *Fantasy* and F-sharp Minor Sonata, thereby inadvertently contributing to the perception by some of Cherkassky as a lightweight. In truth, it was a rare Cherkassky program that did not include a significant musical challenge. Among Beethoven's sonatas, the late Op. 101 and especially Op. 111 were more likely to be programmed than the *Waldstein* or *Appassionata*. A rare and difficult-to-find recording of Op. 111 made in the 1950s shows Cherkassky on his best behavior, reverent without even an occasional wink, totally controlled, and favoring slower tempi than those to which we are accustomed. A lyrical interpretation of the third variation in the second movement, instead of the jazzy but anachronistic one we have come to expect, truly flows from the music that preceded it.

It was Cherkassky's inability to be comfortable when recording that led Nimbus Records in the 1980s to offer him a very liberal and unusual setting in which to work. He would go to company headquarters in Wyastone Leys, Wales, settle in at their castle, record when he felt like it "without those horrid red and green lights!" go for walks in the surrounding park, and eat breakfast in the kitchen. "They say play it like a concert. . . . If there's a wrong note, don't worry about it. They might go over certain spots but you don't have to keep stopping. I make better records that way. If you have to keep stopping it gets boring."[6] The setting suited him well and he stayed with Nimbus until 1988 when he transferred to Decca.

The ten CDs issued by Decca/London in the 1990s also failed to include much of his serious repertoire, but they surely constitute the most complete, compelling, and accurate representation of Cherkassky's repertoire. All taken from live BBC performances, except for two concerto discs, and the live eightieth birthday recital in Carnegie Hall, these historic recordings even capture the audience's approving laughter in one or two of his encore specialties. Cherkassky was delighted by this series of discs, produced with the oversight of the late Peter Wadland and British music critic Bryce Morrison.

Live recordings of the Rachmaninoff Third Concerto from 1957 and the Prokofiev Second Concerto in 1991, released in 2002, give fascinating glimpses of Cherkassky interacting with the music, the piano, the conductor, and the audience. The Rachmaninoff, two minutes faster than a slightly sluggish 1994 studio recording, is filled with whimsical voicings and unexpected relationships. Of course, in 1957 expectations for this then rarely played piece were very different from today. It was not until the following year that Van Cliburn's triumph in Moscow made the Rachmaninoff Third Concerto the chosen vehicle of every aspiring virtuoso. Rudolf Schwarz and the BBC Symphony follow the pianist gallantly until the very last page when the ensemble comes noticeably unglued, but not enough to detract from this arresting if wrong-headed performance. Unlike Rachmaninoff and Horowitz, Cherkassky played the piece without cuts, though he followed their example in using the original, shorter but more mercurial, cadenza. As for the Prokofiev Second Concerto, his 1991 performance with the London Philharmonic, Kent Nagano conducting, was the only time Cherkassky played the work in the last fifteen years of his life. It never occurred to him that there was anything out of the ordinary about an eighty-two-year-old restoring this massive work to his repertoire, and only for a single performance! He played it as one might expect, making music and excitement without pounding the giant cadenza or reducing the second movement to a scramble, although in all fairness, vintage Cherkassky is hardly what we think of as vintage Prokofiev.

Happily, the BBC is continuing to release live performances, and unauthorized or private recordings may surface from time to time in addition to the Cherkassky recitals from Lugano, Salzburg, and San Francisco that have already appeared and which, like the Decca BBC releases, give such a true and appealing representation of Cherkassky's art. Let buyers beware should they stumble upon a Library of Congress listing of a King recording, 395–512, titled "Shura at the Piano," issued in Cincinnati in the 1950s, featuring Shura Cherkassky playing pop tunes such as "Blue Moon, "Foggy Day, and "El Cumbanchero," with Jack Lesberg, bass, and Terry Snyder, drums. Later in the 1950s, a second recording of pop music featuring "Shura at the Piano" was also issued. A complicated trail led to the discovery that the Shura Cherkassky named on the Library of Congress record listing, was actually Shura Dvorine, a 1943 graduate of the Peabody Institute in Baltimore, who studied there with Alexander Sklarevski. Following graduation he made a highly successful Town Hall debut in New York (his name spelled Devorine in the reviews), followed by equally acclaimed classical recitals through the remainder of the 1940s. The same photo of Shura Dvorine, as in the publicity for his Town Hall flyer, produced by his New York management, American-Canadian Concerts and Artists, appears on the record jacket of the King recordings. In a conversation with me, Mr. Dvorine revealed that he had been named Shura by his father who was a great admirer of Shura Cherkassky. The Dvorine family lived in Baltimore at the time of the child prodigy's debut there in 1923, and Shura Dvorine, as a very young child, was taken to meet Shura Cherkassky. A curiosity in this situation is the genuine Shura Cherkassky's reaction to a pianist playing Gershwin and Porter in the dining room of the Hotel Krasnaya in Odessa in 1987. After listening intently he went up and talked to the gentleman at length. When he returned to the table I asked him if he ever did that kind of playing, to which he responded, "I used to but not anymore."

Throughout his life Cherkassky maintained that there were two things he detested: cocktails and studio recordings. Fortunately for posterity, Cherkassky's resistance to recording was not as extreme as Josef Hofmann's, who did not want to record because he did not want any one interpretation of a work to be considered definitive. Cherkassky, as Hofmann, also believed that any composition could be approached interpretatively in any number of ways, and since he and Hofmann had a level of technique that would allow them to do anything they wanted interpretatively, only the live recital provided the opportunity each sought to present something fresh and compelling. For Cherkassky the recording studio further denied him his inherent need for spontaneity:

> It's very difficult because you can't be too spontaneous. You're afraid to make the slightest false note. When everything's correct the inspiration goes. You can't lose yourself. I'm very self-conscious when I record. I am so much happier in live recording. Something goes wrong if I don't have an audience. In recordings when you stop and have to play it again it loses its spontaneity.[7]

Indeed, Cherkassky maintained he was always more restrained on disc: "I think I am less naughty. If I take liberties and then listen to the playback, I myself am shocked." For this reason he always said he was much more content in live recordings where he was inspired by the warmth and view of the audience.

While Cherkassky was uncomfortable with the recording environment, record producers and engineers were inevitably delighted by the lack of complication he brought to the recording setting. Adrian Farmer, in his notes to Nimbus recording 45018 (1983) featuring works of Stravinsky, Mendelssohn, Debussy, Morton Gould, Tausig, and Rachmaninoff, describes the ease with which Cherkassky went about his work:

> There are some recording sessions that seem to go off extremely well at the time, and leave everyone with a sense of having achieved that elusive goal of capturing on tape something of lasting value. And yet, six months later, when you take the tapes down from the shelf and listen again you wonder where the magic has gone. Where is the excitement you remembered? It has disappeared. Chances are it left along with the artist. His infectious musical personality was very real during the time he was with you, but such is the peculiar chemistry of recording that not one part of it managed to get through the microphone. All you are left with is the notes, no music.
>
> There are other sessions which tire you out, where the artist gives you endless, and usually unnecessary repetitions of his music. Eventually when asked, "Now have we got it" you answer "Yes" out of desperation. If the truth be known, you lost the ability to judge long ago. In your mind you consign it all to the rubbish bin, reasoning that anything that takes so long to get down can't be of much value as a performance anyway.
>
> Just as you are beginning to wonder if it is all worth the effort along comes the third type of recording artist. He is very rare indeed, practically an endangered

> species. He plays his music once, maybe twice—(though never more than once on the same day)—gives you very few headaches and makes music of such generosity of spirit that you forget you are recording at all. You put down your pencil and listen. You are in the company of a great artist, the measure of whose greatness is that they suspend all critical judgment, freeing you from the role of critic and producer, and offering instead a complete musical experience; private, intimate, but with an intensity that dominates and ultimately transcends the recording medium.
>
> Shura Cherkassky is without doubt one of these last. He is never predictable, frequently outrageous, with a wicked sense of enjoyment that constantly emerges in the playing.[8]

I observed the ease with which Cherkassky recorded when I attended the 1994 Rubinstein D-minor Concerto recording session at Walthamstow Assembly Hall, London. Cherkassky would have simply played through the work without a hitch, recording it in one take, had the conductor, Vladimir Ashkenazy, not stopped the orchestra to correct balance or phrasing or to make specific recommendations to one of the flutists. When all was done the pianist was not particularly satisfied with the recorded result, saying, in reference to a live performance of the same work that had taken place the previous evening in Royal Festival Hall, "You saw what Cherkassky can do when he has an audience!"

Even though most of Cherkassky's recordings were made late in life under theoretically ideal studio conditions and with optimal fidelity, most of his best recordings were made in less than ideal live concert conditions or in the pre-stereo era when he recorded far less extensively. Opinion is divided as to the merit of the Nimbus discs. Harold Schonberg heartily endorses them, but others reluctantly conclude that the Nimbus discs do not show Cherkassky at his best. They say that much of the color and variety that were the essence of his playing were engineered out, and the playing itself was often careful to the point of being inhibited. According to John Guinn of the *Detroit Free Press*, "Cherkassky's art deserves better sonic ambience than Nimbus provides."

Listening instead to recordings of live performances, such as the San Francisco recital of 1983 and the magnificent Chopin B-minor Sonata of 1985 in the Phillips "*Great Pianist Series*," the "eightieth" birthday recital from Carnegie Hall in 1991, and the BBC recordings from the 1960s, 1970s, and 1980s, we hear a pianist different from the one captured in the Nimbus studios. The eightieth birthday recital recorded by Decca at Carnegie Hall on December 2, 1991, is a remarkable document. Unedited, start to finish, the sound is luminous, the emotion immediate, the unique spontaneity evident, and all are captured in spectacular fashion. On October 7, 1993, the day of Cherkassky's eighty-fourth birthday, this recording received the Gramophone award for Best Instrumental Record of 1993. Gramophone raved: "This is quite simply a glorious recital from first note to last. . . . Those who have hitherto resisted Cherkassky's brand of caprice may find it difficult not to surrender to this occasion."

Because Cherkassky rarely recorded works that he did not perform regularly, there are few complete sets in his discography, the Chopin preludes, scherzi, etudes and polonaises being the exceptions. Among these, the scherzi were staples of his repertoire, the preludes less so, but only a few of the etudes and polonaises appeared on concert programs, and neither complete set of studio recordings pleased him. About the polonaises of 1961 all he would say was, "I had just come back from holiday," implying he was not in his best form; and concerning the etudes of 1955, "not very good," was his opinion, which is not the opinion of the many eminent pianists who find this recording arresting. While these comments must be evaluated with the understanding that Cherkassky rarely, if ever, praised any of his performances or recordings, he was for his own reasons clearly dissatisfied with these particular efforts on his part.

After hearing more than eighty live performances, plus numerous rehearsals and practice sessions over a twenty-year period I gained a fairly clear sense of what Shura Cherkassky's playing was all about. Even so, listening to more than seventy years of recordings and repertoire over the course of one month, for the purpose of writing this book, gave me a new perspective on his extraordinary art. Notwithstanding his great interpretive freedom, there emerges a statesman of the piano who never changed the notes the composer had written or left anything out for pianistic convenience. Not even the most innocent octave doubling ever appears, and there is none of the tinkering we find in Hofmann's playing. The sole extravagance we might find in his vast recorded legacy is the addition of some lovely counterpoint in Godowsky's *Alt Wien*. Cherkassky's most egregious textual error is a deliberate doubling of the tempo in the final cadence of the Chopin B-minor Sonata recorded live in 1985 and a similar telescoping of the final cadence in the Chopin B-flat Minor scherzo.

Curiously, the composer whose music is consistently recorded in the most straightforward way is Franz Liszt's. Cherkassky's 1950s recordings of the E-flat Concerto and *Hungarian Fantasy* are all but definitive, as is the *Twelfth Hungarian Rhapsody*. His Liszt performances are vividly characterized, though they lean more to the elegant style of Mischa Levitzki than the heaven-storming Horowitz approach. Still one cannot avoid being stunned by his physical command of the B-minor Sonata. The last two of his three recordings of this work were made at age seventy-six, one of them live. Only Arrau at eighty-two and Arthur Rubinstein at seventy-eight were older when recording it, with Arrau certainly showing his age. We find Cherkassky, who was not much younger, in top form especially in the final octave peroration, and at less than twenty-nine minutes approaching the speed of the young Horowitz recording rather than that of the mature Arrau.

But in his playing of Liszt, as in his vast romantic repertoire, Shura Cherkassky was never attracted to display per se. Whether performing the *Don Juan Fantasy*, *Islamey*, or the *Brahms-Paganini Variations*, accuracy, detail, and style were never sacrificed for mere speed. He played very few etudes other than Chopin's, preferring the richness, complexity, and musical variety of transcriptions and virtuoso works like *Islamey* or the Liszt rhapsodies to the one-dimensional aspect of most etudes. The excitement generated by his playing came not from speed or volume, but from the breathtaking clarity, ease, and style with which virtuoso roulades were dispatched.

Along with so many compelling performances there are inevitably a few misses. His three Brahms-Paganini recordings, in spite of their musicality and ravishing details, in some parts sound labored and slow. His *Petrouchka*, so often a blockbuster in performance never quite convinces in any of his six recorded versions. Perhaps this should not be a surprise because Arthur Rubinstein, to whom Stravinsky dedicated the piano transcription, dazzled audiences with it for fifty years but never agreed to record it because of his facilitations and omissions.

Fortunately, Shura Cherkassky's recorded legacy is available to all who would make their own judgments and choose their own hits and misses. But for every moment that disappoints or even offends, there will be many more that surprise and delight, for Cherkassky was an artist who was never on autopilot. "Many people like my playing. Others may not. But I do not believe that anyone can call me boring."

Notes

1. *Journal Herald* (Dayton, Ohio), 20 October 1979.
2. *Journal Herald*, 1979.
3. *Journal Herald*, 1979.

4. Nell S. Graydon and Margaret D. Sizemore, *The Amazing Marriage of Marie Eustis and Josef Hofmann* (Columbia: University of South Carolina Press, 1965).

5. Graydon and Sizemore, *Amazing Marriage of Marie Eustis and Josef Hofmann*.

6. Classical Records, 1 November 1986.

7. *Milwaukee Sentinel*, 1991.

8. Adrian Farmer, liner notes, courtesy of Nimbus Records, Wyastone Leys, United Kingdom.

CHAPTER TEN

Onstage

> Shura Cherkassky, known from last year as a storming dervish combined with a melting westerly breeze, appeared with ovations.
>
> —*Nya Dagligt Allehanda*, October 29, 1939

What made it possible for Shura Cherkassky to sustain a stage and recording career of unprecedented length? Question him about this and he would answer, "Don't ask me about anything I do. I don't know how I do what I do." Neither did anyone else. The only thing clear was that meticulous practice was the bedrock of every Cherkassky performance. As an adult he often recalled that even as a child he was a ferocious worker and extremely scrupulous in his practice for which he had "abnormal" patience. A Baltimore cousin, Sadie Ginsberg, with whom he was very close as a child, recalled, "He had a quality which most artists have; an inner motivated drive for the thing they must do. Shura had that always, the necessary thrust." The result of that thrust was so daunting to some that it sent one particular music student away from the piano forever. "If I can't play the piano like that, I want to play the harmonica," was the reaction of Larry Adler, son of a Russian-born plumber, who lived in Baltimore at the same time as the Cherkassky family and studied piano at the Peabody Institute. Happily for Adler, he went on to become a harmonica player of worldwide renown, living in Britain from 1948 onward following his criticism of the House Un-American Activities Committee and his refusal to take a loyalty oath.

Happily for Cherkassky, he went on working tirelessly at his art four hours a day, two in the morning starting promptly at 10:15 a.m. and then again in the later afternoon for another two hours. From childhood onward he was unable to practice without a clock present, and he often quoted Hofmann as saying, "If you can't do it in four hours, you can't do it; beyond that time one's mind grows stupid and confused." On weekends he did four hours in two days, and treated the sixth and seventh, and eighteenth and nineteenth of every month like the weekend days of Saturday and Sunday. Any minutes of practice time lost to a telephone call or any other interruption were meticulously written down, scheduled to be made up. And they were. "When I say I'm going to practice four hours, I don't mean three hours and fifty-nine minutes!" If he lost thirty minutes of practice time in New York before a flight to Los Angeles, the thirty minutes would be made up promptly upon his arrival in California, and although he often said he never even wanted to *look* at a piano while on vacation, the truth was otherwise. He simply could not be without that which he loved most, and he always managed, if the vacation was the least bit extensive, to have a piano in his hotel room (see figs. 10.1 and 10.2).

In later years he worked with a tape recorder while he practiced and was very honest in saying that he was shocked with some of the liberties he took. While he was interested in listening to playbacks, his technique was so secure, and his confidence in his musical point of view so firm, that he rarely tried out pieces for other pianists. For a brief time in the early 1960s he did play for Solomon, the English pianist who was Cherkassky's polar opposite as an interpreter and whose career was ended in 1956 by a massive stroke (though he lived on for thirty-two years to age eighty-six). In regard to the tryouts for Solomon, Cherkassky publicly stated Solomon was "astute" in judging him, but privately told me that "he didn't get very much out of playing for him," and that although Solomon made recommendations for his programs, it was always Cherkassky's decision that determined the final result. One must conclude that whomever Cherkassky might have played for, their influence on him was negligible.

While taciturn concerning most aspects of his life, Cherkassky spoke

158, The White House,
Regents Park,
London, NW1 3UP, England.

June 4, 1990

My dear Betty,

... The reason I always go to Bangkok? Where else in Europe can I find a Hotel on the beach where they allow a piano? Nowhere as far as I know unless in a private home, which I don't like. Bangkok has everything all at once, therefore again I will go there in August where I can work and at the same time enjoy Bangkok....

Figure 10.1 Letter, June 4, 1990.

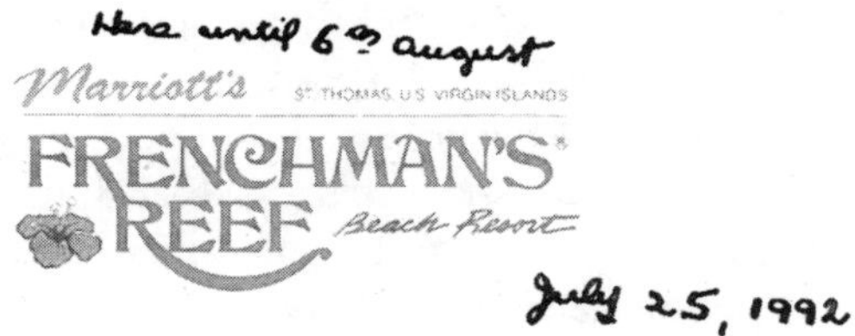

July 25, 1992

My dear Betty,

The weather is superb. plenty of real hot sun, hardly any rain (3 short ones that lasted 5 to 10 minutes). Mr. Temple told me he will give me a key to a room where there is a piano. so from 31st for 6 days I will not exactly practice but play through lightly on pieces and passages that I feel less at ease with, so when I get back to London, I could start properly.

Thank you for calling Mr. Temple. Perhaps (if you think it's wise), you call him again to be reassured about practing in a room where I can lock all doors with key completely. I prefer a bad piano where I am alone, rather than being in a beautiful room where people pass through.

Figure 10.2 Letter, July 25, 1992.

freely of how he worked at the piano. Iron discipline was the foundation of all his practice, and his routine was always the same: place the score on the music rack and then begin to play very slowly and mezzo forte according to an exactly laid-out plan. A certain number of minutes were allotted to selected sections from various pieces on any given program: not a minute more; not a minute less. Technical matters were also approached every time in exactly the same way with exactly the same mind set, placing each finger very precisely on each key, making sure that the fingers were absolutely centered, never overlapping other keys. The American pianist Leonid Hambro recounted that Cherkassky told him that practicing in this way meant that in performance if a finger slipped a fraction in any direction, up or down, right or left, it would still be virtually impossible to play a wrong note. Hambro also remarked on Cherkassky's sight-reading ability, describing it as phenomenal, a high compliment from one whose ability in that area was reported to be absolutely astonishing. In his own words, Cherkassky described how he worked:

> When I practice, I play like it was the first time I ever saw that particular music. Each time I discover something new in the music even if I have been playing it for seventy years. . . . I'm always searching for new ways to express the music—maybe something new with the pedals, or with a new tone, or even technically with some new fingering. I'll be playing a piece twelve or thirteen years, and suddenly I'll say, "My God, it's better with the fingers like that." Or I'll discover something in the chord structure. It's endless the way you can learn.[1]

Commenting further on his practice routine, he frequently said one could tell when pianists were getting older by the way they played chords. They weren't clean anymore and this came from not being able to center the fingers on each key. Asked if he learned this way of practicing from anyone, he said no, but that one of his classmates at the Curtis Institute, Lucy Stern, a pianist he greatly admired, worked in the same manner. He also practiced as Hofmann did, and he said, quoting Hofmann, "I do not resort to regular finger, wrist and arm exercises, but extract and study from works of musical and pianistic merit passages which need special attention."[2]

Four years before he died when asked if he still carried out the routine of his youth, he replied:

> Of course I still need to practice. How can you ask? If one doesn't practice, you notice immediately in two or three days. Not quite accurate. Not quite assured. Even if one can play, the mental attitude is wrong. If I hadn't practiced I couldn't possibly play as well as I could.[3]

Impatient with everything except his work, Cherkassky preferred privacy when practicing since, as he put it with a mischievous smile on his face, people thought that when he practiced he was the piano tuner and that he really couldn't play. Franz Mohr, who was head piano technician for Steinway and Sons in New York City for thirty years, recalled his first assignment as a young man in Germany, when he was sent to tune for a Cherkassky concert. Mohr was awed by the pianist and asked if it would be possible to stay in the artist's room and listen to him rehearse. Cherkassky responded that he could, also assuring Mohr, it was the most boring thing in the world to watch him practice. Mohr described how Cherkassky then proceeded to play very slowly, concentrating on one finger at a time, and playing scales so slowly as to be almost unrecognizable. Orchestral players often had similar experiences in regard to Cherkassky's sound outside of a performance. Often, when the only orchestral rehearsal was on the morning of an evening performance, Cherkassky would play with what he called "half voice," and those in the orchestra who happened not to know his playing would look at each other in dismay. Then at the performance I would watch in silent amusement as the same players visibly reacted when the diminutive pianist played in what he called full voice. It was as though thunder and lightning had struck.

Throughout his life Cherkassky preferred, actually demanded, pianos with heavy actions on which to practice. One of the beneficiaries of this preference was my Steinway B on which he practiced on various occasions, once for an entire week. This grand dame, which had been as truculent as a Mack truck for all its life, turned into and remained the most responsive and malleable instrument thanks to his ministrations. Indeed, his joy in conquering any piano's problems and revealing its myriad possibilities led one reporter, following a concert at the Amsterdam Concertgebouw in 1988, to observe:

> He has totally tamed that large black animal, the grand piano, and has for the past half a century traveled round the world with it in his pocket. It obeys the master's slightest command; it tiptoes on velvet paws, it cascades with lightening speed, and at the slightest signal from its master it alters its speed, changes colour and appearance, and goes on to perform a feather-light summersault.

Franz Mohr, speaking of pianists and their varying tastes in instruments, related that Cherkassky was extremely easy to please in his choice of a concert piano, unlike Horowitz and Rubinstein, each of whom had very specific requirements. The former required an extremely light instrument with an action that went down with about 46 grams and had an uplift of 30 grams, while Rubinstein, who wanted greater resistance to his fingers, preferred an action with 65 grams and 24 grams. Mohr, who was the exclusive tuner for Horowitz, frequently begged the maestro to use a practice piano with a heavier action, a suggestion that Horowitz initially resisted but to which he finally agreed. Subsequently, using a lighter instrument at a dress rehearsal for an upcoming Carnegie Hall concert, Horowitz was delighted, telling Mohr that having practiced on the heavier instrument, the lighter one felt "like going on vacation." While Cherkassky was so easily satisfied with pianos, this was not the case in regard to the piano bench, which had to be adjustable, and it could take as long as an hour of fiddling before the bench was deemed exactly right. He didn't sit at the same height throughout any recital, and for example, he sat lower to play a Chopin nocturne, than he did to play other works.

The transcendental technique that remained with Shura Cherkassky through the last performance of his life at age eighty-six was the result not only of consistent and painstaking hard work, but of one other factor rarely considered: his total lack of conceit. If ever there was a pianist who heeded the axiom Be humble before your art, it was Cherkassky. He took nothing for granted, was extremely self-critical, seriously considered any criticism given, and rarely, if ever, complimented himself. The mystery of his prowess broadens when one considers he never mentioned structural or harmonic analysis, never referred to his absolute pitch or, heaven forbid, to relaxation techniques as support mechanisms. Yet his memory was infallible, his speed and endurance phenomenal. While attention was often called to his gnome-like appearance, his barrel-like muscular structure that served his playing needs perfectly rarely drew comment. He was strong as an ox, and I clearly remember Cherkassky once taking my arm as we crossed a street so that I felt certain my arm had been crushed beyond repair. Claudio Arrau, great artist that he was, for all his analysis, calculation, and choreographing of elbows and wrists, failed in both memory and power well before the end of his career. Perhaps he should instead have emulated the so-called quirky ways of his colleague from Odessa.

Moving from the practice-room to the stage, his preconcert ritual was always the same: sleep late, practice some, eat a huge lunch, nap from 3:30 to 5:00 p.m., rise, dress, "Don't talk to me unless I talk to you," and arrive at the hall at least forty minutes before the performance. Before any concert he described himself as, "not nervous, but impatient. I am very demanding, you know. Is the soap there? Is the piano there? There must be a piano in my hotel room, unless I am staying only a day. And I like to sleep in the afternoon so the front desk must call me."[4] He loved to recount the time the front desk clerk of a particular hotel in Canada did not ring him as ordered, and he slept peacefully until he was awakened by a call from a desperate concert manager wondering where he was. Cherkassky leaped from bed, showered, cut himself shaving, dressed while simultaneously trying to stop the bleeding from the razor cut, and then raced to the hotel elevator only to find a child who was already on board and had pressed the buttons for a stop at every possible floor!

When asked if he ever felt nervous about playing in public, Cherkassky's answer was always the same: "*Never!*" This stood in marked contrast to Josef Hofmann who freely admitted,

> In spite of more than 50 years of playing in public, I very seldom feel entirely relaxed when performing before others. A certain tension exists which may be ascribed to nerves, which in reality is due to an accelerated mental and physical condition. If not too extreme, this attitude fosters inspiration and efficiency, but when it reaches the point of over-ecstasy it becomes negative and greatly interferes with one's artistic effort and results.[5]

For Shura Cherkassky, worry concerned practicalities, never the music. His concert attire, tailored in Hong Kong, allowed extra room in the armholes to facilitate use of his tremendous power. Concert socks were black silk and one entire afternoon was once spent on Zurich's famed Bahnhofstrasse shopping for the perfect pair of *socken*, with a stop at Sprüngli for a dish of his favorite muesli. Backstage, two fresh towels, two programs, two rolls of unwrapped toilet paper, the right amount of fruit and hot tea, *very* hot tea, were absolute requirements, along with a piano on which to practice. It was essential to his routine that he practice before the performance and during intermission. Five minutes before going onstage he would sit in a chair, place his raised feet on another one, close his eyes and start counting backwards. When this ritual was completed, before he walked onstage he always tried to find someone to spit on his cheek. When asked if this was an old Russian custom, he laughed and said, "I think it's just *my* custom." Stepping onstage, always with the right foot first, he strode briskly to the piano, standing briefly before bowing unsmilingly to the audience. Once seated on the bench that had been meticulously placed and adjusted for height beforehand, he silently chose an even number, perhaps 24, then started to count it to himself, looking up at the audience halfway at 12, then back to the keyboard to count the remaining 12, and on the stroke of 24 he would start to play, off on his labor of love, sitting ramrod straight, moving minimally and without gestures of any kind.

Once the performance began, Cherkassky's computer-like brain translated mundane practice sessions into performances that were seemingly effortless acts of creation, each one bringing its own delights, its own ecstasies. Described by some as an iconoclast, he spun a glittering web of sound, infusing his superb mastery of texture with interesting voicings, sophisticated pedaling, roaring power, and whispering nuances, all of which were united in a special blend of clarity and incandescent color that left his audiences by turn awed, bemused, and deeply moved. His ability to achieve the latter was amply demonstrated at a 1987 Leningrad recital where members of the audience wept unashamedly as he played Chopin's F-minor Nocturne, Op. 55, No. 1. Even Cherkassky, who spoke rarely of his playing, couldn't help noticing the reaction in Leningrad and again in Moscow, on May 17, 1987, when he repeated the nocturne in the conservatory's big hall. He told Detroit music critic John Guinn of the *Detroit Free Press*,

> After playing the Chopin F Minor Nocturne, the people gave me an ovation you would not believe. It was the next to last piece on the program, but they responded like I just played the Rachmaninoff Second or the Tchaikovsky B-flat. I had to get up three times to acknowledge applause. Something happened there. It was something special. I don't think I could play it that way again.

As Guinn noted, *that* was exactly the point.

Cherkassky's imagination was boundless. "Expression is primary. Why else play?"[6] he would say. Boredom was to be avoided at all costs, and he could amuse and distract himself and his audiences with what for other pianists were merely trifling details relegated to the background or even the trashbin. He often spoke of intuition in regard to his performances, describing himself as an intuitive person who onstage engaged in his favorite activity: "An emotion comes to me, I play and I communicate." For many listeners, a Cherkassky recital was an exercise in ultimate seduction. It was also akin to taking an ocean voyage, never knowing at the outset which oceans would be navigated to arrive at one's destination. The only certainty was that one would pass through calm seas and raging storms, observing dazzling prisms of color along the way.

Even as a child Shura Cherkassky knew he belonged in large halls, preferring them to intimate settings where he felt he could not express the spontaneity that was an essential part of his very special gift. "Either I practice and practice or I play in large halls"—with nothing in between really suiting him. He particularly enjoyed an opportunity to perform in New York's Carnegie Hall, Tokyo's Suntory Hall, or Amsterdam's Concertgebouw where his power of projection could make his beautifully focused sound reach the farthest corners of the house. The more complex the work he was playing, the more he reveled in its performance. He found nothing technically difficult save Chopin's Etude Op. 10, No. 2, a fact that brought a satisfied smile to his face as he recounted, "So did Horowitz and Rubinstein." In the last year of his life he was learning Ligeti's Etude No. 13, *L'escalier du diable*, a technical maze for most, a kindergarten game for him, but in his words, difficult to internalize.

He often spoke of the spontaneity that was a hallmark of his performances, saying that he didn't know what he was going to do on the spur of the moment, which is exactly what he liked best. He didn't believe in analyzing a work, and he had no special method; everything came naturally. Taking particular pride in being unpredictable, he said he never played a work twice in the same way and that even five minutes before going onstage he didn't know how he was going to play. People who heard him at different times often said he sounded like different pianists. "When I play a concerto the conductor will say to me, 'Why didn't you do it that way this morning at the rehearsal?' "[7] When conductor William Steinberg asked that exact question, the pianist replied, "But *that* was the rehearsal!" Cherkassky clearly understood his spontaneity was key to his attraction to audiences. "In the long run that is what keeps audiences coming back for more—the chance to hear something out of the ordinary. Not to hear exactly what they heard the last time, or a faded copy of what some other artist did years ago."[8]

Such an approach resulted in Cherkassky's never duplicating any one performance, but this was not an indication of idiosyncrasy or eccentricity. Rather, for Hofmann and Cherkassky, the artist who never played twice in the same way was one who could do so because he had the technical control that gave him absolute freedom of expression. For Cherkassky and for Hofmann, spontaneity was the soul of art and was often referred to by Hofmann as "improvising the interpretation." To come before audiences and duplicate onstage exactly what had transpired in the practice session was not acceptable to Hofmann or his star pupil. Improvising the interpretation presupposed the artist's mind and taste to be so well trained as to allow him to rely on the inspiration of the moment. But in back of all there had to be a logical plan of action.

This spontaneous approach in performance led to risk-taking interpretations that gave significant importance to the player in relation to the composer. On those infrequent occasions when Cherkassky wasn't playing to his own expectations, this same spontaneity got him into trouble, causing him to break a line, change tempo, or toy with the rhythm. It also gave fodder to the critics who described his playing as idiosyncratic or inconsistent or distorted. However, it was not unusual to read that Cherkassky did this wrong or that wrong, but that the performance was magical anyway. A great part of

Cherkassky's genius was his ability to convince his listener, no matter how odd or unorthodox the performance might seem. A case in point was his Royal Festival Hall performance in 1951 of Rachmaninoff's Second Piano Concerto with the London Symphony Orchestra under the direction of Royalton Kisch. A reviewer for *Musical Opinion* wrote:

> The soloist in Rachmaninoff's C minor Piano Concerto was Shura Cherkassky whose treatment of the work was unconventional to the point of waywardness; it was impossible to subscribe to his views on *tempi*, such as the very deliberate pace adopted for the opening theme of the first movement, excessive haste in the *piu animato* section of the *adagio*, and dalliance with the second subject of the finale, where the application of *rubato* seemed too liberal; yet on the other hand, it was a deeply felt reading that never allowed attention to waver; the articulation in the rapid passages was exemplary and exhilarating, and, when he did play in *tempo*, the pianist's vehemence and verve swept the music along with an irresistible impetus; as sheer piano playing the performance was masterly in its combination of brilliance, power, delicacy, and great variety of colour.

Obviously, Cherkassky's control over the instrument was such that he was able to do whatever he wanted with the music, and while there were those who might not agree or might even strenuously object, they could never say he was unsuccessful at what he set out to do. While he believed the performer must not ignore the composer's wishes, he also thought it was up to the player to add something. A bit of the unorthodox was a good thing, as he saw it, the lifeblood of a good performance. He admitted to often thinking while onstage, "Shall I surprise them and play this passage *piano* or shall I shock them and play it *forte*. I think I'll be naughty and shock them." He played for the moment, and it was the anticipation of these moments that created the palpable silence before he began any piece. His interpretations breathed new life into the tried and true repertoire, leading London critics to wax eloquent. In 1954 a reviewer for *Musical Opinion* wrote,

> Even when Cherkassky provokes disagreement, his views on the music are expressed with such compulsive conviction and ardor that unremitting attention is exacted from his listeners. . . . To achieve this is no mean feat, and vastly preferable to the deferential attitude towards the text of more orthodox but musically mindless pianists who can be heard by the score throughout the year.

For Cherkassky, the centerpiece of piano playing was sound. His was legendary, consistently described as ravishing by critics around the world. From childhood on he played with it, toyed with it, teased it, and took enormous pleasure in showing his audiences what the modern concert grand was able to do under his hands—and feet. The latter mixed and shook the pedals to create an astonishing array of sound, which became a trademark of his playing. He said that Horowitz told him that "Everything has to sing, even when one plays fast passages. Always sing, not just play the notes. Even in big, bravura passages. Sound, sound is the most important." Cherkassky agreed, saying, "Everyone plays the right notes. I want sound." That was precisely what he found lacking in many of the younger pianists of the twentieth century: a luscious, singing tone as well as daring and individuality.

> There are many, many good pianists today. They play very well but they play the same way and it's just not interesting. They don't have very much to say and some seem afraid to express their feelings. I come out of a concert and five minutes later I forget that I've even heard them. . . . Everyone talks about the sound I make, and yes, whenever young people play for me I don't care how fluently they play the notes, I listen for the sound they make. If they don't have that sound, if it doesn't sing or something, then even that wonderful playing of the notes doesn't mean too much.[9]

He noted that not many performing artists before the public were able to follow Horowitz's ideal of making the piano sing, adding that when they played fast, it was just mechanical. Hofmann thought in the same terms, believing that a single note struck by Chopin or Liszt on the most beautiful piano available would not touch a hearer, while a single note sung, by Caruso for instance, would make an instantaneous appeal to the mind and heart of an audience. While calling the piano an inhuman instrument, he also nominated it for the finest of instruments because "you can do with it what you like. All its sounds are equal to begin with, but by means of expressive touch and careful manipulation, it will say whatever you want."[10] Chicago Symphony conductor Daniel Barenboim, for whom Cherkassky had great esteem, heard the elder pianist on numerous occasions. Concerning Cherkassky's performances, Barenboim commented to me in an interview,

> At his best, when the playing was not willful, and this is not a criticism—anybody who has a personality is willful at times and the personal touch gets out of hand, and he was no exception—but when it was under control it had a magnificent sense of color and *always* great beauty of sound. No matter how powerful the sound it never got rough and you never heard the wood of the piano. He always got to

> the end of it, [the sound] always round and always beautiful and of course always with a great amount of color.

When the subject turned to interpretation, in 1994 Cherkassky told a reporter for the *Corriere della Sera* that he had always remained

> faithful to my personal understanding of the music. When I play, I play with the heart. Many people reproach me for taking certain liberties with my performances. But these are always permissible. They have nothing to do with the fact I passed my eighty-second birthday last October. It is necessary to remain faithful to the spirit of the music which one plays, to the intention of the composers, rather than to a particular instrumental detail.

Continuing this train of thought, he observed,

> If you play everything that is written in the music and you observe every mark the same way every time, how do we know if the composer lived today, he wouldn't have changed it? You should sort of change sometimes, you keep alive that way. The changes are a product of mood when you grow older. When you've been playing a piece over and over again, you may see something you haven't seen before. I'll be in a mood and find some different gradation, wonder if I should use less pedal here, or play it lighter there.[11]

Just as sound and interpretation were matters of primary interest to the inheritors of Anton Rubinstein's tradition, so too was the treatment of repeats, the use of rubato, the concept of authenticity, and the meaning of style. Never was a repeat played as a mirror image, but rather it was an occasion to present the music from another point of view. Concerning authenticity and his use of rubato, Cherkassky recalled,

> I used to do much more rubato than I do now. I've been criticized for being too liberal but it's good to dare because otherwise it becomes boring. Perhaps I used to exaggerate rubato too much. Then I tried to curb it, but I still don't believe in playing everything too strictly, including Bach. Everything should have a beauty in it. I don't believe in being authentic exactly as it's written in the music.[12]

He was just as emphatic concerning style: "I don't believe in such a thing as style. What is it? I suppose it's a compliment to be called a romantic, but I just don't get it. You play with intuition, with what you know. What you know, you communicate to an audience. That is all. *I just play the way I feel.*"[13]

Cherkassky's dazzling expression of individuality flew in the face of what was politically correct, musically speaking. He brought to his performances the most important ingredient of all: the ability to communicate human emotion. "Maybe it's a question of human relations. That's what we're doing when we play the piano, you know—establishing human relations with the audience, trying to make a psychological connection."[14] And he made this connection with consummate technique, by which I do not mean how perfectly he played, but rather how he used colors in all their varying tints, how he let the music breathe, and how he allowed sensuality in its most honorable dress to step to the foreground enveloped in glorious sound.

He also had clearly expressed views on the matter of competitions:

> I don't believe in contests, I cannot judge any musician. Somebody could be very good, but he might lose in a competition. I've seen a loser become much better than the winner after a few years. The prize will help at the beginning of the career, but it doesn't live forever. It's the work that tells, not the prize.[15]

He believed that if he were a young artist beginning his career all over again, he would never win a competition, a fact of which he was quite proud: "That is a compliment to say so. My playing is too individual. I never play it safe." Of his own experience as a judge for the finals of the University of Maryland William Kappell Piano Competition, a task to which he reluctantly agreed, he was amused by the fact that "I have to write down, 'one,' 'two,' 'three' for each of the finalists. Imagine that! One of my colleagues who will also judge told me he will not write one for *nobody*. But who knows?" It pleased Cherkassky to learn that Arthur Rubinstein also had difficulty comprehending the scoring of contestants. Asked to judge a particular competition and score the participants from one to twenty, the famed pianist graded most of the entrants zero, a few twenty, and none in between. When asked why he had scored in such an extreme manner, Rubinstein replied, "Simple. Either they can play the piano or they cannot."[16]

Cherkassky heard his first concerts in Odessa as a very young child, recalling one given by Simon Barere, whose playing he did not forget: "A fabulous technician!" Like Shura's mother, Barere had been a pupil of Essipova at the St. Petersburg Conservatory before completing his studies with Felix Blumenfeld. Then there was Pollini, whom Cherkassky said he admired, though he didn't like his playing because he was so exact, "like a photostat." In a similar vein, he was not enchanted by Arrau's interpretations, saying that they didn't touch his soul. Of Guiomar Novaes he was ecstatic in his praise, saying, "That sound. Oh my God, it was the closest thing to Hofmann. I can never forget that sound."

Concerning Earl Wild, he wrote me on November 17, 1992 (see fig. 10.3). Cherkassky also had thoughts about Ivo Pogorelich, which he expressed in another letter to me (see fig. 10.4). As for the young Evgeny Kissin, believed at that time to be smothered by his mother and his piano teacher, Cherkassky reserved judgment (see fig. 10.5).

Tatiana Nicolayeva was greatly admired by Cherkassky for her perform-

158, The White House,
Regents Park,
Bondon, N.W.1 3UP, England.
November 17, 1992

My dear Betty,

...Earl Wild' playing is excellent. I do not care for that Rhapsody, it is not one of the best, Gershwin encores excellent, again I do not care for those embelishments, however he is an excellent solid pianist - top class....

Figure 10.3 Letter, November 17, 1992.

158, The White House,
Regents Park,
London, NW1 3UP, England.

June 4, 1990

My dear Betty,

I agree with you about Ivo Pogoreli(
He is not just "another pianist". He has individuality, originality, superb pianism, and he "dares" (like I do) to play differently even unconventionally sometimes which might provoke some concervative musicians.

Figure 10.4 Letter, June 4, 1990.

158, The White House,
Regents Park,
London, N.W.1 3UP, England.
March 2, 1993

My dear Betty,

Perhaps you are right about Kissin, his mother and his teacher travel everywhere with him, he is now about 20, and he should be doing things alone musically, of course I don't know the details, and who really knows him to know if its all for the best.

Figure 10.5 Letter, March 2, 1993.

ances of *The Art of the Fugue* and the *Diabelli Variations*, which were described by him as first class. Cherkassky's appraisal was very different from that of Sviatoslav Richter who thought her playing of the *Diabelli Variations* was one in which "she understands virtually nothing of what she's playing. Such tempi are harmful to your health; the rest is boring and prosaic."[17] Cherkassky deeply mourned Nicolayeva's sudden death in 1993, but took comfort in the words of her son who told him that his mother had died peacefully and as she wanted, "in connection with music."

Among the younger generation of pianists, one artist he did single out was Martha Argerich, describing her passion and her sound as "genius, sheer genius." For her part, Argerich responded in kind, saying she "adored Shura, as a musician, as a pianist and as a man." When I asked to what Argerich attributed his celebrity, she cited his all encompassing repertoire and his incomparable sound, which she said he could adapt to any surroundings, producing an ideal result. Following her own rapturous performances of two concertos in Carnegie Hall in October of 2001, she commented, "I loved Shura. He was a magician as well as a musician."

Cherkassky also knew and greatly respected Arthur Rubinstein, whom he described as "an extraordinary fellow" who was very liberal in his thinking and who talked about everything under the sun except music. The latter characteristic greatly pleased Cherkassky who, contrary to some interviewers' reports, had little interest in having conversations about music, even though it was the greatest passion in his life.

But when all was said and done, it was Horowitz alone who entirely captured Cherkassky's mind and soul from the time of his youth to the end of his life: "*Oh*, that sound. How can one not admire this pianist? As soon as he sits down at the piano, you recognize that sound of his." Cherkassky never had anything but superlatives for Horowitz, recalling a performance in Carnegie Hall of the Rachmaninoff Third Concerto: "As I was listening I actually thought I was going to faint. I had to take a long walk afterward to clear my head. I was absolutely crazy. . . . Nobody reached the heights Horowitz did in that concerto."[18]

The two pianists were friends, and during his New York engagements Cherkassky would visit Horowitz in his East Ninety-fourth Street townhouse. They spoke Russian and enjoyed exchanging tidbits about people they knew. Horowitz in turn had the utmost respect for Cherkassky. Tom Frost, who worked for Columbia Masterworks for twenty years and who recorded Horowitz from 1964 to 1973 and from 1984 to 1989, stated that "Horowitz never commented on his contemporaries except for Cherkassky whom he singled out as an exceptional pianist."

The torrents of feeling Cherkassky was able to pour forth onstage flowed from his belief that the private life of an artist was an integral part of his musical personality. For him the two were an indivisible whole without which the special relationship between the artist and the audience could not be created, a relationship that, in his words, could be considered somewhat sadomasochistic. One's private life had to have character. Character was for Cherkassky what made an artist, not technique. And perhaps, though rarely defined or even alluded to, character is what ultimately shines through this pianist's playing by reaching, touching, moving, exciting, lulling, and cajoling audiences around the world. He often said the most important thing was to learn to know oneself not only in music, but in life, and that the most profound change had come in his career with the realization that music was everything in life for him. He also wrote of his frustrations and how he thought they influenced his playing in a letter to me in May of 1991 (see fig. 10.6).

Since Cherkassky freely admitted in conversation after conversation that he didn't know how he did what he did, why do some pianists of infinitely less musical insight attempt to analyze his playing? A great part of the spell Cherkassky was able to cast onstage came precisely from the ease and naturalness of what he was able to do at the piano, an ease that during his concert-playing life delighted believers and disarmed skeptics. There were those who disagreed with what he did, but none ever denied his ability to do it. Ultimately, how he did what he did was of no consequence. Only the ingenuous could think themselves able to analyze something so genuine, so per-

The Peninsula
Hong Kong

May 21, 1991

My dear Betty,

Now I decided to stay here until 28th as I have suite with piano, few nice people (still not exactly what I want(but that is a vicious circle). Who can help me? Not by talking alone. Perhaps these frustrations help me to play better? As no matter what, I NEVER for a second let any thoughts interfere with my work, perhaps that is why I get now more acclaim. I never forget what Raymond Lewenthal told me - "You can do one or another". He was right.

Figure 10.6 Letter, May 21, 1991.

Lydia Schlemenson Cherkassky, 1872–1961. A graduate of the Imperial Conservatory of Petrograd, she once played the Tchaikovsky Variations for the composer. COURTESY OF THE CURTIS INSTITUTE OF MUSIC, PHOTOGRAPH COLLECTION #609.

Lydia, Isaak, and Shura Cherkassky in Odessa, the Ukraine, 1911. From the family album of Judy Bender of Arnold, Maryland, whose mother, Sadie Dashew Ginsberg, was Shura Cherkassky's first cousin.

No. 61 Pushkinskaya, the site of the family apartment in Odessa.
COURTESY OF THE AUTHOR.

Baltimore, 1923. Shura Cherkassky with his manager, Frederick Huber.
COURTESY OF THE HEARST CORPORATION, BALTIMORE NEWS AMERICAN COLLECTION, UNIVERSITY OF MARYLAND AT COLLEGE PARK.

April 17, 1923, and a line waiting outside Albaugh's Ticket Agency in Baltimore to purchase tickets to Shura Cherkassky's concert. COURTESY OF JUDY BENDER.

Shura Cherkassky, 1924. COURTESY OF JUDY BENDER.

With Josef Hofmann at Hofmann's studio at the Curtis Institute, 1927. COURTESY OF THE CURTIS INSTITUTE OF MUSIC, PHOTOGRAPH COLLECTION #609.

Josef Hofmann's class, 1926–27. Top row, l–r: Olga Barabini, Lucille Munro, Joseph Levine, Edith Braun, Esther Polvogt, Martha Halbwachs (Massena), Harry Kaufman, Edith Bly, Edna Wood, and Gerald Tracy. Bottom row, l–r: Vera Resnikoff, Martha de Blassis, Abram Chasins, Lucy Stern, Jeanne Behrend, Shura Cherkassky, Angelica Morales, and Ercelle Mitchell. COURTESY OF THE CURTIS INSTITUTE OF MUSIC, PHOTOGRAPH COLLECTION, #609.

With his parents in Durban, South Africa, 1931. COURTESY OF THE CURTIS INSTITUTE OF MUSIC, PHOTOGRAPH COLLECTION #609.

Playing for factory workers in Russia at the Electrocombinat, March 1935. COURTESY OF HENRY STEINWAY, STEINWAY AND SONS, NEW YORK CITY.

Japan Tour, 1935, Shura with Geisha friends.

During the California years, 1940–49, Cherkassky and his mother resided in Los Angeles at 1418 ½ Sierra Bonita Avenue. COURTESY OF THE AUTHOR.

Mr. and Mrs. Shura Cherkassky in Finland, November 1946. COURTESY OF THE INTERNATIONAL PIANO LIBRARY, UNIVERSITY OF MARYLAND AT COLLEGE PARK.

Shura Cherkassky during the 1950s: successful, expensively dressed, and still unhappy. COURTESY OF THE CURTIS INSTITUTE OF MUSIC, PHOTOGRAPH COLLECTION #609.

Shura Cherkassky's piano in his London flat at the White House Apartment Hotel. COURTESY OF THE AUTHOR.

Shura Cherkassky's desk in his London flat, with his much-used typewriter and ever-present photo of his mother. COURTESY OF THE AUTHOR.

Explaining his cataract operation to the opera star Jessye Norman, 1990. COURTESY OF THE AUTHOR.

October 1991, enjoying his "80th" birthday celebration at the home of his American manager, Harold Shaw. COURTESY OF THE AUTHOR.

December 1992, with Wanda Horowitz and the author following his performance at the Memorial Concert for Vladimir Horowitz, Steinway Hall, New York. COURTESY OF THE AUTHOR.

July 1994, with friends Charles Cumula and Richard Casper, poring over reviews following his appearance at the Mostly Mozart Festival in New York. COURTESY OF THE AUTHOR.

December 1994, flanked by the author and Vladimir Ashkenazy following a recording session of the Rubinstein D Minor Concerto at the Walthamstow Assembly Hall. COURTESY OF THE AUTHOR.

November 10, 1995, backstage at the Rudolfinum in Prague following the last performance of his life. COURTESY OF THE AUTHOR.

sonal, and so beyond the realm of the ordinary. Describe it, admire it, challenge it, appreciate it? Certainly. Dissect it? Impossible. The British critic Bryce Morrison summed it up well when, on the occasion of Shura Cherkassky's eightieth birthday, he was asked to write a celebratory tribute, which he found almost impossible to do: "I found myself chasing quantities as elusive as quicksilver. Pin them down and they wriggled away with the pin. Cherkassky would have been delighted with my dilemma, rejoicing to the end in a life-affirming caprice that defied neat analysis or a tidy sense of category."

And what of the Hofmann influence on Cherkassky's pianistic abilities? In large measure a myth developed, perpetuated by a media that ignored the history of its own writings. One has only to read the multitudinous reviews of the child prodigy's debut year in America to understand that every facet of the playing attributed to the teaching of Josef Hofmann was completely in place before a single lesson was taken with Hofmann. Cherkassky was acutely aware of this chronological anomaly, stating, "Very, very many have said that I am like Hofmann. But they said that when I was a child prodigy, even before I went to study with him, that I resembled him, so afterward they said it all the more."[19] Indeed, Cherkassky himself clearly summed up Hofmann's true mentoring when he said, "Hofmann was a great electrifying personality, a sort of supervisor for me. But he really wasn't what you call a teacher." What influence existed was exerted by virtue of an indefinable like-minded intuition that entwined these two people.

During the last decade of his concert-playing life Cherkassky spoke of his lifelong fidelity to his own musical identity, summing up over seventy-five years of playing before the public with these simple words: "I don't say I play better or worse that anyone else, but part of my success is that I'm different. I don't think there's anyone else quite like me."

There certainly wasn't!

Notes

1. Carnegie Hall, archives, 1989.
2. *Sunday Call* (Newark, N.J.), 7 November 1937.
3. *Guardian* (London), 10 October 1991.
4. *Globe and Mail* (Toronto), April 1983.
5. *Sunday Call* (Newark, N.J.), 7 November 1937.
6. Carnegie Hall, archives, 1989.
7. *New York Times*, 29 March 1981.

8. *Citizen* (Ottawa), 26 April 1982.
9. Carnegie Hall, archives, 1989.
10. *New York Journal*, 13 March 1898.
11. *Seattle Times*, 19 October 1982.
12. *ABC Concert Guide*, "The Elusive Intuitive," 1992.
13. *Sun Sentinel*, 25 October 1992.
14. *Chicago Tribune*, 28 October 1988.
15. *Nation Review* (Bangkok), 24 July 1984.
16. John Train, *The New Money Masters* (New York: HarperBusiness, 1989), 167.
17. Bruno Monsaingeon, *Sviatoslav Richter: Notebooks and Conversations* (Princeton, N.J.: Princeton University Press, 2001), 328.
18. David Dubal, *Remembering Horowitz* (New York: Schirmer, 1993), 320.
19. *Globe and Mail* (Toronto), 14 April 1983.

CHAPTER ELEVEN

A Conductor's Nemesis

With Shura, all you can be sure is that you can't be sure.

—Gerard Schwarz, conductor

Part of Cherkassky's success was, as he said, the fact that he was different. It was also a major part of the problem he ran into when dealing with conductors. Throughout his concert-playing life Cherkassky appeared with many of the world's leading orchestras and conductors starting with his appearance in 1923 with the Baltimore Symphony Orchestra. Yet his orchestral engagements and reengagements were sparse in comparison to the length of his career and the acceptance he received as a solo artist. Certainly the cause was not audience response, all of whom signaled their approval, but rather conductor reaction to the notorious spontaneity of an artist who, on more than one occasion, caused problems, musical and personal, for those who perceived themselves only as directors and never as colleagues in a shared adventure. Not that orchestral leaders didn't have legitimate concerns. Michael Lankester, conductor of the Hartford Symphony, summed up his experience directing a performance of the Rachmaninoff Third Concerto in 1990 with the wonderfully apt description, "Following Shura is like trying to push a string uphill and keep it straight."

Cherkassky treated a concerto performance much as he did a solo recital: as a happening rather than a reproduction of what had taken place at rehearsal. He had a take-no-prisoners attitude and it was not unusual to hear him choose his own tempo while the conductor struggled to regain the lead and the orchestra fell uneasily in place. His imagination and creativity in performance led many conductors to react as did Erich Leinsdorf whose description of a meeting and a Cherkassky concerto performance in 1953 summed up the frustration of many of the orchestra directors under whom Cherkassky played:

> During my visit to Israel, my soloist was the pianist Shura Cherkassky. We took our meals together. Cherkassky managed, between mouthfuls, to ask more questions than any sage could have answered. Everything interested him. Who had bought what and with whose money. He was a one-man cross-examiner. His pianism was flawless, his musicianship of the worst, having mastered the finger portion to such an extent that he could, and did change everything else from one performance to the next, what was loud today might be soft tomorrow, and what went presto on Tuesday might be taken slowly on Wednesday. If he had played Beethoven or Mozart, I might have gone crazy, but fortunately he played only rhapsodic composers such as Liszt, who should not be treated this way either, but can stand such "interpretations" with less ultimate damage. Liszt himself was allegedly free with the compositions he played.[1]

Yet Cherkassky himself made no apologies for following his own muse.

> Yes it's true, lots of conductors don't like it [his unpredictability] and I can't blame them. They're right. They rehearsed the score one way and then I'd play it another in concert. They want to know why suddenly I play *forte* instead of *piano*. Conductors in the past were more individual like the soloists and could cope with such changes. But not now.[2]

Cherkassky's wonderful wit surfaced on many occasions as he described various concerto performances of his career. About Gunther Herbig he stated, "I can't remember anything bad and that's already good." When one conductor asked Cherkassky why he played a piece so fast, with a twinkle in his eyes he replied, because he could. He loved to recount, while demonstrating at the piano, a performance of the Rachmaninoff Third Concerto under a Greek conductor who simply stopped at the end of the second movement following the piano flourish, completely ignoring Rachmaninoff's *attacca* as well as dominant chord crying out to move on to its resolution. After standing silent with his arms folded across his chest, the self-satisfied conductor finally cued the orchestra to begin the last movement, causing the soloist to remember the experience with hilarity for the rest of his life.

One not so amusing incident occurred while Cherkassky was playing the same concerto in Solingen, Germany, in 1957. During the course of this performance the conductor, Werner Sahm, dropped dead just before the cadenza in the first movement. The deceased was carried to the artist's room backstage and his demise was announced to the audience. Cherkassky returned to his dressing room where a diehard fan approached the pianist asking for his autograph. Shocked, Cherkassky replied, "Get the hell out of here. Don't you know there is a dead person next door?"

Concerto playing certainly is not every soloist's cup of tea. "If I never played with orchestra again I wouldn't mind at all." This was the carefully considered, measured response of sixty-four-year-old Jorge Bolet, then at the height of his career, when asked if he preferred playing concertos or recitals. Vladimir Horowitz didn't mince words either when asked his reaction to orchestral engagements: "No! Too many wrong notes from the back. I'd rather make my own mistakes!" Understandably impatient with conductors who could not match his vibrant personality, Horowitz played shockingly few concertos, and then with only the best orchestras and conductors. He loved Szell and Ormandy, and he respected his father-in-law, Arturo Toscanini, but disavowed their collaborations: "They were *his* performances, not mine."

If anyone had reason to feel frustrated by conductors and straight-jacketed by orchestral ensemble it was Shura Cherkassky. Yet curiously, he never expressed anything but satisfaction and pleasure about orchestral dates. He was even perfectly pleasant in situations that would drive other more temperamental artists to frenzy. One such example was given by Lolita Mayadas, director of administration for the Florida Philharmonic, who had engaged Cherkassky in 1980 for a performance of the Prokofiev Second Piano Concerto with Brian Priestman conducting. One hour before rehearsal it was discovered that the required piano was not on stage but in another building across town. Instead of creating an unpleasant scene, the rehearsal went forward as scheduled with the pianist from Odessa unperturbed. Mayadas recalled, "No problem. He sang his way through it," adding it was quite startling that anyone could *sing* their way through the Prokofiev Second Concerto.

While his unpredictable musical temperament made him, for many conductors, a difficult subject to follow, his foolproof technique, imagination, and infallible memory produced performances that were exciting and arresting. Conductors should have seized upon this unique artist's giant personality with relish. But many didn't because they simply weren't willing to accept risk, or worse yet, the possibility of being upstaged. The absence of conductors who could be his champion was a major roadblock during his entire career.

In spite of his willful reputation, Cherkassky did perform under the major conductors of the world both before and after World War II. His orchestral engagements following the war and up to the end of his life fifty years later included collaborations with many distinguished conductors, some of whom were able to deal with his spontaneity in performance, and some who were not: Ashkenazy, Commissiona, Dorati, Dutoit, Fruhbeck de Burgos, Gergiev, Giulini, Haitnik, Herbig, Karajan, Kempe, Leinsdorf, Leppard, Macal, Mazur, Navarro, Ozawa, Rattle, Rodzinski, Rostropovich, Schmidt-Isserstedt, Schwarz, Maxim Shostakovich, Sinaisky, Slatkin, Susskind, Temirkanov, Sir Alexander Gibson, Sir Charles Grove, Sir John Pritchard, Sir Malcolm Sargent, and Sir Georg Solti. Prior to World War II, he played under the baton of the foremost European conductors, among them, Ansermet, Scheneiviogt, Vazy, Beerdisjew, Wiklund, Sirop, Strasser, and Van der Pelz.

Two conductors with whom Cherkassky worked particularly well were Vladimir Ashkenazy and Gerard Schwarz. Ashkenazy accompanied him in Sheffield, England, in December of 1994 in a performance of the *Rachmaninoff-Paganini Variations* and subsequently in Walthamstow Assembly Hall at a recording session of the Rubinstein D-minor Concerto. A performance of the latter was given at Festival Hall in London on the evening before the recording session. When I asked Ashkenazy how he dealt with Shura's "muse," which was likely to drop in on him at any moment, Ashkenazy replied that the Royal Philharmonic players had warned him about Shura's tendency to be unpredictable, and when he worked with Shura he was particularly attentive and alert in that direction.

> Being a pianist myself helps me enormously when I accompany pianists—and these two points contributed to a situation whereby I had almost no problem getting things together organically with Shura. It was a real pleasure working with Shura both personally and musically. He was totally unpretentious and honest and his command of the instrument was really a fascinating phenomenon—he was one of the last pianists of the "other" era and there *was* room for him!

Ashkenazy and Cherkassky were indeed compatible artists and compatible people as well, as was evident in their first encounter backstage in Sheffield, England, in the artist's dressing room prior to the rehearsal of the *Rachmaninoff-Paganini Variations*. Great camaraderie and genuine mutual understanding prevailed as the two discussed tempi, entrances, and color.

Numerous successful collaborations took place with New York City's 92nd Street Y Chamber Symphony under the baton of Gerard Schwarz, who once stated with the insight of long experience,

> The only thing you can be sure about Shura is that you can't be sure. . . . He's a wonderful man but an idiosyncratic one. When you're playing with him he will get mad if he looks up and you're not looking at him. If you don't pay attention to him he'll punish you with an unexpected *rubato*.[3]

In one rendering of Chopin's Second Piano Concerto, Cherkassky and Schwarz produced a performance that a critic described as glowing with beauty and fresh ideas, but that caused the pianist great consternation when the flute entered wrongly in the second movement creating a conflict for the soloist. Should he follow the flutist or come in on the right beat? He chose the former but then spent the entire evening following the performance regretting his decision, saying with the closest thing to a pout, "She did it first. She did it first." Commenting on Cherkassky's interpretation of the Chopin concertos, Schwarz recalled: "I did a tour with him a few years ago with the Chopin F-minor Concerto. We did seven performances and each night it was completely different, ranging from emotionally reserved to sheer flamboyance."[4] Dazzling performances were given of the E-minor Concerto as well, leading one New York critic to sigh, "It's doubtful even George Sand heard it better performed."

Two other conductors who looked favorably on Cherkassky's work were Leonard Slatkin who said he wished he could have worked with Cherkassky more, and Daniel Barenboim who deeply regretted he never had the chance to conduct one of his performances.

Cherkassky played most of the concerto repertoire, winning particular critical acclaim for bravura interpretations of Tchaikovsky, Rachmaninoff, and Rubinstein as well as for his haunting and technically stunning renditions of the Chopin concertos, the *Là ci darem la mano Variations*, and the *Andante Spianato and Grand Polonaise*. He also ventured into Mozart territory playing the D-minor Concerto, K. 466. The July 1990 performance of this work at New York's Mostly Mozart Festival was praised for its exquisitely shaded playing, its carefully controlled execution, and the wisdom behind the conception. Using the Beethoven cadenzas to great effect, Cherkassky gave a performance of taste and balance with just enough originality to make the interpretation memorable. Of the Beethoven concertos he favored the Fourth, which he played with understated eloquence and a rare understanding of the whole. His performance of the concerto under Sir Malcolm Sargent at Royal Festival Hall in 1964 was described as one with "extraordinary rhythmic zest and clarity, coloring the music with immense skill . . . every detail finely moulded. The slow movement was perfectly controlled, portraying a perfectly sustained arch from first note to the last." He omitted the third Beethoven concerto from his performing repertoire because of his unwillingness to make any compromise with the broken octaves in the last movement, which his small hands had difficulty negotiating. Even as he believed that dynamic shapes and voicings were subject to the spirit of the moment, purists were no more rigorous than Cherkassky about never changing or rearranging the actual notes. Never mind that so scrupulous an artist as Alfred Brendel resorted to the widespread and sensible strategy of playing alternating octaves instead of the awkward original that Beethoven had written for his third concerto. The composer's Fifth Concerto was another story, with Cherkassky delivering the *Emperor* with granite-like power, making the familiar sound seem newly composed, albeit with total respect for the master who had created it.

Moving into full-fledged Romanticism, his performance of the Liszt E-flat Concerto was "probably the most authentic performance of that work you're likely to hear this side of heaven or hell, depending on where you think Liszt ended up," wrote John Guinn of the *Detroit Free Press* in 1986.

> In most hands Liszt's music can seem loaded with glib technical tricks, cheap emotional content and vapid, overblown gestures. Cherkassky's interpretation which was absolutely secure technically, eschewed all such vulgarity by concentrating on the music's worthwhile elements: its salient harmonies, its lyrical melodies, its judicious balance of ferocious bravura and gentle reflection.

Liszt's *Hungarian Fantasy* glittered as well and was lavished with rubatos and hair-raising climaxes. And Cherkassky's performances of the Schumann A-minor Concerto were delivered in a manner that elicited kudos from the Stuttgart press for the memorable solution he provided in his interpretation of the finale.

> Only the *ritornelli* were rendered fiercely, fortissimo in an almost baroque manner, while the interim episodes assumed a style reminiscent of a romantic piano piece. This way the movement attained quite a new formal structure and the traditional impression that even after a thousand bars Schumann had not managed to solve the problem of the Finale, should now be eliminated from the annals of the work as superfluous ballast.[5]

The Brahms D Minor, reviewed by critics as magnificent in conception and performance, was set forth with poetry and pointed brilliance, with a fierce, sprawling first movement giving way to a tender adagio, culminating in a bold rondo finale. To his performance of the Saint-Saëns Concerto No. 2 in G Minor, which he first performed in Vienna in 1978, he brought dazzling fingerwork and an infectious rhythmic bounce.

In the realm of the modern, Cherkassky was among the first pianists to regularly perform the massive Prokofiev Second Concerto, delighting in its brilliant force and twentieth-century idiom. Interestingly, he never played Prokofiev's First or Third concertos, each of which would seem so well suited to his pianistic and musical personality. Instead he chose the composer's Second Concerto, delivering a blockbuster performance of the piece in 1961 in Carnegie Hall at age fifty-two, and in 1991, at the age of eighty-two, playing what many considered to be an utterly individual, mesmerizing performance captured in a live recording at London's Festival Hall with Kent Nagano conducting. He shared the same enthusiasm for the Strauss *Burleske*, which he so aptly described as "a wonderful work, but not for the pianist," and for the Shostakovich First Concerto, which he played as early as 1935, as well as for the jazz elements of the Ravel *Left Hand* Concerto, and Gershwin's *Rhapsody in Blue* and Concerto in F.

The most unusual piece in his orchestral repertoire was Hofmann's *Chromaticon*, written under the pen name Michael Dvorsky, under which Hofmann also penned a fictitious biographical sketch. Dvorsky was allegedly a young Frenchman in delicate health who had been born in Pau, France, in 1890, the son of a Polish father and a French mother. Purportedly living in San Sebastian, a Spanish watering place, he wrote piano pieces, orchestral pieces, and two concertos, of which the *Chromaticon*, described as a "Symphonic Duologue for Piano and Orchestra," was the first. The initial performance in America of the *Chromaticon*, by Hofmann and the Cincinnati Symphony Orchestra under Dr. Ernst Kunold, took place in Cincinnati, November 24 and 25, 1916. It was again performed by Hofmann the following January with the Philadelphia Orchestra, conducted by Leopold Stokowski. In March of 1917 a letter was published in *Musical America*, dated February 22, 1917, c/o Señor Don Federico, Camino de Lugariz, San Sebastian (Antiguo), in which "Dvorsky" repudiated the contention that pianist Josef Hofmann had adopted a nom de plume and was actually the composer of the *Chromaticon*:

> Editor, Musical America, New York
> Sir: I have learned from a friend living in England that you published in your esteemed paper an article about my Concerto for piano with orchestral accompaniment, the "Chromaticon."

> Reading between the lines, it is clear that you believe Mr. Josef Hofmann, the celebrated pianist, to be the composer of the "Chromaticon."
>
> As I do not know whom to reproach for such an insinuation—it is impossible to think that an artist of the rank of Mr. Josef Hofmann should have spread such reports—I refrain from accusing anybody.
>
> Only I have to inform you that it is indeed I who am the composer and that I sent my manuscript to Mr. Josef Hofmann, hoping he would play it. I was encouraged to do this because Mr. Josef Hofmann had played several of my short piano pieces a year or two ago.
>
> Therefore, you will not only be doing me justice, but I shall regard it as a particular favor if you abstain in the future from making such insinuations as you make in connection with the "Chromaticon."
>
> Kindly accept, sir, the assurance of my most distinguished sentiments.
>
> —Michel Dvorsky[6]

A representative of *Musical America* was dispatched forthwith to check on the address of Michel Dvorsky's letter and wrote back to the publisher that he could assure him that such a person did not exist, or at least had never lived in that district. Finally, in 1918 Josef Hofmann came forth to dispel the mystery of Michel Dvorsky, stating that he chose to introduce his latest compositions under a nom de plume in order to obtain the unbiased opinion of the public.

Cherkassky's first performance of the *Chromaticon* took place at Newport News, Virginia, with the Virginia Philharmonic on April 19, 1980, in a program re-creating Hofmann's Golden Jubilee Concert at the Metropolitan Opera in 1937. The performance by Cherkassky, which was repeated the following day at the Kennedy Center in Washington, D.C., and two days later in Norfolk, Virginia, was greeted with rave reviews; the composition, with divided opinion as to its merits. Apparently Hofmann had an even stronger opinion about his own work, as is evident in a comment relayed to the *New York Times* critic, Harold Schonberg, in April of 1976, when he wrote a review of Hofmann's Golden Jubilee Concert of 1937, which Hofmann had privately arranged to have taped. The concert included solo works as well as the Rubinstein D-minor Concerto and the *Chromaticon*, and in 1955 Columbia Records released part of the recording of the event. Schonberg reviewed the recording, and in the course of writing his criticism he disparaged the *Chromaticon* as a composition, which resulted in a certain telephone call:

> "How nice of you to remember Hofmann's playing," a woman's voice said. "We were so pleased. It is so good to know we are not forgotten."

> "Who is this?" Schonberg asked.
> "Why, Betty Hofmann."
> "Where are you phoning from?"
> "Los Angeles."
> . . .
> "Why didn't you like the *Chromaticon*?" asked Hofmann's wife.[7]

According to Schonberg, she then spent ten minutes giving an analysis of the work. It used all twelve notes of the scale. It was highly advanced for its day. It was a masterpiece of piano writing. And on she went in the same vein for half an hour. But ten minutes after the conversation ended, Schonberg's phone rang: "This is Betty Hofmann again. I just wanted to tell you I phoned Josef in Long Beach, and he told me to call you right back and tell you he agrees with you. The *Chromaticon* is really a terrible piece of music."

Notwithstanding Cherkassky's respect for the classical canon, his interest in the contemporary, and his attraction to the offbeat, it was in the Romantic standards, especially the Rubinstein D Minor, the Tchaikovsky First and Second, and the Rachmaninoff Third Concerto, that Cherkassky pulled out all the stops, galloping start to finish in true thoroughbred fashion. He reveled in their throbbing power even as he spun their melodies with the delicacy of fine lace, making his performances quintessential displays of the heroic manner of Russian playing traceable to Anton Rubinstein.

Throughout his career he championed Tchaikovsky's Second Concerto in G, Op. 44, which became a signature work in his repertoire. Continuously overshadowed by the First Concerto in B-flat, the Second was neglected mainly for its immense technical demands. It was also regarded by many as being weak compositionally, with the focus too much on the piano and too little on the orchestra. As one observer wittily put it, "It is no wonder that the orchestra lost our attention, Tchaikovsky put it there only to keep the pianist from feeling lonely." Tchaikovsky's biographer, Herbert Weinstock contends that the disappearance of the G Major, Op. 44 from concert programs was

> without sense or justification. . . . Each of its three movements contains excellent musical ideas put into action with assurance and originality. To perform it once to every ten playings of the B-flat minor would be to hurt no one and to increase the musical enjoyment of many.

Cherkassky firmly believed in the work and was supported in his view by the conductor Walter Susskind who had this to offer:

> Anybody, who gets to love the Fifth Beethoven Symphony will probably, if he were in a mind to compare it, be less pleased when hearing the Fourth Symphony for the first time. There are towering works in every composer's output which, when compared with slightly lesser ones, will probably create a certain sense of disappointment. The composer who has written nothing but towering masterpieces hasn't been born. What I feel about this concerto is that generally—in Tchaikovsky biographies and histories of the concerto—it gets too tough a treatment, possibly because it cannot be rightly compared in excitement and invention with the First Concerto. But, I'll give you another example: The cello concerto by Dvorak is one of the most beloved of the romantic concertos. Well, he also wrote a very fine violin concerto which, had he never written the cello concerto, would be considered a towering work. . . . I think this odious comparison to the towering masterpieces is dangerous. . . . It would be a sad world if we only . . . went to a concert when they played the Fifth or Ninth of Beethoven—or only the first Tchaikovsky.[8]

Reveling in the difficulties of the G-major Concerto, Cherkassky seized the singing melodies, expressive content, and the bountiful opportunities it offers the soloist to display virtuoso skills in endless roulades of scales, cascading arpeggios, and blocks of sonority requiring huge power. The notoriously difficult cadenza was tossed off as nothing with the two-handed trill bringing the first movement to an electrifying conclusion. Cherkassky chose to play Siloti's abbreviated version of the second movement, saying he got bored accompanying the long solos for the violin and cello, which also of course took attention away from the solo piano part. When he played the concerto under Gunther Herbig in Detroit in May of 1986, the performance was described as quite capricious in its tempo and dynamics. Herbig preferred a square pace and accompanied pedantically, often oblivious to Cherkassky's attempts to elasticize the phrasing, an unfortunate situation since the pianist's individuality thrived on spontaneous rapport.

One of the more unique performances of the Tchaikovsky Second Concerto took place in South Africa in 1963 when Cherkassky's appearance in Johannesburg's city hall earned him the headline: "Pianist dives under piano—audience gasped as he suddenly vanished." The following article describes what happened.

> Celebrity pianist Shura Cherkassky performed on and under the piano during a Tchaikovsky concerto in Johannesburg last night.
>
> Twice during the third movement he dived under the keyboard while the orchestra continued playing and fixed the pedal which had worked loose and was

> not responding to his foot. The audience gasped, but on both occasions the pianist was back on the stool and the pianist carried on.
>
> The South African Orchestra, under Frits Schurman, continued without a hitch, and Cherkassky gave a brilliant performance. At the end the audience called him out again and again. And he threw kisses at them.
>
> The trouble had started at the end of the first movement of Tchaikovsky's Piano Concerto No. 2. A mechanic was called to repair the pedal and the pianist carried on. But, during the third movement at the end of a solo passage, the audience was astonished to see Cherkassky dive under the piano while the orchestra played on.
>
> He "surfaced" for his next solo passage but a few minutes later was down on his knees again crouching under the keyboard. He was almost out of sight. Would he get back on his stool in time? He did, with a second or two to spare, and then finished the work amid terrific applause.[9]

Cherkassky explained afterwards that a screw had come loose in the pedal and that another pianist might have given up but he felt he simply had to fix it. "The second time down I was able to fix it to hold for 30 seconds more to the end of the work. This had never happened to me before. I was so excited that I felt I had to kiss the audience. So I did. I've never done *that* before."[10] Another critic noted Cherkassky played with terrifying power and pace combined with exquisite loveliness, and with such fire and flourish in the finale that it set the audience shouting.

As for the Second Concerto's more famous sister and its alternations between bravura and intimacy, Cherkassky and Tchaikovsky's First Concerto were a perfect pianistic fit. The work was a staple of his repertoire from early youth to the end of his days, and the headlines it earned him ranged from the ecstatic to the colorful, such as, "Cherkassky cripples concerto." On occasion, fitting in with a conductor's intentions created a problem for Cherkassky, as in one performance with the St. Louis Symphony in April of 1984 when the soloist decided to take matters into his own hands:

> It seemed the tempo set by guest conductor Garcia Navarro was not quite fast enough for this septuagenarian virtuoso; the ascending sequence of chords with which the pianist made his entrance in the sixth bar was like the crack of a whip, not only driving the music into high gear but also announcing, simply by virtue of its overwhelming physical power, that from that moment on he and he alone was in charge of the proceedings.

The headline of this review in the *St. Louis Globe Democrat* read, "Shura Cherkassky in St. Louis Symphony triumphs."

In the spring of 1991 Cherkassky sent me a letter in which he described the reaction of the audience and of the conductor, Mitslav Rostropovich, to his performance of this work in Evian, France (see fig. 11.1). While Cherkassky's performing repertoire included at least thirty-three concertos, only three Beethoven and two Mozart concertos predated the Romantic era. Of them all, he admitted, in a rare statement of preference, to loving best Rachmaninoff's Third Concerto, which received its first performance with the composer as soloist with the New York Philharmonic under Mahler in 1909, barely six weeks after Cherkassky was born. As a child Cherkassky had greatly admired Rachmaninoff, citing him in 1923 as his favorite among the moderns. In 1928 he heard Rachmaninoff play "a Liszt sonata" (almost certainly the *Dante* Sonata, which was part of Rachmaninoff's touring program in 1928) and never forgot it, saying that although he didn't think others would play it in the way Rachmaninoff did, he personally found it arresting. In the early stages of his career Cherkassky performed the Rachmaninoff Third Concerto in a powerhouse, blockbuster style, clearly heard in a live recording from London in 1957 under Rudolf Schwarz. At the age of eighty-six he played Rachmaninoff's Third with a brilliance that was not blinding but illuminating, in an elegant and assured style, blending all with exquisite poetic phrasing. The opening statement was presented as the softest murmur, its repetitions dressed always in new finery but with Cherkassky's gorgeous sound omnipresent. Spacious singing lines ruled his playing of the second movement, and crackling intensity the third.

In 1986 a critic for the *Ottawa Citizen* wrote of Cherkassky's performance of this piece that "This was music making on an exalted level and the entire

The Peninsula
Hong Kong

May 21, 1991

My dear Betty,

Just a few lines as have few free moments. In Evian the success was so extraordinary after Tchaikovsky 1 with Rostropovich, I came out <u>seven</u> times with cheering standing ovation including three times with Rostropovich who kep on kissing and hugging me in front of audien After Prokofieff in London there was a fantastic review in Daily Telegr in London, rave, even writing about my walk saying I don't look a day older that I did 20 years ago, etc.

Figure 11.1 Letter, May 21, 1991.

performance was bathed in the nectar of the gods." It is particularly fitting that Shura Cherkassky played the Rachmaninoff Third Concerto in the last public performance of his life in Dvorak Hall at the Rudolfinum in Prague, Czechoslovakia, on November 10, 1995.

Notes

1. Erich Leinsdorf, *Cadenza* (New York: Houghton Mifflin, 1976), 156.
2. *New York Observer*, 27 February 1995.
3. *Baltimore Sun*, 17 November 1991.
4. *Baltimore Sun*, 17 November 1991.
5. *Stuttgarter Zeitung*, October 1984.
6. *Musical America*, 31 March 1917.
7. *New York Times*, 18 April 1976.
8. *Journal Herald* (Dayton, Ohio), 20 October 1979.
9. *Johannesburg Rand Daily*, May 1963.
10. *Johannesburg Rand Daily*, May 1963.

CHAPTER TWELVE

The Last Romantic?

> I just play the way I feel.
>
> —S. C.

Critics frequently described Shura Cherkassky as the "Last Romantic," an artist whose playing was a throwback to turn-of-the-century pianism, when what a pianist wanted to do with the score was just as important as what the score told him to do. In 1977 Harold C. Schonberg of the *New York Times* described Cherkassky as

> a romantic who makes music in a very personal manner . . . a dazzling technician . . . [who] represents an old style of playing, in which color, technique and beauty of sound were of paramount importance. He has grown up in that style and he is one of the last to keep it alive.

Ten years later, in 1987, Schonberg reiterated his opinion, writing,

> Mr. Cherkassky is thus one of a handful of musicians who reflect the Romantic style. In a day when interpretations are highly standardized, he goes along in his own highly idiosyncratic, personal manner. It is a style that is sometimes too perfumed for some people's tastes. But it is also a style that is poetic, can rise to authentic grandeur, can convey the emotional content of the music without neglecting its structure, and can make the younger generation's playing sound like pebbles rattling in a tin can.

This sentiment was echoed by the well-known music critic and biographer of Maria Callas, John Ardoin, who wrote in the *Dallas Texas News* in 1991,

"The principal difference between Mr. Cherkassky and the young firebrands burning up the keyboard is that his prowess is always wed to a rich interior vision of what a piece of music should be and what it must say."

While he never accepted the title bestowed on him, the "Last Romantic," claiming he did not even know what Romanticism really was, he freely admitted his playing reflected instinct and feeling. *Instinctual* was the expression he most regularly used to describe his performances, adding that the connection was subconscious and not meant to be analyzed or calculated. "It's instinctual. If you analyze, you lose spontaneity." He also didn't think it was sufficient for a pianist to be a great musician, saying it was possible to be a great musician and not be able to play. What was important was to be able to play and to *feel*. "When I play, I have no poetic or fantastic thoughts in my mind, such as many pianists say they have. It is merely the thought of making the music as beautiful as possible. The music itself is the sole consideration."[1]

To call Shura Cherkassky a Romantic pianist or the last Romantic pianist is simultaneously correct and misleading. It is correct if we agree Romantic means a style of playing that is mercurial, passionate, risk-taking, vividly colored, and deeply subjective; misleading if we believe such descriptions of his performances of nineteenth-century repertoire exclude the possibility of his giving valid performances of other music with just as much distinctiveness. Correct as well is the Romantic label if we agree that the great Romantic pianists are admired not for their scholarship, strict observance of the score, or adherence to a still undefined Romantic tradition but for their individuality and personality, while the great classical pianists are judged and praised on their ability to honor an established classical canon, an ability that is based on research, scholarship, and strict adherence to the score. Serkin, Brendel, and Arrau, among others, repeatedly articulated their goal of submerging their own personality to better identify with the intent of the composer, thereby creating a relatively homogenized group of performers. While Cherkassky never specifically stated the opposite goal, a long lifetime of performances and recordings make clear that for him, as for Horowitz, Rachmaninoff, and others, it was exactly that personal slant, which the performer brought to the music, that mattered most. This personal difference is not something that can be easily described, let alone taught or imitated. Pianist Alexis Weissenberg has explained it well, saying, "Horowitz doesn't try to be interesting. He just is." The same may be said of Cherkassky. The intellectual content on which some pianists claim to base their interpretations was as he saw it a purely theoretical and unproven ingredient and an unsatisfactory basis for a performance. This is not to imply that his brain was not the controlling force behind every performance. In spite of his statement that he did not know how he did what he did, he obviously knew perfectly well what he was doing when he did it.

Applicable too is Cherkassky's last Romantic label if we accept the fact that no future pianist will have a direct link to any of the Romantic giants as Cherkassky did to Rachmaninoff, and through Josef Hofmann to Anton Rubinstein, but at the same time the label is misleading because Cherkassky could never be the last of anything since he was unique. No one ever called Rudolf Serkin or Alfred Brendel the "last classical pianist" since we assume there will continue to be great classical pianists even though any direct link to the classical era is long gone. Will there be other pianists with musical personalities so powerful that they will be legitimately compared to Horowitz or Cherkassky or Friedman? One can only hope so.

If one accepts the classic-romantic dichotomy, what comes as a surprise is the considerable overlap in the core repertoire of Cherkassky and the great classical pianists. After Beethoven, the composer most frequently performed by Serkin was Chopin, while Brendel continued to program the Liszt B-minor Sonata long after he had abandoned the many other Liszt works that he recorded in his youth. What is not the least bit surprising is the totally different mindset that Cherkassky, Serkin, and Brendel brought to the execution of this common repertoire, a mindset that perhaps is our justification for describing Cherkassky as a Romantic pianist, no matter what he played. In spite of the vast difference between him and them in approach and style, Cherkassky never spoke of Serkin, Arrau, Brendel, or especially Schnabel with anything less than respect. The only reservation he expressed was to describe them as "sometimes a bit *ac-a-dem-ic*" (always pronounced as though it were four separate words).

With uncommon exceptions, a night in the concert hall with Shura Cherkassky was a rare listening experience. The historical record supports this statement with extraordinary unanimity of voice. Anyone with the opportunity to read more than two thousand reviews and commentaries written by critics all around the globe and over the span of Cherkassky's more than seventy-five-year career would be obliged to conclude that the criticism lavished on his playing was overwhelmingly favorable. Even when the criticism was hedged, it was positive: "Quirky or sublime, weird or whimsical, maddening, disturbing or deeply penetrating—and as often as not all of these at once: a Cherkassky recital is not to be missed," wrote Dominic Gill in the London *Financial Times*. While reviewers and listeners could find themselves perplexed, in disagreement, or even annoyed by some passage or some work in a Cherkassky performance, a bad review was the exception, and a genuinely indifferent response to his playing nearly impossible to find.

Impossible that is, except in Boston, a city that never embraced Cherkassky after initially acclaiming his debut there in 1923 and again in 1925, and where he performed only rarely in the last fifty years of his life. One might expect some to be offended by Cherkassky's freedom and caprice, but one is given to wonder how Ellen Pfeifer in the *Boston Herald* could find his playing "so boring, so utterly neutral in expression, so monochromatic in style and mood" in 1988, and an "emotional blank" two years later. This unprecedented description of his playing might be dismissed coming from a writer who also found Horowitz in 1976 "a boring guest" whose "music making is downright odd," and who "doesn't really understand what is happening." Curiously, Pfeifer's criticism is echoed in Anthony Tommasini's *Boston Globe* reviews of the same Cherkassky performances. Lamenting the pianist's "casual, all in-a-day's work approach" in 1988, Tommasini thought he sounded "stylistically neutral" and "bored" two years later, although he did concede, unlike his colleague, that the audience had been "knocked dead" by Cherkassky's performance. Even more perplexing is the indifference of Boston's principal music critic, Richard Dyer, who found so much to praise but had no enthusiasm for an earlier Cherkassky recital in Newport, Rhode Island, in 1987.

If Cherkassky was boring in Boston, this surely was not the case in the rest of the world. Accolades to his pianism, and above all to his imagination and the excitement it provoked in the concert hall were the norm, as the record amply demonstrates. Of course there were specific performances that missed their mark. When they did Cherkassky was the first to recognize this, often asking on the way to a postconcert supper, "What didn't you like on the program?" and "What did you think was the best?" He thought carefully about any criticism offered because he knew that his muse sometimes did not speak exactly as he wished, just as he was aware that a flight of fancy to one listener could be labeled a distortion by another.

Since he prided himself on never playing a piece twice in the same way, it is an exercise in futility to attempt to describe the quicksilver qualities that made his playing so special. Examples of his approach, so different in the basic repertoire he shared with other pianists, came in his renderings of Beethoven as well as of Chopin and Liszt. Consider, for example, the way in which he floated out the opening chords of the Beethoven *Sonata quasi fantasia* in E-flat, Op. 27. Long overshadowed by its more famous opus mate, the

Moonlight, this curious work, infrequently programmed even by Beethoven specialists, was a staple in Cherkassky's programs and was applauded by audiences and critics alike for the flowing and deeply colored lyricism, alternating with explosive power, with which he delivered the piece. The last recital of Cherkassky's life featured the Sonata Op. 101, rendered with poetry, serenity, and urgency—a work he chose, after long indecision, over Op. 111, which earlier he had preferred. In an article published in *BBC Magazine* in 1995, one month before he died, he reflected on Op. 111, saying, "I don't feel so much in harmony with it as I once did. If I played it now, I would play it more straight. I used to put too much feeling into it. It's a wonderful work, which few can play. Backhaus could, of course, and Schnabel." Cherkassky also played all the Beethoven sonatas with popular nicknames, and while he never played the *Diabelli Variations*, he did perform the undeservedly neglected *Eroica Variations* and the equally overlooked Sonata Op. 90, as well as the rarely heard *Dressler Variations* composed in Beethoven's youth. He brought to this music his customary devotion to sound, emotion, imagination, and virtuosity, and gave a particularly compelling reading of the *Eroica Variations*. Before ending this piece in a masterful unraveling of the complexities of Beethoven's fugue, he would etch the theme with deceptive simplicity, and then richly color each of its fifteen variations.

If his approach to Beethoven did not please Serkin aficionados, his Bach must have left them apoplectic. An unashamed Romantic in this respect, he never hesitated to play Bach-Busoni or Bach-Liszt, Bach-Tausig, or even Bach-d'Albert, whether in Carnegie Hall or Peoria, saying he considered transcriptions absolutely legitimate music for concert programs as long as they were done well, and adding that he thought Busoni to be the very best of all Bach arrangers because he didn't substantially change the structure of the music. In his performances of Bach-Liszt he brilliantly solved the problem of transforming music written for the organ into music for the piano by using massive sonorities and a huge color range, and by presenting a clear and logical demonstration of Bach's linear designs. As a young man of eighteen he told an interviewer for *Etude* magazine that he was immensely fond of arrangements of Bach by Liszt, Tausig, and Busoni, and that he liked fugues and thought audiences did as well when they were well played. His own ability to separate five simultaneous voices, while maintaining line and infinite shades of color, was simply astonishing. When asked in the 1980s if he didn't actually prefer playing fugues, he paused thoughtfully and then said with a twinkle in his eye, "Not always." But in truth, contrapuntal and linear playing were as natural to him as any virtuoso roulade. Perhaps it was this ease in contrapuntal playing that gave him the freedom and the need to search out and highlight the inner voices others left unobserved and with which he often converted a monophonic Romantic repertoire into multilayered contrapuntal inventions.

His untranscribed Bach repertoire, which included the *Italian* Concerto and the *Chromatic Fantasy and Fugue* (favorites of an older generation of pianists), the partitas and English suites, as well as the individual preludes and fugues, was always presented without apology as piano music. He eschewed the terraced dynamics and pedal-free imitations of the harpsichord favored by purists, often using the pedal to create great swirls of sound, as in his performance of the *Chromatic Fantasy*. Among the partitas he was especially partial to the long and demanding one in E Minor, in which he honored the niceties of Baroque practice, all the while incorporating a Romantic disregard of them.

Throughout his career, it was a rare Cherkassky program that did not begin with a significant work by Bach or Handel, or by even earlier composers such as Rameau and Lully. No one who heard him play the *Gavotte Varié* by Rameau or the *Suite* by Lully (actually transcriptions by D'Anglebert of dance movements by Lully) can doubt his absolute commitment to such early music. These two seventeenth-century gems engaged as much of his vast technical arsenal as any Romantic barnburner. Superbly detailed, highly nuanced, elaborately ornamented, and sparsely pedaled, his performances of these pieces inevitably generated surprise in that they could be so arresting.

If he violated the stereotype of the Romantic pianist with his enthusiasm for early music, there was nothing atypical about his avoidance of the classical era. One will search in vain through the programs of Hofmann, Rachmaninoff, Rosenthal, Paderewski, or any other Romantic pianist for any significant presence of Haydn or Mozart. When they appeared at all, they were merely a change of pace or a breathing space between more "substantial" fare. The only Mozart and Haydn in Hofmann's historic twenty-three recitals in St. Petersburg in 1916 were the A-minor Rondo and the F-minor Variations. If a classical concerto was needed, it was usually the Mozart D Minor, K. 466, or the A Major, K. 488. Several Mozart sonatas can be found on programs prior to World War II, but Haydn was usually represented by the "small" E Minor, Hob. XVI/34, or the "big" E-flat, Hob. XVI/52. Tellingly, one finds no one complete Mozart or Haydn sonata in the prewar recordings by any of the virtuoso pianists except the 1932 Horowitz recording of the Haydn E-flat Sonata. Cherkassky's nearly foolproof musical compass almost certainly steered him away from such music, which offered too little legitimate opportunity for him to exhibit the uniqueness of his musical personality. Let the record show, however, that while Mozart's *Turkish* Rondo was a frequent encore, ever so slightly tarted up with inner voices, his renditions of Haydn and Mozart works, when programmed, were delivered simply and with grace.

For certain performers the pianistic and mental step from Lully or Bach to Schubert can be long. Yet in his programs Cherkassky shifted effortlessly. Had those who were quick to dismiss Cherkassky's intellectual powers at the piano listened with an open mind to a live performance of Schubert's A-major Sonata D. 959, they might have rethought their appraisal. Virtuoso brilliance combined with soaring melodies and a grand sense of architecture marked his interpretation of this work, which he played with a rare understanding of its many moods. To the A-major Sonata D. 664, he brought a much richer color palette and characterization than most of his colleagues, including those who claimed to be specialists in the Viennese manner. His playing of the *Impromptus*, Op. 90, could be problematic, depending on how much he did or did not toy with the rhythm, but there could be enchantment in them as well, as in the third of this group, when he would shape the melody in a manner that made the bar-line disappear so the whole piece gave the illusion of being suspended in air. And even in Schubert he could find occasion to employ his pixyish sense of humor, as in his rendering of the *Moment Musical* where he deftly showed the audience Godowsky's parade of inner voices.

While he played the staples of the conventional nineteenth-century Romantic repertoire, there was nothing predictable about the way he played them. Consider, for instance, his interpretation of the Liszt B-minor Sonata, which he first performed in 1926 at the age of seventeen. Critics described the conception as demonic, the delivery as heroic and dramatic. They also wrote that his playing of the piece included a dimension of tenderness not found in most interpretations, and that beyond its mechanical wonder, his performance that evening in 1926 revealed an imagination that was individual and mature far beyond its years. As he went through life he played the work regularly, with a rhapsodic freedom that paid little heed to the overall structure of the piece, a failing that most listeners and even many critics were happy to overlook. In the last year of his life, at the age of eighty-five, a performance in Italy of the sonata led one critic in the *Corriere della Sera* of 24 January 1995 to observe:

> Let us note the obvious facts of Cherkassky's prodigious technical ability which places him at the limits of the incredible. Not only does Cherkassky demolish the

> fastest passages with total nonchalance and is able to allow himself astonishing octave passages in the Sonata by Liszt, but, above all his control of sonority is measured to the millimeter. . . . But what does mere technical prowess count when we find ourselves before such a musician? It is the subtlety, the visionary interpretations, the impalpable grace and the elegant phrasing demonstrated by Cherkassky that leave one breathless. We have never heard the Sonata by Liszt so deconstructed, so abandoned to bursts of improvised, fleeing and mournful beauty.

In addition to the B-minor Sonata, Cherkassky would focus his energies on Liszt's transcriptions and rhapsodies, tossing them off with an ease that was astonishing, as in the arrangement of Wagner's *Tannhäuser* overture. Even though he played this repertoire with the fearlessness of an acrobat without a net, in Cherkassky's hands the music of Liszt became renderings of high artistic order rather than a bag of circus tricks meant to dazzle. Huge rounded phrases and haunting lyricism were combined with an intellectual control over effortlessly delivered pyrotechnics. At the height of bravura playing, lyrical sound poured forth. He roared and whispered and did so with infinite tonal variety and unflagging energy. Cherkassky's rendering of the "Là ci darem" interlude from the *Don Juan Fantasy* was once described as "coming near to out-singing the human throat."

At his best, Cherkassky was acknowledged to be one of the greatest Chopin players of all time. His performances were described as radiating a luminous beauty and an immediacy that gave the impression he had just thought up everything he was doing. Through Chopin he spoke eloquently, in true bel canto style, sometimes with elegant understatement, at other times with determined fire. While he was often described as the last of the belle epoque salon virtuosos, his playing of Chopin was also recognized for its utter freedom from the stylistic impositions of any age. In his book *Chopin Playing*, James Methuen-Campbell cites Cherkassky as a master Chopin interpreter with his

> attention to the polyphonic side of the music, marvelously detailed phrasing, and a grasp of the overall shape of the work. . . . Many have remarked that he takes liberties with Chopin, but it is often his departures from routine interpretation that bring the music to life. . . . He is like a magician at the keyboard, conjuring up near-miraculous sounds that the most assiduous listener may hear only once in a lifetime from another pianist.[2]

Cherkassky was one of the few pianists to play Chopin's early C-minor Sonata, written as an exercise in composition for Chopin's teacher. He brought to his rendering of the B-minor Sonata an interpretation of the largo that was described by Berlin critics as "the pinnacle of pianistic perfection." His performance of the B-flat Minor Sonata led John Ardoin in the *Dallas Morning News* of November 9, 1989, to comment that "The sustained mystery of the first movement of the Chopin Sonata and the hushed drama of its funeral march were among the most overwhelming pianism I have ever been privileged to experience," while Donal Henahan writing in the *New York Times* stated that the pianist did not so much disregard the score as twist it imaginatively to his own purposes. Rarely played works such as the *Bolero*, *Allegro de Concert*, *Tarantelle*, and the *Là ci darem la mano Variations* were distinctively characterized, while the waltzes, mazurkas, nocturnes, scherzi, ballades, preludes, and etudes were delivered with an appropriate poetry or bravura and unfailing tonal splendor.

In sum, Cherkassky's Chopin playing was certainly anything but mainstream and led another reviewer in 1981 to write in the *Los Angeles Times*:

> Because the pianist and many in his audience had known and lived with this music for so long, the revelatory aspects of his playing had to stun the listener. . . . His rhapsodic playing of the two *Nocturnes* and the two *Impromptus* combined velvet tone with deep songfulness, lightness or articulation with sonorities either weighty or delicate, and deliberate thoughtfulness with sudden blurring.
>
> None of this emerged as willful or arbitrary. Instead, it charmed. Within each context, it all made musical sense. Technical considerations in Cherkassky's playing do not exist; he may choose tempos according to mood, ambience, *zeitgeist* or the position of the stars. The net result is that his choices are valid, as valid as any consensus, tradition or computer printout because they communicate and because they are musical. In the end one does not argue with musicality.

If any composer was an ideal foil for Cherkassky's Romantic temperament, it was Robert Schumann. Cherkassky was a natural Schumann player with his special brand of poetry, his way with a phrase, his ability to move seamlessly from one mood to another, and his knack for capturing subtle emotions. Schumann's *Kreisleriana*, Op. 16, a signature piece in Cherkassky's repertoire, was performed with an emotional intensity that allowed this set of eight thematically unrelated pieces to build coherently to a serene release in the closing bars. Dominic Gill, in a 1985 review in the *Financial Times*, said,

> Schumann's music and Cherkassky's concerns meet precisely at a magical point—in a region of dappled half-lights, sly glances, sudden reversals and ambiguities, breathless delicacies of inner voice, innuendos of tone. And always with

> ardour: Cherkassky's reading of the fifth and seventh sections was as wild with fantasy and flying with colour as it was rich in subtle inflection.

The pianist's performance of *Carnaval*, the *Symphonic* Etudes, and the *Fantasy in C Major* received the same rhapsodic, imaginative treatment and attention to detail. A far cry from the delivery favored by many of his colleagues, Cherkassky's *Carnaval* swept the audience along with his commitment, making each of its musical portraits come vibrantly to life. One critic wrote that at the end one was left with the impression that this was exactly how the composer wanted his work to sound.

While one would expect Cherkassky to be at home in Schumann's virtuoso G-minor Sonata, it was in the unwieldy sprawl of the giant F-sharp Minor Sonata that he really came into his own. Unconcerned by the problems of its clumsy form, he reveled in its unfolding moments, creating performances that were arresting, however unorthodox. For him, the proper exploration of such a work depended on what Theodor Adorno described as the "process of losing one's way and finding it again."[3]

Of all the standard Romantic composers, Brahms was the one Cherkassky performed least, programming only three major works and some incidental pieces. His execution of the *Paganini Variations*, while a technical tour de force, focused on the musical elements of each variation, resulting in an interpretation described as one of great maturity. On the other hand, a combination of elegance and power, a surprising emphasis on inner voices and accompanying figures, a monumental sonority, and a brilliant clarity in the concluding fugue marked his performance of the *Brahms-Handel Variations*. This particular set of variations suited him extremely well with the opportunities it offered him in the repeats to indulge his highly personal and chameleon-like approach to touch, dynamics, and pedaling.

No performance of any work in Cherkassky's repertoire, however, drew greater disagreement than the Brahms F-minor Sonata. Consider Harold Schonberg's opinion, for instance, as it appeared in the *New York Times*:

> He really should not have played the Brahms F minor Sonata. Mr. Cherkassky's style consists of impeccable finger work, a constant breakup of the line with a stop-and-go effect, immensely long ritards inserted all over the place, a search for inner voices, and all kinds of delicate pedal effects. Thus instead of the grand sweep of the gnarled Brahms sonata, we had a collection of teased details. Mr. Cherkassky did not play this sonata. He tickled it. Tempos were sluggish, ritards were dragged to the rim of the universe. Never has one heard a more eccentric reading.

A polar opposite point of view came from *San Francisco Chronicle* critic Robert Commanday:

> No question but that the totality of the F minor sonata was crucial to him. This really is a symphony for piano, the grandest and last piano sonata that Brahms, only 20, would write. Cherkassky produced it in all of its deep power and passion but conveyed remarkably clear impressions. This was transcendental Brahms. Cherkassky developed the Andante's song themes with a haunting touch. The first one had the effect of a circle slowly returning and rolling forward, the other acting as its complement, the second of the pair of embracing lovers described in the line of poetry Brahms had affixed to this piece. The Scherzo was demonic, the Intermezzo severe and Beethovenian, the finale powerful.

During the Australian tour of 1928 Cherkassky told a reporter, "Chopin first made me feel deeply but I could not understand Brahms until recently." He was then not yet nineteen years old.

Ever curious and ever wanting to share new experiences with his audiences, Cherkassky delved into aspects of the traditional repertoire that were quickly rejected by other pianists. A case in point is the Tchaikovsky Sonata in G Major, Op. 37, which he played with as much passion and bravura as the Liszt B-minor Sonata. Carl Maria von Weber's Sonata No. 4 in E Minor, no longer considered a major work, became a surprising disclosure of things to come under Cherkassky's hands. Donal Henahan in the *New York Times* commented, "the opening movement of the Weber also managed to sound like Chopin, an historical impossibility but perhaps the key to Mr. Cherkassky's individual style." The little-played Grieg Sonata, an attractive, conventional, and enjoyable if minor work, appeared rarely on the programs of other major pianists, but Cherkassky programmed it quite frequently. Curiously, however, the piece was also admired and recorded by Alicia de Larrocha and Glenn Gould, two artists who pianistically and musically shared no other common denominator with Shura Cherkassky.

Among the Russian composers represented in Cherkassky's repertoire were Balakirev, Glazunov, Glinka, Khatchaturian, Mussorgsky, Prokofiev, Anton Rubinstein, Scriabin, Tchaikovsky, Rachmaninoff, Stravinsky, Shostakovich, Liadov, and Medtner. The *Islamey* of Balakirev, with its formidable clusters of double notes, was played with uncontained color and visceral power. Mussorgsky's *Pictures at an Exhibition*, a collection of sharply contrasted, highly individual vignettes, was custom-tailored to the pianist but could, on an off-night, sound stilted and even, to some ears, dull. Another staple in Cherkassky recitals was Stravinsky's *Petrouchka*, which he played boldly with swirling colors and great forward thrust. When he performed the piece for the composer, Stravinsky suggested that he play the "Danse Russe" fortissimo while holding the soft pedal, to give a special effect. In spite of numerous successful performances of the work, Cherkassky worried incessantly that his third movement of *Petrouchka* was too slow, but then he would laugh and say, "Igor said Arthur played it too fast," referring to Igor Stravinsky and Arthur Rubinstein. The Stravinsky suite was also the linchpin for a favorite Cherkassky story: Invited to a dinner party, Cherkassky declined saying that he was much too busy with *Petrouchka*. "Never mind, you can bring him along too," responded his would-be hostess.

Cherkassky's love of transcriptions introduced his audiences to many little-known gems of the repertoire as well as the tried and true. Many believed the most extraordinary delivery of all the transcriptions he played came in his rendering of Paul Pabst's paraphrase of Tchaikovsky's *Eugene Onegin*. Cherkassky gave a heart-wrenching performance of the piece in his native Odessa in May of 1987 in which his Russian soul shone through with luminous clarity. The applause would not stop. When he was presented with a tape of the Odessa recital he wrote me with the comment shown below (see fig. 12.1). He gave another mesmerizing account of the work at his eightieth birthday recital at Carnegie Hall in 1991.

In exploring Cherkassky's vast repertoire one should note that because his notions about repertoire were largely formed in a world very different from the latter half of the twentieth century, he was never seduced by that era's compulsion for completeness and never felt obliged to learn every work by

158, The White House,
Regents Park,
London, N.W.1 3UP, England.

November 11, 1990

My dear Betty,

Last night for the first time I have listened to the casette from Odessa that you gave me! Why did you keep it a secret for so long? And do you have also caseetes of my Leningrad and Mosco recitals? Can you imagine how emotioally shocked I was when during the applause I have heard several times your conversation with Elsie?? This casette is precious. The "Eugene Onegin" I thought I was at my best form should I play it again next season?

Figure 12.1 Letter, November 11, 1990.

one composer. It is easy to underestimate the impact of the LP and the CD on this vast expansion of the standard concert repertoire, an expansion that made the complete works of almost every composer conveniently available and increasingly familiar to anyone with a stereo set, CD player, or radio. This was not true in Shura Cherkassky's youth. Only the Beethoven sonatas and the works of Chopin found their way in toto into any pianist's repertoire, and even then only rarely. It is also easy to forget that earlier in the twentieth century, touring artists could easily spend two or three days a week sitting on a train, losing precious practicing time. For the contemporary pianist, however, jet travel and a vast worldwide network of super highways have made touring much less of an interruption in practicing, therefore making it easier for the performer to maintain a large repertoire or to prepare the complete repertoire of Scriabin, Rachmaninoff, or any other composer.

For Cherkassky, however, the determining factor in this eclecticism was his insatiable curiosity and his clear grasp of what he liked and what was right for him—which made it very unlikely that he would learn a piece just for the sake of completeness when he could otherwise explore different music by diverse composers and learn something that really interested him. For example, Cherkassky was a pioneer in playing the music of Godowsky, but he programmed fewer than ten of the composer's works. During the last decade of the twentieth century, three different pianists each recorded the complete Chopin-Godowsky etude transcriptions (all fifty-three of them) as well as a broad selection of other works by the composer-pianist. In an interview given to the *New York Times* in 1989, Cherkassky remembered Godowsky.

> [A] pedantic man. I played for him the Albéniz Tango that he arranged, and I think we must have spent half an hour on it. He would keep saying, "No, play it this way" or "Not quite that way" or "Bring out this line." I still play some of his transcriptions. His arrangement of Strauss' Wine, Women and Song is wonderful, but you know, even in that one, there are too many notes—too much counterpoint, and too much interlude between the melodies.

Even a work like the Rachmaninoff Second Concerto, which he played often in the first half of his life, was dropped when its attraction for him faded. Given some of the recorded mismatches between performers and repertoire, one wishes other players were as scrupulous in their choices as Shura Cherkassky was during his lifetime.

Another striking feature of Cherkassky's repertoire, along with its vastness, was a breadth that took it beyond the Romantic category in which he tended to be pigeonholed. He played music by at least seventy-three composers and arrangements by at least fifteen transcribers, and he was constantly seeking out additions to his repertoire. Somewhat surprisingly, certain staples of the literature were not all learned in his youth. In 1966 he took up for the first time Mozart's Concerto in G Major, his Sonata in A-minor K. 311, and the Beethoven Third Concerto, which he admired and enjoyed but did not perform. In 1966 he also learned the Ravel *Concerto pour la main gauche* and several pieces of Messiaen. A tape of the Ravel taken from a live radio broadcast from Edinburgh can be found in the National Sound Archive of the British Library.

When he was choosing programs for any performing season Cherkassky liked variety, and he avoided the one-composer syndrome, except when he was programming Chopin. He said that he "didn't think about them [programs] very much. I think only of the music, of good music, and I don't confuse it with politics or nationality." He had no preferences, stating there was too much good music for him to say he preferred one piece to another. In any program he shifted with ease from the old to the new, from the calm to the volcanic, from the serious to the humorous. Constructing programs was done with the aid of a repertoire book that contained a listing, in meticulous columns, of all the works he played and had played in public. Each listing came complete with opus number and timing, making it possible to quickly come up with the two programs he supplied to presenters for each season. Following his death, his repertoire lists came into the possession of his London agent who later reported, unfortunately, that they had gone "astray." Along with two programs for each season, Cherkassky also suggested seven concerti, the final choice depending on conductor requests and the pianist's own preference. His preference for the Tchaikovsky G Major in Japan in February of 1988, however, was ignored when the conductor "wouldn't have it, absolutely wouldn't have it."

Wise decisions made in the use of his time were another factor contributing to an enormous repertoire that extended from the harpsichordists to Boulez. "I like modern music. If you practice it, it doesn't sound strange. I like to study modern music because it keeps you young." Cherkassky's attitude was clearly the antithesis of Hofmann's, who told the *New York Times* in 1915, "I am one of those who is perhaps known unfavorably, I do not doubt, for not playing much modern music. That is because I do not believe that modern music, taken by and large, is on the same level mentally, emotionally or artistically with what has gone before." Clearly, for Cherkassky, the challenges offered by twentieth-century works were just as easily solved as those in the Romantic repertoire. The Barber, Bartók, and Prokofiev seventh sonatas were delivered in a vigorous style, with sharp dynamic contrasts and preservation of the angularity that characterize these works. His performance of the Bartók sonata in 1968 was described in the *London Times* as a "towering interpretation . . . a supreme moment in Mr. Cherkassky's career." Stravinsky's *Petrouchka* and Messiaen's *Ile de feu I* and *II*, from *Quatre études de rhythme*, were audacious in their conception and execution. Stockhausen's *Klavierstuck* IX, a touchstone of postwar avant-gardism composed in 1961, became one of the great successes of his recitals in the 1980s and 1990s, particularly when paired with Schulz-Evler's *Arabesques on the Blue Danube Waltz* as a recital finale. The latter was played with all the elegance of old-world Europe and made a stunning contrast to the Stockhausen. I, II, III, and IV in the Stockhausen set make extraordinary demands on the performer by requiring the simultaneous execution of precise dynamic levels and intricate time subdivisions; V, VI, VII, VIII, IX, and X in turn allow the player to judge relative values instead of absolute ones. *Klavierstuck* IX begins with the repetition of one dissonant chord 142 times, followed by different groupings such as 85 or 13 ranging in sound from *ffff* to *pppp*. This construction offered Cherkassky a perfect opportunity to demonstrate to the listener his astounding control of color. While I was visiting Cherkassky in his hotel suite in Pasadena, California, following a concert there in 1989, he asked me to listen to him play the Stockhausen, but only after he had handed me an index card with the diverse groupings of the repeated chord meticulously mapped out. The artist then stood in the surroundings of his deluxe suite calling out from memory, in a manner reminiscent of a school child reciting before his teacher, the number of repetitions in each group. Any mistake led to a return to the beginning and another try at it. Only after this was accomplished to perfection did he play the piece, and then three times in succession, 681 repeated chords in all! Following the tryout Cherkassky wrote me (see fig. 12.2). And the critics thought his performance of the piece was great, citing Cherkassky's mastery of infinite shades of color, and "quicksilver touch which lent an elfin playfulness to a piece whose percussive abstractions might seem to rule out such pleasantries." Applauded as well was the eighty-year-old's intellectual curiosity in learning the work.

Another staple of his modern repertoire was the Berg Sonata No. 1, this composer's only work for piano solo, written in 1908, one year before Cherkassky was born. His conception of the piece was intellectual rather than emotional, despite its Romantic underpinnings, and his performances of the work were consistently described as revelatory. So too with his playing of the

HYATT REGENCY MAUI
ON KAANAPALI BEACH
200 NOHEA KAI DRIVE
LAHAINA, MAUI, HAWAII 96761-1990 USA

808 661 1234 TELEX 708 667 6030
TELEFAX 808 667 4499

January 4, 1990

My dear Betty,

I am glad that you saw me practice Stockhausen in Pasadena. I haven't done that to anyone else. I think it is a great piece for the piano.

Figure 12.2 Letter, January 4, 1990.

1936 Hindemith Sonata No. 3 in B-flat, a work combining terse architectural logic with Romantic lyricism. A ringing tone, precise articulation, and continuous musical clarification of all the lines defined Cherkassky's performance of the piece. In 1994 when he programmed the work in Germany, his performance was described in the *Sueddeutsche Zeitung*, as "an historic moment, in which the music became sensual and alive. Formal strength and structural modernity entered into marvelous harmony with the gentle magic of romantic sound."

Straying beyond the confines of well-known repertoire, Cherkassky religiously hunted out the unknown. On May 29, 1949, at California's Ojai Music Festival, he premiered Homer Keller's Piano Concerto, composed in 1949 (Keller, 1915–1996, was a student of Howard Hanson at the Eastman School and of Arthur Honegger in Paris); and in 1962, in San Diego, California, Cherkassky presented the little-known *Fifteen Little Variations* by composer Nikos Skalkottas, a student of Arnold Schoenberg. Lenox Barkley's *Polka* and *Two Preludes*, Op. 23, were programmed as a tribute to his love of things British, along with Richard Rodney Bennett's *Five Etudes for Piano Solo*, and Benjamin Britten's only solo-piano piece of length, *Holiday Diary*. Luciano Berio's *Three Pieces from Encores* occupied his attention in 1992 as well as the *Three Page Sonata* by Charles Ives: "I know it pretty well, but there are six lines I just can't remember. I have to read it at night; I have to take it to bed with me. I just hope nobody comes with the music!"[4] He didn't have to worry; his wonderfully delineated and deftly colored performance was reviewed as enthralling, making a highly persuasive case for Ives. During the last year of his life he was also learning Ligeti's Etude No. 13, *L'escalier du diable*. In a more traditional vein, he was equally at home in Leonard Bernstein's *Touches*, Aaron Copland's *El Salon Mexico*, Japanese pieces by Okumura, and various morceaux by Abram Chasins. Ultimately, Cherkassky approached contemporary music with the same attitude with which he approached all music: "Modern or old, music should be beautiful. I could play Berg or Messiaen or Stockhausen differently—drier, dispassionately. But then it sounds like algebra."[5]

One can question the musical judgment of ending a 1983 recital in Miami with a group of pieces by his longtime friend, Mana-Zucca. On the other hand, one cannot help but admire the loyalty and thoughtfulness of the aging Cherkassky, at long last receiving in America the acclaim that had eluded him for nearly fifty years, paying posthumous tribute to his friend who, like Cherkassky, had outlived her early success but unlike him had never experienced a renaissance. Born Augusta Zuckermann in the early 1880s, she had enjoyed considerable success before the war, especially as a composer of songs, two of which appeared in almost every singer's repertoire: "There is Joy in My Heart" and "I Love Life." The latter sentiment she took seriously, living into her nineties until her death in Miami in 1981. A piano student of Busoni and Godowsky, Augusta Zuckermann performed with the New York Symphony under Walter Damrosch, eventually changed her name, and took up residence in Miami where she became a leading musical figure. In the early years of her life she once played for Josef Hofmann a piece titled "Memories," composed when she was ten years old. Hofmann, who didn't like the composition, told her to come back "when she really had something to say." Years later Mana-Zucca asked her friend Shura Cherkassky to learn "Memories" and play it for Hofmann. He obliged and Hofmann then said, "Tell Mana that now she has something to say." Cherkassky often programmed Mana-Zucca's works, with "Memories," "Fugato-Humoresque on *Dixie*," and "Zouaves Drill" among the most frequently performed, and he played them with patrician elegance or dazzling bravura as required. These pieces became staples in his repertoire not just because the composer was his lifelong friend but because he truly believed in her music.

No Cherkassky recital was complete, however, without the delicious musical bonbons he served up at the end and to which he gave the same exquisite care he showed the towering masterpieces in his repertoire. "Most pianists play their serious pieces in the first half, then in the second half they play all the 'bonbons.' But my programs are different. In my programs the second half is just as boring as the first half." Thus did Arthur Schnabel, the piano world's intellectual leader in the prewar era, whimsically defend his always serious and often challenging recitals. In those days, unlike today, Schnabel's programs were the exception. Rosenthal, Rachmaninoff, Hofmann, de Pachmann, and Horowitz regularly programmed all sorts of confections that would now be scorned as "salon music," and they always planned their programs to end with a string of encores carefully calculated to delight and impress rather than enlighten and exalt. Often they could not wait until the end to unleash the encores, which frequently started at intermission and sometimes appeared after a particularly well-received group or piece in the middle of the program. It was not unheard-of then even to do a literal encore, that is, in performance to immediately repeat a work that had provoked particular enjoyment from the audience. In his Carnegie Hall recital of January 1935 Josef Hofmann played no less than sixteen encores, five during the recital and eleven at the end, turning the concert into a near marathon that lasted more than three hours. Few recitalists then would have concurred with Edward Said's statement, "Encores, in my opinion, are appalling, like food stains on a handsome suit."[6]

Whether the straight-laced programs of today represent merely changing times or greater intellectual maturity is uncertain, but what is clear is that piano recitals were far more numerous and better attended in the era of the encore, the era during which Shura Cherkassky came of age and formed a style of programming that shunned the one composer or complete-works-of recitals. This formative experience doubtless explains why, unlike some of his more parsimonious colleagues, Shura Cherkassky was neither stingy nor coy about encores. As long as people cheered, and they always did, he was happy to play. Six or seven encores were not unusual, which gave him ample opportunity for variety and experimentation. Since this part of his program could represent as much as a quarter of the playing time at a Cherkassky concert, it is not surprising that these bonbons in some ways defined his playing. (How often have listeners at a Schnabel, Serkin, or Brendel concert even mentioned an encore except perhaps to note that there was none?)

As an encore, nothing could quite equal the impact of Shura's raucous romp through Morton Gould's *Boogie-Woogie Etude*. Never mind that Cherkassky and Gould were contemporaries who died within weeks of each other; never mind that Shura was a young man in America at the time boogie-woogie became popular; there was still something stunningly incongruous about the Last Romantic abandoning his nineteenth-century image for a toe-tapping, foot-stomping, eye-popping boogie-woogie romp. Whether in Carnegie Hall or Suntory Hall, the audience simply went wild when he performed this piece.

While Shura's impish good humor always bubbled just below the surface, when it was time for encores there was invariably some piece in which it would unabashedly burst forth. It is difficult to imagine a more vivid musical comedy than his rendering of the Shostakovitch *Polka* from *The Age of Gold*. The Chaplinesque antics with which he poked and plucked every dissonance unfailingly brought guffaws from even the most reserved recital crowd.

His Romantic temperament made Cherkassky as adventurous in his choice of encores as he was in his other repertoire. For every Chopin piece or classical gem played as an encore, there was some work that few, if any, listeners could identify. His own *Prélude Pathétique*, always played with such aching beauty, invariably found people asking, "What was *that*?" Once described as a "rummager in the attic of nineteenth-century junk," he enjoyed searching out rarely played gems of well-known composers from every era, among others Rachmaninoff's *Elegie*, Stravinsky's *Circus Polka* (perhaps too long and too sophisticated to really succeed as an encore), and Sibelius's *Romance*. But it was the unknown that pleased him most. The technical obstacles found in a rollicking transcription of "The Irish Washerwoman" by Mildred Couper ("someone I knew in Los Angeles") were conquered gleefully.

Perhaps Cherkassky's greatest daring in selecting encores was his fearless determination to revitalize works that others thought were overplayed and hackneyed. He did not accept the common understanding of the word *hackneyed*; to him it just meant a work had been played too often in the wrong way by the wrong artist. The Paderewski *Minuet*, de Falla's *Ritual Fire Dance*, Sinding's *Rustle of Spring*, Liadov's *Music Box*, Daquin's *Cuckoo*, Rubinstein's *Melodie in F* were all encores that he played as though they were brand new. One could really understand the once great popularity of the Rubinstein *Melodie* when one heard Cherkassky arch it so beautifully across the vast reaches of Carnegie Hall. The same might be said of Debussy's *Clair de lune* and *Arabesques*, and other "student" pieces that he illuminated though the simplicity of his statement. One doubts, however, that any student ever played *Rustle of Spring* with so much virtuosity or to such striking effect; and if in the process *Rustle of Spring* was transformed into a gathering storm of summer, no one ever seemed to mind. Paradoxically, while it was his unchecked whimsy that made so many encores so delicious, it was his absolute sincerity and conviction that made these old chestnuts sound not hackneyed, but honored.

Godowsky's *Swan* was played with incomparable sheen. No living swan ever floated more serenely above the intricacies below than Cherkassky's *Swan*.

Although he always projected a look of almost frightening concentration while performing, never, even in the most ravishing phrases, did one find him staring at the ceiling or making agonized grimaces. He loved making music, he loved playing the piano, he loved performing, but he believed music should be heard and seen without distraction. Only in the encores did he acknowledge the humorous value of the kind of movement he eschewed elsewhere. However, let it be clear that even in encores he never tried to make piano playing look difficult and he never projected his emotions in facial expressions or bodily contortions. Emotion was expressed only through the music. But fun was fair game in the encores. He ended his stylish and sophisticated performances of the difficult Rachmaninoff *Polka* with a conspicuous, extended-pinky dive-bomb from great height to strike a completely unexpected middle D. Then after holding that note just enough too long, he continued with the roundabout cadence that amusingly ends the piece.

Unwilling to compromise his artistic vision, Shura Cherkassky was born and died a soloist. He had no interest in performing chamber music, let alone accompanying, but he did venture into the chamber music repertory by playing the Rachmaninoff Cello Sonata, which was recorded in 1934 with cellist Marcel Hubert. He also admitted to playing privately the Kreutzer Sonata with Mischa Elman. When I commented it was too bad it had happened in private, Cherkassky replied, "Oh no it wasn't."

However Romantic his temperament or musical style may have been, Cherkassky's repertoire was vagabond. He roamed the centuries choosing a menu of pieces representative of every era. He had no favorite composer, no preferred piece, and felt comfortable with all composers except Debussy, about whom he said, "I don't know why, but I don't think I'm quite fit for Debussy." He simply loved music, and with great energy, curiosity, and enthusiasm he studied the new, to perform with the old. As a consummate individualist, Cherkassky gave his audiences performances that were unpredictable and exhilarating, placing him in a tilt with prudish performers whose own lack of daring and imagination forced them to seek refuge in "authenticity."

In the performance of Romantic repertoire it was expected that the performer would bring his mind, his heart, and his personality to the music. He would become a partner with the composer, while making beautiful sound, tonal variety, and imagination the foundation of every performance. Tempo rubato was an art in itself and was never used to break the line, but rather to add interest, to call attention to some particular inflection. Instead of being free to the point of eccentricity, as it was sometimes claimed, Cherkassky's playing had logic and control without the impersonal aspects of rigidity and separation from emotion. The literalists, who disregarded Cherkassky and the original point of view he gave to each and every piece he played (instead of bowing to what might be the then-current musical fashion), obviously gave short shrift to the notion that Baroque and Classical composers, as well as the Romantic ones, wanted their music rendered as more than a literal reproduction of pitches in rhythm.

Certainly composers can convey architectural and tonal intent on paper. But what of artistic intent? Cherkassky understood that the score was the beginning and not the end. And therein lay the irresistible seduction of Shura Cherkassky's artistry. His gift of creativity was in play each and every time he took the stage, and his audiences were inevitably treated to revelations of personal insight, all of which added up to recitals that were consistently provocative. Until the end of his life he remained adamant that if the composers of yesterday were playing their own compositions in the present, they would change some aspect of the interpretation. Inevitably, any Cherkassky recital stimulated extended discussion, argument, and reevaluation of other pianists' interpretation of the same pieces. His technical prowess, his voluptuous tone, his way with hidden voices and the pedals, and the sincerity and generosity of feeling with which he played, to quote British critic Bryce Morrison, left "many bewitched, some bothered and a few bewildered, but none bored."

He communicated the emotions we share in life, and therein lay his special secret. He took us with him and he made us reach with feeling into the depth of our being. We laughed, we cried, we wondered. We felt sad, we felt happy. We felt excited, exhilarated, joyous. We felt romantic. No emotion was beyond us. Which is exactly what Shura Cherkassky wanted: "Music is a part of life, not separate, and I want to bring out those personal things that make you laugh, that make you cry." And that is precisely what he did. As did Franz Liszt, who said,

> For the virtuoso, musical works are in fact nothing but tragic and moving materializations of his emotions; he is called upon to make them speak, weep, sing, and sigh, to re-create them in accordance with his own consciousness. In this way he, like the composer, is a creator, for he must have within himself those passions that he wishes to bring so intensely to life.[7]

Diminutive in size, Shura Cherkassky was a giant at the piano. Just as he was a brilliant raconteur in life, so too was he a fascinating storyteller at the piano, a narrator whose playing, for the vast majority of his listeners, did not distort the writing, but illuminated it. The fertility of his imagination was astounding and in looking past the notes he followed Goethe's dictum that one can only comprehend a work of art properly if one is capable of contributing something of oneself.

Shura Cherkassky gave completely of himself to his art. He didn't make music. He lived it!

Notes

1. Carnegie Hall archives, 1989.
2. James Methuen-Campbell, *Chopin Playing* (New York: Taplinger, 1981), 167.
3. Theodor W. Adorno, *Sound Figures* (Stanford, Calif.: Stanford University Press, 1999), 47.
4. *Times* (London), 27 October 1991.
5. Carnegie Hall, archives, 1989.
6. Edward W. Said, "Remembrance of Things Played: Presence and Memory in the Pianist's Art," *Harper's*, November 1985, 69.
7. Franz Liszt, *Gesammelte Schriften*, essay on Clara Schumann, 4:189–206.

CHAPTER THIRTEEN

The House of Steinway

Long live Steinway, the only piano.

—S. C.

An unsung hero in the life and career of Shura Cherkassky was the Steinway piano, his instrument of choice. Throughout his concert-playing career he searched for pianos that were "inspiring" and concluded that such pianos existed only at Steinway and Sons. Soon after his arrival in America he had the opportunity to try the instrument, previously unknown to him, and subsequently gave his whole-hearted endorsement to the piano, which he then used almost exclusively for seventy-two years of performances following his American debut in 1923. The year after this debut he sent a letter to Steinway and Sons.

> Dear Sirs:
>
> Since my arrival in America I started playing the Steinway and I realize now that I could not possibly use any other instrument but the Steinway, which to me means "The Piano." It is wonderful! Only thus can I express my opinion, my thoughts . . . my gratitude to that divine Medium of Art which has brought me closer to my gods—my favourite Masters.
>
> —Shura Cherkassky

Not only Cherkassky's hands, but also his feet received a workout in performance. "Look at my shoe, look at my shoe," he often said, calling attention to an inevitable scratch on the left shoe that came from bracing against the pedal in concert after concert. Actually he delighted in the disfigurement since it gave him the opportunity to shop for new shoes. The pianos on which he practiced, including the two-pedaled rented grand in his London apartment, had the stiffest possible action because, as he reasoned, "If I can play on that then any concert hall piano will seem easier." Like all concert pianists, the matter of the perfect piano for use in performance was of prime concern to Shura Cherkassky. His dissatisfaction with any instrument other than the Steinway was clearly and colorfully expressed in a 1935 letter written to Mr. John Eshelby, who at that time was the Steinway representative in London (see fig. 13.1).

When in 1951 through no fault of his own Cherkassky's name became attached to other makes of piano, he wrote an indignant, explanatory, and apologetic letter to Alexander Greiner, head of the Concert and Artist

c.c. for A.W.G.

COPY OF LETTER FROM:-

SHURA CHERKASSKY,

C/o Schklowsky,
Palatori 1,
Neitsyt Niemi,
Viipuri,
Finland.

to:-
Mr. John Eshelby,
Steinway & Sons,
London.

8th May, 1935.

Dear Mr. Eshelby,

Thank you very much for your kind letter. I have just arrived here in Viipuri three days ago from Russia staying there longer than I planned. On the spur of the moment I decided to stay for the May celebrations, and it was worth staying. You must be having also quite an exciting time in London now.

Thank you so much for forwarding all the mail. I appreciate it more than I can tell you. I will pay you for all the mail understamped and the expense of the telegram.

You ask me to tell you about pianos I used in Russia. In Moscow it was Bechstein, but I am sure it must have been a hundred years old. In general pianos in U.S.S.R. are dreadful. It is shameful not to have one decent piano in a city that plays such an important part now - Moscow. Leningrad was the only city that had a beautiful piano - also Bechstein. I believe Schnabel brought it from Germany five years ago. Altogether I found Leningrad the most wonderful place to play in. It is full of old culture and tradition.

Figure 13.1 Letter, May 8, 1935.

In Kharkov it was "Becker", in Odessa "Blüthner". Both atrocious pianos. Of course I had trmendous success everywhere, and enjoyed my tour and trip. I have had a truly marvellous time, travelled all over European Russia. You must see that Russia gets at least six Concert Grand Pianos. They are just as much in need of good pianos as they were in need of bread in 1921.

Now about music in Russia. Speaking frankly I have found that music in Russia is not on the same level as their dramas, ballet, opera, theatres - these are superb. I have not heard any first class concerts although I have gone to the very best that were there. Moscow orchestra (symphony) is medicore, while Leningrad Leningrad is good, but does not compare with any of the American orchestras.

Now about composers - yes, I consider Shostakovitch a genius. He has a style of his own. There are Jelobinski, Poloninkin, etc., but they write trash. Shoporin is not bad. There is so very, very much to say about Russia. I'll wait until I see you in London.

Of course I want to play in London. I will be in London in July on my way to South America. I would be so grateful if you could arrange for me to play Shostakovitch Concerto. Its a very effective work and I know it will cause a sensation. Please let me know what you can do. Mr. Holt would arrange concerts, but he wants money, and as you know I have not made any money in Russia (only roubles).

With warmest regards from myself and mother, I remain,

Very sincerely yours,

(Sd.) Shura Cherkassky.

Figure 13.1 Continued.

Department at Steinway in New York (a position held by Greiner from the 1930s to 1958 when he was succeeded by Fritz Steinway). The writing is quintessential Shura Cherkassky, as shown in figure 13.2. Upon the retirement of Alexander Greiner and the succession of Fritz Steinway to his position, Shura Cherkassky wrote a letter of congratulation in which he once again reiterated his belief in the Steinway piano (see fig. 13.3).

On the matter of the Bösendorfer piano the pianist had similarly strong views. Scheduled to play the opening concert on the University of Washington's President's Piano Series, a series inaugurated to showcase the Bösendorfer Imperial concert grand piano, Cherkassky appeared neither impressed nor pleased by the instrument. In an interview given to the *Seattle Times* he told music critic Joel Cohen he would rather play a Steinway or a Yamaha. "I have always been a Steinway man, with Yamaha my next favorite though it hasn't got the soul of a Steinway." While admitting that the Bösendorfer could be considered the Rolls Royce of pianos, he also found the Bösendorfer

Bordeaux, 13 December 1951

FILE Shura Cherkassky 12/17/51

Dear Mr. Greiner,
I was very happy to hear from you. and there
certainly is a mixup. I am a Steinway artist and very
proud of it, and for me there is no other piano
that exists. I believe I have figured out why my name
is mixed up with Chappel (awful piano) piano. The only
time I ever in my life played on it when I played for
a British film last March at Elstree (outside of London)
and there was a Chappel piano there to play on. There
was no Steinway, although probably I realize now, I
should have insisted on it — but that's that! But,
what infuriates me, what right do they have to
put my name in connection with Chappel? And in
an advertisement in the English magazine. This is
an offense and I could take measures against it.
What would you advise me to do? I have only worked
4 days for the film "So little time" — it is being
released in February with screen credit. In future I
shall be more careful. In Paris it is quite true that I
do not play on the Steinway as I gave recitals in
salle Gaveau where one is not allowed to play on
anything but Gaveau! It is allowed at salle
Pleyel, but I did not play there. When in October I
played with orchestre Colonne at Théatre Chatelet,
they automatically had a Gaveau there. I have
discussed all this with Mr. Kühne in Berlin
who tells me that I must talk it over with
Mr. Stark. But what can he do against
such situation? Last night as well, I played
here with famous French conductor Paul Paray
at Grand-Théatre. There was a Gaveau. Tomorrow
night recital in Nice — I know there is Gaveau there
at the Casino Municipal as well as in Menton.
France is funny that way. What can I do to
be able to play on a Steinway everywhere? Would
you write Mr. Stark about that? In Spain,
in Barcelona I had a Blüthner, in Valencia a
Bechstein already on the stage. In Las Palmas,
Canary Islands, of all the places, they had
an extraordinary, magnificent concert grand
Steinway. I believe I explained everything. I wish
it was all up to me. I am sure you understand
wishing you and Mrs. Greiner all the best for 1952. With
kindest personal regards. Very sincerely yours,
address:
4, rue Quentin-Bauchart, Paris (8e), France. Shura.

Figure 13.2 Letter, December 13, 1951.

HOTEL PLAZA
12, AVENUE DE VERDUN
NICE (A.-M.), France.
TELEGRAMMES: PLAZOTEL-NICE
TELEPHONE: 889-41 - 8 LIGNES

RECEIVED
AT GENERAL OFFICE
SEP 1
Ans'd

September 13, 1958

My dear Mr. Steinway,

I have received your letter, and should have written before, but I have been so much "on the go" that I have been neglecting all the correspondence shamefully. My best congratulations that you became the manager of the Concert and Artist Department. I know that you are just the right man for it, and I do hope I shall again have the pleasure of seeing you. You probably know about my activities in Europe, and elsewhere. I am kept very busy, and do not wish to force the matters about playing in the States. This will come naturally, also mostly because of my records, which I understand are selling considerably well in America now. Should you at all come to Europe be sure to let me know.

With warmest personal regards, also to everyone, and long live the Steinway the <u>only</u> piano.

Very sincerely yours,

Shura Cherkassky

I just came back from a pleasure trip to the Orient, Japan, Manila, Hong Kong, Bangkok, India, Tehran (not playing there).

C. & A. FILE — Cherkassky

Figure 13.3 Letter, September 13, 1958.

to offer greater physical resistance to the hand than other pianos, making it more difficult to play. "I prefer the Steinway, its general sound. I don't know if the Bösendorfer is brilliant enough [in tone] for a concert hall, but I'll try to make it be." By all accounts he did exactly that at the Seattle performance.

Even the venerated Steinway wasn't infallible, however. There was the loose pedal of that South African concert in 1962, and a hammer that broke during a 1987 concert at the John Harms Center in New Jersey. Clickety-click, clickety-click, went the G above the staff during a performance of the Grieg Sonata in E Minor. After trying valiantly to plow ahead, the pianist finally stopped, asking for help. Management was unable to locate the piano tuner who, as it was later discovered, had gone out for coffee. Ever the consummate performer, Cherkassky played to the end, click and all, to the respectful amusement of an admiring audience.

Nothing better demonstrates his preoccupation with the sound of the piano and his indifference to mechanical concerns than an evening at Avery Fisher Hall in New York City when, unknown to Cherkassky, stagehands placed the wrong instrument on stage for his performance. Following a brilliant rendition of Beethoven's *Dressler Variations*, the first piece on the program, Cherkassky went offstage and returned with the stagehands pushing into place the piano he had originally chosen, one selected for its particular sound.

In addition to the concert grand on stage, Cherkassky insisted on a practice piano in his hotel room while on tour, and also one backstage in his dressing room at every performance. He said he could not play in concert unless he had a piano in the artist's room on which to warm up, and he didn't mind in the least what the piano was like. It could be old, rotten, and out of tune. It was just necessary to have something to bang on. He really didn't think that was asking a lot, and he relished telling the story of a Toronto appearance where, when he arrived backstage prior to the performance, he found himself without a piano on which to practice. Going through the building he located one in an upper floor studio but found the same room locked when he returned during the intermission. Insisting that he could not go forward with the performance unless he could practice on that piano, the door was finally unlocked and Cherkassky extended the intermission not only to practice but to insist on quiet time before going back on stage. He recalled that he returned for the second half and gave one of the best performances of his life of the *Rachmaninoff-Corelli Variations*.

Beyond the use of the Steinway piano in concert, two important events in the life of Shura Cherkassky were also associated with the house of Steinway. The first was the Steinway gala of 1988; the other, a tribute to Vladimir Horowitz at Steinway Hall in New York City in 1992. In 1988 Steinway built its 500,000th piano, a nine-foot grand in a highly ornate case designed by Wendell Castle that contained the names of the 832 pianists and 90 ensembles on the Steinway roster. Coordinated by Richard Probst, director of Steinway's Concert and Artist Department, and David Dubal, program director of WNCN, the celebratory concert for this event covered a broad span of musical literature but concentrated heavily on composers of the nineteenth and twentieth centuries. The program ended with a performance of Schumann's *Carnaval* by twenty of the twenty-three pianists, each of whom played one section, except for Cherkassky who played "Chopin" and returned to substitute for an indisposed Vladimir Feltsman in the "Finale." He then caused a sensation in a performance of Hofmann's *Kaleidoskope*. His sound, energy, point of view, and enormous projection thrilled the audience. Hofmann had composed *Kaleidoskope* to be played by one of the greatest piano techniques in the world: his own. But anyone who heard Cherkassky play *Kaleidoskope* that evening would have to wonder if Hofmann could have possibly played it better than his one-time pupil.

Cherkassky's second Steinway-centered event took place when Wanda Horowitz decided to arrange a private memorial concert in New York City in honor of her late husband, and only one pianist was considered by her to play the tribute. That pianist was Shura Cherkassky. Described by Cherkassky as one of the proudest moments of his life, he considered the invitation as very, very important and most unusual. Horowitz was for Cherkassky a god.

> [He was] something that happens once in a hundred years. When I first heard him do you know what happened to me? I was up in the gallery in Carnegie Hall when he made his debut and I was absolutely hypnotized. I wanted to be just like him. I wanted to know what kind of life he leads. I was quite obsessed. It was the sound he made that really excited me.

On the evening of October 28, 1992, at Steinway Hall on West Fifty-seventh Street in New York City, before a group of specially invited guests, the lifelong admirer of Vladimir Horowitz played a program of Chopin, Rachmaninoff, and Liszt. Following the performance, a delightful dialogue developed between Wanda Horowitz and the evening's pianist, with Mrs. Horowitz reading a letter written by Cherkassky in answer to her invitation to give this concert in honor of her late husband.

> Wanda Horowitz: I feel I've become the Steinway speaker. But I want to thank you very, very much Shura—and I'm very glad that you accepted because I know how much you admired my husband.
>
> Shura Cherkassky: I couldn't have had a greater honor in my whole life.
>
> Wanda Horowitz: I wanted the people here to know what you wrote me after I asked you to play. I hope I can see. Between the eyeglasses and your handwriting! (Much laughter from the audience.) He says he is greatly honored! Etc., etc., etc. (More laughter.) "It is beyond any words that I feel as you well know that Mr. Horowitz was and is living in my soul. There was no one who surpassed him and nobody will. He will remain unique!"

The reading was followed by an ebullient Wanda saying,

> And now I want to tell you something very cute and very true. Do you know how the public has the fault of going to a pianist and asking "Mr. So and So, what do you think of Mr. So and So?" Of course you can never have the right answer because how can you say, "I don't like him?" And so I think that because my dear Shura is very sincere he used to say a little bit what he thought. Somebody said, "Shura it's not good, if they ask you, 'Do you like Mr. So and So?' to say no. Say something nice." So Shura then said "he's a very good pianist, he's very talented, I like him very much." Then one day someone said. "Shura, have you heard Mr. Horowitz' recital?" And Shura said, "That was marvelous, that was unique. And this time I *mean* it!"
>
> Now I want to tell *you* Shura, this time *I* mean it. I enjoyed *your* concert very much. And I know how much it meant to you.
>
> Now you may kiss me, because I am older than you.

Later in the month while at home in London, Cherkassky received a tape of the performance. Rarely satisfied with himself, he wrote me (see fig. 13.4).

The music is gone but the House of Steinway so venerated by Shura Cherkassky perpetuates his memory in its pantheon of great artists with a stunning photograph of Shura Cherkassky seated at his beloved Steinway (see fig. 13.5).

During his 1935 tour of the Soviet Union, Shura Cherkassky didn't get his wish to play a Steinway. But by the time of his return to his country of birth in 1976, Steinways in the USSR were the equal of any in the world, so that on his 1987 Soviet Union tour he could revel in the instant response and glorious tone of his favored instrument, which he lovingly declared to have the soul of a woman.

158, The White House,
Regents Park,
Bondon, N.W.1 3UP, England.
November 17, 1992

My dear Betty,

Yesterday I did get the cassette finally of Horowitz memorial concert. Ever so many thanks for sending it. I listened to it at once. It is good but I am a tiny bit dissapointed with my playing. Polonaise is not steady or rhythmical enoguh, the phrasing at the end are too quick (the bad habit that I have and tring to get rid of), Rachmaninof is exacellent but could be more gradations and conrasts between sounds Rhapsody almost no adverse critisisms, but Scriabne is superb. I could lean much from that cassette. It is, a valuble, one and Mrs. Horowitz's speach, etc. was thrilling...

Figure 13.4 Letter, November 17, 1992.

Steinway & Sons
109 West 57th Street
New York, N.Y. 10019

Wednesday evening, October 28, 1992, at 6:30

Steinway & Sons
Presents

SHURA CHERKASSKY

CHOPIN	Polonaise in F sharp minor, op.44
RACHMANINOFF	Barcarolle in G minor, Op. 10 Prelude in G sharp minor, Op. 32, No. 12 Polka de W.R.
LISZT	Hungarian Rhapsody No. 12
SCRIABIN	Etude, Op. 2, No. 1

Mr. Cherkassky wishes to dedicate this evening's performance to the memory of Vladimir Horowitz.

Shura Cherkassky plays the Steinway piano

Figure 13.5 Steinway program, October 23, 1992.

CHAPTER FOURTEEN

On Tour, USSR, 1987

> I constantly think of Russia. It is deep in my mind and heart.
>
> —S. C.

In the spring of 1987 Shura Cherkassky invited me to join him on a three-week concert tour of the Soviet Union. These were remarkable days in which he showed himself to be much more than a pianist, allowing emotion to bubble freely to the surface, marveling at the happenings around him, and reacting intensely with sadness or joy or wicked wit to the human encounters along the way, which touched him as much, perhaps more, than his pianistic triumphs.

Curiously, he who never looked back and was blatantly bored by reminiscing, continually called attention to these weeks, asking to be told again and again about this or that in the journey we had shared. When he learned I was writing an article about the tour he sent a letter in which he wrote:

> I bet it will be read with great interest, as I know (but be careful!) you have enough material to say some unusual things! . . . I constantly think of Russia. It is deep in my mind and heart and I recall all the things we did. Even the annoying things did not seem too bad, and now they even seem funny.

Recollections of the trip taken from the author's journal as written in 1987 follow.

May 1987

This trip was destined.

As a music student in New York City, my piano studies took place with

William Harms, a truly gifted though somewhat reclusive pianist who had studied with Mollie Margolies, an assistant of Rudolf Ganz, before entering the Curtis Institute in Philadelphia as a full scholarship student of Moriz Rosenthal. While studying with Rosenthal, Harms came to the attention of Abram Chasins who recommended to Hofmann that he hear the young student. Following an audition Hofmann gladly accepted the pianist from Kansas who joined his class at the same time Shura Cherkassky was studying with Hofmann. Harms made his orchestral debut with the New York Philharmonic, played under such notables as Stokowski, Reiner, and Iturbi, and performed in concerts across the United States to critical acclaim but never made a full-fledged career while his friend Shura went on to worldwide recognition.

Throughout my years of study with Harms our conversations would inevitably turn to the subject of great pianists, and the question was always asked if I had ever heard Shura Cherkassky. "No," was my reply. "Well you *must*," I was told. The years passed but never forgotten was Harms's admonition that if one really wanted to hear the piano played one must hear Cherkassky. Finally, in March of 1976 the chance came. The *New York Times* announced an upcoming concert at Hunter College in New York City and, quite simply, the experience of hearing him that evening left me in a combined state of astonishment and delight. Backstage, following the concert, my thanks for his performance received a very warm response and to use Shura's words, "We clicked." Thus began a friendship that lasted until his death in 1995. When Shura extended an invitation to me to join him on his 1987 Soviet Union tour, the idea seemed far-fetched but my reaction quickly passed from "out of the question" to "maybe" to "how could one not?" before crystallizing into a firm "yes." Sitting in Avery Fisher Hall the night of March 4, 1987, listening to him play a thrilling concerto performance I knew I would be going to Russia. There were gasps from the audience as he passionately thundered through the first movement of the Rubinstein D-minor Concerto then gentled down and played a poignant, singing, heartfelt, slow movement before taking off on a final rousing last movement. While the audience stomped and cheered, my husband and I raced backstage to congratulate him. His response to our unabashed exhilaration at his playing was "Do you think we could have some ice cream?" Champagne and fireworks seemed more in order, but ice cream and conversation it was until 4:00 a.m. at New York's all-night restaurant Brasserie where it was settled that later that morning a visit would be made to the Aeroflot office on Fifth Avenue to start planning our Russian adventure.

Shura was greatly amused by our conversation with Aeroflot in which our request for information about airline schedules between New York and Moscow received the response: "There are no published airline schedules." When asked about approximate costs the agent replied, "There are no published air fares." Exasperation setting in, we asked if Aeroflot had any airplanes. "We cannot give that information," came the answer. With a polite thank you to the agent and a knowing nod and wink from a New York policeman stationed in the office for security we left, and our questions were answered two blocks south on Fifth Avenue at Swiss Air where a characteristically courteous and efficient agent looked in his computer and promptly gave us complete schedules and routings on various airlines as well as fares for the trip.

The machinations that went on for the next two months are storybook stuff. Although I would be joining Shura's entourage once I was inside Russia, technically I would be traveling as an independent American tourist, something not at all encouraged by either the U.S. State Department or by travel agents. *Hazardous* was the word frequently used to describe such plans. "The group is the only way to go" was the repeated mantra.

After exploring all the options I made the decision to travel as an à la carte tourist entering the Soviet Union via Helsinki using Finnair as my carrier. On Sunday May 9 Flight 810 hurtled down a Kennedy airport runway at 8:50 p.m., exactly as scheduled, while the "William Tell Overture" played over the plane's loudspeakers. Descending into Helsinki some seven hours later to Wagner's "Ride of the Valkyrie," we were informed that ours would be the last flight into Helsinki that morning before the airport closed due to weather. The lounges were consequently crowded with passengers waiting for delayed incoming and departing flights, and in the midst of that crowd, after randomly choosing an empty seat, I began a conversation with the couple sitting next to me, a delightful pair from Los Angeles who were on their way to Russia to visit relatives. Mr. and Mrs. R. were eighty and seventy-eight years old respectively, and when I told them the reason for my trip was to join the pianist Shura Cherkassky on his concert tour, Mrs. R. exclaimed "Shura, *Shura* Cherkassky?" It turned out that Mrs. R. and Shura, who had not seen each other in forty years, had been childhood playmates after their families immigrated to America and settled in the same New York neighborhood in 1924. She remembered him as an independent and very stubborn child determined to succeed at whatever he tried to do.

Late that afternoon the flight to Leningrad was called and the full impact of going to Russia wiggled its way into my consciousness. Would it really be as dreary, dull, and oppressive as the journalists told us? When we landed and deplaned, there was a noticeable quiet among the passengers as we moved ever so slowly through passport control before entering the drab baggage claim area where the military was very much in evidence and customs inspection was uncommonly thorough. Particular note was made of passengers' jewelry, not an encouraged part of Soviet dress because of its association with wealth and the aristocracy. Even more detailed inspection was made of every piece of reading matter, in my case a biography of Vladimir Horowitz and a Russian grammar book to which extra scrutiny was given since it contained maps of Russia and pictures of locomotives and airplanes.

Finally, when I was cleared to go, a government agent escorted me to a private black car, which then sped toward Leningrad along a spacious highway surrounded by open green fields dotted with towering white birches. The hotel chosen for me by the Soviet government was the Pulkovskaya, a "deluxe" modern hotel without bath towels as they were known in the West but with very attractive public spaces, quiet and comfortable rooms, and an excellent Service Bureau Staff whose command of English was outstanding. They explained their particular concern for my welfare by telling me I was the first à la carte tourist in the twelve-year history of the Pulkovskaya Hotel. One of the more colorful moments of the trip, which caused Shura to react with hilarity, came the following morning when a note was left for me at the hotel's front desk from a Mr. Carter saying, "Dear Elizabeth, Your husband called last night. He is worried about you. Please call him." Unfortunately, the concern of the Service Bureau Staff for its guests was not shared by the hotel's telephone operator who, when my husband had called the previous evening and asked to speak with his wife, was told, "No such person in Pulkovskaya Hotel." A loud Bang! followed, and the telephone went dead. Three attempts on his part and still, "No such person in Pulkovskaya Hotel." Bang! Bang! Bang! On the fourth try the hotel operator agreed to ring the room of another guest whose name was Carter, thinking my name had been misspelled. It hadn't. A man's voice answered and Mr. Carter from Baltimore, Maryland, agreed to try to find my husband's wife for him.

Shura's first concert of the tour was scheduled for May 15 in Leningrad, truly an imperial city, where softly colored palaces lined the wide boulevards, canals gave the promise of sparkle, and the river Neva, normally filled with excursion boats at that time of year, remained frozen thick by an artic wind in spite of the calendar saying it was May. My days were spent exploring the beauties of the city while the rich musical life of Leningrad filled the evenings. There was a production of *Le Corsaire* at the Mariinsky Theater by the

Kirov Ballet that Shura particularly wanted to attend and the task of getting tickets was assigned to me. As I spoke with the Service Bureau Desk, a petite and very beautiful woman standing nearby, who spoke perfect English, offered her help. Addressing the staff in fluent Russian, she assured me they had great sympathy for me and would do everything they could to find two tickets. This vivacious woman and I then found ourselves going on the same tour to Pushkin, the summer residence of the czars. Her elegance suggested she was someone of special circumstances, but who? As we parted at the end of the tour and said our goodbyes she handed me her visiting card. Only after she had gone did I see that the morning had just been spent with the former ambassador from Bulgaria to the United Nations. That evening Shura and I enjoyed a brilliant performance by the Kirov Ballet while seated in two of the best seats in the house. We felt certain we knew who had made this possible.

On the day before the Leningrad performance, I met Shura in his hotel suite at the Europeiskaya, a downtown hotel in old-world style, located directly across the street from Philharmonic Hall. As I approached his room he stepped into the corridor with the fingers of one hand pressed across his lips and the other hand pointed at the ceiling, indicating his room was bugged. Be careful of what you say was the clear message. It was in his hotel suite that I was introduced to Toya, a representative from Gosconcert, the state concert agency, that controlled all concert performances in the Soviet Union. Toya would be traveling with us for the duration of the trip, and informed sources had warned us that all employees who were allowed to associate with foreigners reported to the KGB. In CIA terms, she was our *handler*. Superb is far too modest a word to describe her command of English. Her vocabulary, turn of phrase, and American accent were simply phenomenal, which may be the reason why, in the past, she had served as an interpreter for such personages as Indira Gandhi, Thomas Hoving of the New York Metropolitan Museum of Art, and Jacqueline Kennedy Onassis. Toya was one of those Soviets for whom Mother Russia was all, and her unfailing patriotism had to be admired. She was also an individual of strong opinions and will, and in the weeks ahead there would be some fiery exchanges among the three of us. She was absolutely convinced AIDS was an invention of American germ warfare, and that given the opportunity Vladimir Horowitz would have defected during his 1986 tour of the Soviet Union.

Leaving Shura's hotel we crossed the street to the concert hall and went backstage where Shura minutely examined every nook of the space that would be his nest for the hour and a half before he went on stage the following evening. We then proceeded to the auditorium, a breathtakingly beautiful space in its dress of pale blue silk, deep blue velvet, white marble columns, and magnificent crystal chandeliers. On stage three pianos were available to choose from and a decision was quickly reached as to which it would be: a Hamburg Steinway. Shura then practiced, and it fascinated me in its usual way, with no exercises to warm up and no practicing in rhythms or anything of the sort, just simple, straightforward, slow playing of the pieces at a mezzo forte level, always in control and never once giving into the temptation to just let it rip. While he worked in this rather nondescript fashion it was still possible to hear distant teasings of surprises that would become full blown in performance.

When the practicing was finished it was time to have tea and sweets and walk along Nevsky Prospekt going in and out of stores empty of goods, and observing Russians of the younger generation flouting the law as they whispered offers of money to well-dressed foreigners in exchange for blue jeans and cigarettes. While walking, Shura noticed a poster announcing his concert the following evening, and it caused him to smile as he read the Russian characters. The wrong program had been printed and a house that had been sold out for weeks was coming to hear works that were not in fact scheduled. Great fun! What wasn't great fun was the news from Toya that Shura had no hotel room in Moscow, the next stop on the tour, contrary to the already confirmed agreements in his contract.

On the day of the Leningrad performance, while Shura rehearsed I went to visit Petrodvorets, the summer home of Peter the Great, and it was there I had a little adventure to which Shura reacted with horror: "My God, you know you are not supposed to approach strangers! What if you had been arrested?" That thought, of course, had never entered my head, when I decided to stay longer at Petrodvorets, rather than return with the rest of the tourists as scheduled. Toward 3 p.m., when it was time to get back to Leningrad, my lack of Russian did me in. Unable to find anyone who was willing to speak with me, let alone give directions in English for public transportation back to the city, I found myself beginning to wonder if I might miss the very concert I had come to hear. While seated on a park bench, figuring how to get out of this self-created predicament, a group of school children passed by. Thinking, there's the answer, I approached one little girl of about ten and asked if she spoke English. "A little," was her reply. Explaining that I wanted to go to the train station, she looked at me thoughtfully, and after a very long pause finally said with a lovely smile, "Yes, to train station, bus three hun-dred fif-ty two numbers." That Russian child will never know how grateful I was at that moment to her and her command of the English language that allowed me to catch bus number 352, get to the station, board a train, return to Peter the Great's city, and meet Shura.

At 6:15 p.m., on the dot, we arrived at the hall where an unannounced, unexpected Russian television crew was on hand to film the event. This was interesting because the BBC had requested permission to come to Russia to document the trip and been denied on the grounds that no hotel rooms were available to house the crew. The Russians had to wait while Shura devoted the next hour and a half to his usual routine of practicing, concentration, and resting. At 7:55 p.m. an escort led me to the hall, not through the usual entrance, but rather through a dazzling reception room adjacent to backstage where French windows, sumptuous blue silk brocade, baroque moldings, glistening chandeliers, and gleaming parquet floors spoke plainly of another time in Russian history. It was in this room that the czar and czarina waited before a performance, entering the hall through what had been their private passageway. The same held true for this American visitor who was taken to the State Box, in other days the Royal Box, and seated where once the czarina had sat.

The sold-out house was in place well before the concert began. No latecomers here. At a few minutes after eight, the president of the Philharmonic Society, an attractive and well-dressed woman, came on stage and as is customary in Russia announced the artist and his program. There had been a strong tug-of-war between Shura and the concert management as to his name. The Soviets insisted he be introduced as Alexander; he insisted on Shura. And Shura it was, not Alexander, who strode briskly to the piano to begin the concert. There were two programs for this Russian tour during which he was scheduled to play five concerts: one each in Leningrad and Moscow; two in Odessa; and one in Riga. In Leningrad he opened with the Bach-Busoni Toccata, Adagio, and Fugue in C Major and followed with Schumann's *Kreisleriana*. The playing that night was powerful and perfectly paced in the Bach with biting clarity in the fugue. Following the Bach there was a chorus of spontaneous bravos from the audience at which point a small, golden-haired child of about eight walked up to the lip of the stage and offered a bouquet of daffodils, which Shura took while bending to shake her hand and say a few words. When the applause finally died down the *Kreisleriana* began, and for the next half hour one could hear rapt silence in the audience. Cherkassky's glorious singing tone was everywhere in evidence, and when he ended he was greeted with an ovation, more flowers, and with a carefully wrapped present laid at his feet by a young man who gave a most respectful bow to the artist.

At intermission tea was served backstage during which Toya made a point of telling us a gentleman in the audience, a specialist in music education, had asked to speak with the Americans and she had told him that would be impossible. Her show of Soviet authority over capitalist independence caused Shura to roll his eyes in evident irritation and also a warning to be silent. Following intermission, the audience heard Stravinsky's *Petrouchka*, a Chopin nocturne and ballade, and finally the Liszt *Hungarian Rhapsody* No. 12. As a solo piano piece, *Petrouchka* was not often played in Russia and this performance, very personal and powerfully projected, not only piqued great curiosity but also provoked much whispering in the audience at its conclusion. When he began the F-minor Chopin Ballade, intensely pianissimo, something he particularly liked to do with the opening of this piece, the effect was arresting. An audience member remarked it sounded as though the angels were calling. Next Cherkassky played the F-minor Nocturne, after which the audience erupted as if he had just played a dazzling virtuoso piece. In some way he had touched this audience in their core, and it was a good many minutes before they would let him continue with the program. Finally came Liszt's *Twelfth Rhapsody*, dispatched with flaming virtuosity, following which he was greeted with rhythmic clapping, shouts of bravo, and cascades of flowers.

Called back for five encores, he played the Albéniz *Tango*, Rachmaninoff's *Polka*, the Scriabin C-sharp Minor Etude, Chopin's *Grand Valse Brillante*, Op. 18, and the Mozart *Rondo alla Turca*. Backstage, after Shura had greeted his admirers, the Russian TV crew took over and an interview began. Later Shura brought the evening to a happy conclusion, hosting a party for a small group of friends in his hotel suite. Caviar, sturgeon, gourmet meats, salads, sweets, and ice cream made a feast appropriate to the occasion. Kefir (a relative of buttermilk) took the place of the traditional champagne, but who cared? Shura had provided all the sparkle and all the bubbles one could wish for that evening. (The newspaper *Tass* subsequently reported that of all the recitals played in Leningrad in the previous months, only the recital of Shura Cherkassky continued to be talked about for weeks on end following his appearance there.)

The next day we were scheduled to leave for Moscow at 1:10 p.m., and we risked missing the flight in order to visit Tikhvin cemetery in Leningrad where Dostoyevsky and some of the most famous musicians the world has known lay side-by-side. The cemetery opened at 11:00 a.m., which left us very little time to visit, get back to the hotel, race to the airport, and catch the plane. But it was a risk well worth taking to experience the feelings of reverence and awe that came from standing before the graves of Tchaikovsky and his colleagues Glinka, Glazunov, Cui, Borodin, Balakirev, Rimsky-Korsakov, Mussorgsky, Liadov, and Anton Rubinstein.

The flight to Moscow was our first with Aeroflot and distinguished itself as a strikingly different airborne experience. Reservations were confirmed the day before departure only and assigned by some mysterious formula worked out by Intourist. Flying from city to city one came to take for granted long, rough rolls on takeoff and ponderous, seemingly powerless ascents. Cabin noise was unusually loud, which may or may not account for the continuous rock music played from takeoff to landing. Safety instructions were given only in Russian, and on flights under four hours juice alone was served with surly service the norm. On the trip from Leningrad to Moscow a group of Italian tourists, whose usual good humor was much in evidence, passed around an umbrella to protect us all from the condensation dripping copiously from the ceiling. Shura's reaction was to comment that he thought it was bad luck to open an umbrella indoors. Still the flight landed safely as did all the others including the one to Riga, which plowed through extremely heavy weather to land in zero visibility.

While Shura waited for news about his hotel accommodation, I checked in at the National, a hotel facing the Kremlin and Red Square. He finally telephoned to say, after all the upset of having no room, he now not only had a room, but a huge apartment in the Sovietskaya, a hotel reserved for diplomats, ministers of state, and the like. He was right. It was mammoth. Numerous rooms with oriental carpets, floor-to-ceiling windows, balconies, and marble columns in the living room gave one the feeling of being on a movie set rather than in a hotel suite. The only incongruous item in the sumptuous surroundings was an upright piano whose trademark however fit the Soviet scene perfectly. It was called "Red October."

The next afternoon Toya accompanied me to Shura's hotel where we found him nibbling fresh fruit and every now and then getting up from the table to quietly try this or that passage on the Red October upright. "Don't talk to me unless I talk to you," he told us. Once he was satisfied that everything was in order we left for the Great Hall of the Moscow Conservatory, a legend to American pianophiles since Van Cliburn won the Tchaikovsky Competition on its stage in 1958. A good part of the world was also privileged to see its gold and white beauty televised in 1986 when Vladimir Horowitz played there as a symbol of improving Soviet-U.S. relations. When we arrived at the conservatory many people were milling around, and as we crossed the courtyard to the entrance an older man, obviously unaware who

Shura was, walked up to him and asked, in Russian, "Do you have an extra ticket?" Shura smiled apologetically and answered, "nyet." Moscow was desperate for tickets because just as in Leningrad the concert had sold out weeks in advance. The halls themselves, however, were strikingly different. While the Leningrad hall was cool, elegant, and patrician, the Great Hall of Moscow was warm and welcoming, with meter upon meter of gold brocade and gleaming, burnished wood enveloping the audience. At precisely 8 p.m. the head of the concert society came on stage and, as in Leningrad, announced the artist and his program.

As soon as Shura started to play it was evident that while this was the same program as Leningrad the performance of it was going to be very different. It was immediately faster and bolder, and as the concert proceeded it was evident the musical demon inside Shura was being allowed out that night. And the Moscow audience loved it. Rhythmic clapping, usually reserved for the end of a program began in the first half, and when the concert ended pandemonium broke loose. After numerous encores the audience still didn't want to let him go and security guards were called to control the crowd as he made his way backstage to a waiting crush of people, including Elena Gilels, daughter of the late Emil Gilels. A midnight supper with the ever-present caviar, sturgeon, and kefir brought a triumphant evening to a festive close.

The next morning we were off to Odessa, shaking up the military at Sheremetyevo airport in the process of doing so. When passing through the security check I set off alarms in every direction. Guards with machine guns were upon me in an instant saying, "Metal? Metal?" With great chagrin out came two objects from my raincoat pockets: a couple of cans of Bumble Bee tuna fish. Before leaving the United States, having been told that food was both terrible and extremely scarce, I had tossed some provisions into my suitcase to tide me through an emergency. Instead they almost created an emergency. Shura found the whole scene very funny; his friend much less so.

As we waited to board the plane for Odessa, Toya pointed out a tall, strikingly handsome military officer. This was an important military attaché from Cuba who would be flying with us to Odessa (a great honor she assured us) and then joining thousands of his Cuban brothers in that port city on the Black Sea. After the attaché had smilingly helped me with my hand-luggage on and off the plane, Shura inquired if he had asked me for a date. I assured him that it must be obvious to the attaché that he (Shura) was my date, which caused Shura to laugh that happy laugh his friends knew so well.

Odessa was the high point of the tour, with Shura scheduled to play two concerts in the city of his birth. The day before the first recital, as guests of the Ministry of Culture of the USSR, we were given a private tour of the Odessa Opera House, Shura's favorite childhood haunt. No wonder. It is every bit as beautiful as the Paris and Vienna houses. A performance of *The Sleeping Beauty* was in rehearsal, and before leaving we were introduced to a graceful sylph of a young woman, Nina Ananiashvili, the newest star of the Bolshoi Ballet. Toya spent a good number of minutes telling us this brilliant dancer would never defect, let alone do anything more than "lend" her talents, with Soviet approval of course, to the American stage for an occasional appearance. Instead, following her performance at the Metropolitan Opera House in New York in July of 1987, which was described by the *New York Times* as the "revelation" of the company, she signed with American Ballet Theater, going on to become its undisputed star.

Shura had left Odessa in 1922 at the age of thirteen, and the emotions created by his return to Odessa at age seventy-eight were very evident on stage. He poured his heart out to his audiences in Odessa, playing in the grand manner of the romantic tradition. But the most unforgettable moment of the entire trip came in the second Odessa program with a transcendent performance of the Pabst transcription of *Eugene Onegin* at the highly ornate Odessa New Stock Exchange, where Liszt had given five of the last six recitals of his performing life in the summer of 1847. It was generally agreed Cherkassky owned this piece, and that evening in particular he made its opening as haunting a statement as one will ever hear in the concert hall. The love theme sang its way to every corner of the house, floating as it were, before dissolving into a delirious swirling rendition of the waltz. The rest of the program consisted of the *Rachmaninoff-Corelli Variations*, played with very little pedal, a commanding Bach-Liszt Prelude in A minor, César Franck's *Chorale, Prelude and Fugue*, and a delicately traced Schubert Sonata in A Major Op. 120. Once again the response was tumultuous, and after the concert reporters from *Pravda* and *Tass* interviewed Shura at length, asking if a Cherkassky festival would be possible in the fall. And so it went through a long line of well-wishers who came to congratulate him on his latest triumph.

Watching Shura during these days, as he returned to the memories of his childhood, was a very touching scene. As we rode from the airport to the hotel he commented, "Oh, there are many more cars today than when I left." He visited his old apartment and met an elderly lady living there who had been a young playmate in the building during his childhood years. He wondered if he had been born at home or in a hospital, and it mattered dearly to him that he find out. The hospital was the answer. A trip to the site of his concert debut revealed that the hall had been converted to commercial use, a fact that saddened him. As he walked up and down Pushkin Street, the main thoroughfare leading to the sea, and stood on the famous Potemkin steps it was clear Shura Cherkassky's Russian origins had been called very much into play.

In order to have more time to explore Riga, it was decided that I should leave Odessa one day ahead of Shura whose concert was scheduled for the following evening. This was a trip that was *not* destined. What should have been a two-hour trip from Odessa turned into an eleven-hour ordeal created by a three-hour unexplained luggage search at the Odessa airport, a missed connection in Moscow, bad weather, and an extremely rough flight. When our plane landed in Riga the fog was virtually impenetrable, and it never did lift, so that by 6:00 p.m. the next day it was obvious there would be no Cherkassky recital in Riga that evening. That night back at the hotel I requested a wake-up call for the following morning, and when the phone rang I groaned inwardly at how quickly the time to get up had come. Picking up the receiver of the squealing telephone, I heard not an operator, however, but Shura saying he was calling to tell me all was well and that he had just arrived in Moscow after waiting at the Odessa airport for thirteen hours for a flight to clear. He was greatly agitated by the fact that Toya had asked him to turn over his passport to her, which he had adamantly refused to do. In between Odessa and Moscow, he said, his plane had landed near Chernobyl, the site of the 1986 nuclear disaster, and he wanted to know if I thought that would have a negative effect on his career. After reassuring him I truly didn't think so, I had the wit to ask, "What time is it?" "Ten to four" (in the morning), he replied. Shura's marvelous spontaneity was once again in play.

Before returning to Moscow I went exploring in Riga, and while walking down one of the main streets I passed the Latvian State Conservatory of Music. On impulse I turned around, walked in, and was greeted by a woman, her arms filled with books. Speaking fluent English, she introduced herself as an administrator. After I had explained my interest in learning about the conservatory she smiled and said she had just that moment come from the school's library where she had been searching for books appropriate to give foreign guests. It appeared I was the first such guest, and she generously gave me a beautifully illustrated book on the history, development, and course of study at the Latvian Conservatory, printed in Latvian, Russian, and English. When Shura saw the present and rifled through its pages he quipped, "Oh, do you think they'd accept me as a student?"

His concerts now finished, Shura decided to take three days off before returning to London, and they were happily spent wandering about, visiting the Kremlin complex of palaces and cathedrals, viewing collections of czarist finery and carriages at the armory, attending a performance of *Der Freischutz* in the red and gold splendor of the Bolshoi Theater, riding the metro while admiring its marble walls, chandeliers, and museum-quality paintings, with Shura all the while lamenting the plight of his fellow Russians as they waited two hours five abreast in Red Square to visit Lenin's tomb, or just as long to purchase nonexistent goods in stores with empty shelves. Only a trip to Melodiya Records resulted in successful shopping, with the purchase of a prized pile of Safronitsky recordings. When I mentioned to Shura how happy I was to have such significant documentation of the Russian style of piano playing he stated, as always, he did not believe there was such a thing as a Russian style and that he never subscribed to any school or method.

As we roamed about he kept remarking on how poorly his countrymen looked thanks to a diet too rich in alcohol and too lacking in fruits and vegetables, and on how shabbily they were dressed, with the women in dark colors, and the men wearing open-necked shirts with medals from the Great Patriotic War decking their jackets. Indeed, in Moscow it seemed psychologically that the Great Patriotic War was still going on. Men walked as though they were marching, the military was everywhere in evidence, the feel was simply of another time. One visit that did bring a smile to Shura's face was to the Moscow Conservatory where we were informed that in addition to the usual courses in music and a major instrument, students were required to study the *History of the Party*. And afterward we went to see Shura's cousin, Tanya Peltzer. At age eighty-four she was Russia's most famous comic actress and a member in excellent standing of the Communist Party. She was also the one who, Shura said with a laugh, received more applause at his concerts than he. Not true!

On another occasion we met a Russian music critic and his wife in their apartment, where we were served beautifully prepared cake and tea. The critic mentioned his plight of not being able to find pins for his badly deteriorated Blüthner piano, which had belonged to the conductor Kiril Kondrashin. All the information was taken down and upon his return to London, Shura arranged to have the proper pins sent along. It also came up in conversation that the critic was a great admirer of Horowitz, whose biography was in my hotel room. When I offered to give it to him Shura cautioned me to be careful as everything Horowitz, his beloved Volodya, had to say about his mother country was not exactly flattering, and possession of the book might cause trouble for his friend. Still it was decided that he should have it and at the end of our visit the critic escorted me back to the National where he waited in the lobby while I proceeded to my room and placed the Horowitz biography in the bottom of an opaque plastic laundry bag on top of which I set a bouquet of flowers Shura had given me. Hoping the disguised book would pass by watching eyes unnoticed, I returned to the lobby, and gave the "bouquet" to our friend, saying for all nearby to hear, "Please wish your wife a very happy birthday!"

On our next to last day Elena Gilels and her husband and young son Kyril entertained us in their home at a late afternoon tea that turned out to be a lavish supper of wonderful Russian delicacies. The conversation was lively and humorous, with all of us using Shura to translate one piano story after another. During our visit we mentioned we had wanted to go that evening to the Tchaikovsky Hall to see the Russian Folk Dance Ensemble, but there were no tickets available. A phone call from Elena Gilels to the theater management immediately remedied that situation and off we went to Tchaikovsky Hall. When we arrived we learned with great displeasure that our seats actually belonged to paying citizens who were rudely dislodged from their places by officials of the hall. Shura squeezed my arm tightly and fiercely whispered, "Say Nothing!" Following the folk dance performance a taxi was nowhere to be found. Seeing a group of tour buses parked outside the theater Shura approached one with a small French flag placed in the windshield. He immediately hopped on board asking, "parlez-vous français?" At the response of "mais oui," Shura proclaimed, "vive la France!" and arranged transportation aboard the tour bus for the two of us back to Moscow center. After returning to the National we enjoyed our last dinner of the trip to the accompaniment of a simultaneously joyful and soulful balalaika orchestra.

Our final day in Russia dawned raw and cold. At 5:40 p.m. a British Airways jet took off for London carrying Shura home. At the exact same moment my Finnair flight took off for Helsinki. When the pilot of our aircraft announced we had left Soviet air space the passengers on board applauded loudly and for whatever reason there was a palpable sense of relief. My thoughts floated back to the Russians we had met privately who showed warmth and hospitality, as opposed to the man in the street who feared contact with foreigners. Still there were exceptions, as the morning in Odessa when a woman walked up to us and asked, "American?" When the answer was yes, she handed me a tiny bouquet of lilies of the valley and quietly walked away, a lovely gesture immediately tarnished by Toya who said that since it was against the law to gather lilies of the valley it was her duty to summon the police and press charges. Fortunately, Shura protested loudly and was able to talk her out of her plan to have the woman arrested for her "crime." Another time while riding the metro in Moscow I sat down next to a lady who was carrying a huge bunch of lilacs, half of which were suddenly placed in my hand. When I tried to express my pleasure and my thanks the woman simply smiled. She got off at the next stop. Without a word, Shura nodded knowingly.

We both agreed, with Shura emphasizing how important travel was, that what appeared to be missing most in Russian society was the stimulation that comes from mixing with other cultures and the kind of happiness that derives from independent thinking, motivation, and achievement. Those who reaped the rewards and security of the system as it stood then would understandably be reluctant to see it change, just as citizens who had spent a lifetime avoiding confrontation with authority would have difficulty in developing other instincts. The educational system gave children little freedom to find their own means of personal expression. Creative analysis was not indigenous to the Russian character; insularity and suspicion were. Was Glasnost real? Was it realistic? Could Mr. Gorbachev and his reforms undo a seventy-year pattern of behavior? We didn't know. We would have to wait for history to tell us the answer.

My plane landed safely in Helsinki and I checked into the Intercontinental Hotel. As I began the adjustment to the capitalist system with all its perks I laughed silently to myself and thought, "Decadent, decadent, decadent!" Later that evening Shura and I talked by telephone, reliving every detail of our three weeks inside the Soviet Union, and speaking of encounters and conversations not written of in these pages. We agreed the trip was the experience of a lifetime. "Would you go back?" he asked. "In a minute," was my instant reply.

After placing the phone back in its cradle I spent a good many hours thinking, So who is Shura Cherkassky, *really*?

CHAPTER FIFTEEN

Understanding Shura

The answer to it all is you have to be yourself.

—S. C.

It is true that Shura Cherkassky was held in awe and affection by many who knew him. It is also true that he was a man badly misunderstood by many others who came in contact with him. Shyness was read as brusqueness; his intense focus on the piano to the exclusion of people was interpreted as callousness; his demands on himself for the perfection he gave his audiences was thought to be self-centeredness; and the routine that kept him perfectly intact until the last six months of his life earned him the label "eccentric." Had his critics probed beneath the surface they would have discovered an individual of substance and integrity, a person totally different from their perception. He was a man who wanted to reach out to people and make relationships, but more often than not, he simply did not know how. Too often it was forgotten that this émigré child from Russia arrived in America speaking no English, attended only a few classes in public school, and essentially did not socialize with other children, in spite of all the public relations hype of his being a "normal American boy." Certainly it is reasonable to ask how anyone reared in this way, above all a genius, could be expected to participate in and respond in an ordinary way to the ordinary events of everyday life. Yet for anyone who extended a helping hand, there emerged a person of extraordinary character, bubbling with life and faithful to a fault, who was as honest and decent as one could hope, and who had the capacity to immeasurably enrich another's life.

By his admission Shura was a very lonely man, a loneliness that was more often than not a result of the awe he inspired. This awe was a double-edged sword for him. While he reveled in thunderous ovations, numerous recalls to the stage for encore after encore, and rave reviews by music critics, he was simultaneously frustrated by this interest in him only as a pianist and never, in his view, as a person. People waiting in backstage lines always made the same boring comments, always asked the same inane questions or worse yet, in the later years of his career, would want to reminisce about pianists and events of fifty years ago. He was adamant about not wanting to look back, saying,

> I'm not terribly interested in archeology or anything that happened many years ago. I like to see something that happens now. It's the same way when I read books or when I go to the movies or when I go to the theater. I like to see something that can actually happen in this present day . . . not fantasy or illusions or history. That's the way I am. I don't like to look back.[1]

Given his childhood circumstances and the struggles of his prewar and California years, it is easy to understand his dislike of remembering. People who insisted on dwelling on the past or talking about only his piano playing annoyed him greatly, as did "those awful receptions after concerts with their little sandwiches or where they put you with people at dinner who mean nothing to you and you will never see again." In letters to me, he expressed his feelings on the subject very clearly (see figs. 15.1 and 15.2).

During late-night suppers following his concerts, he would often wail, "Why, why do they never ask about *me*?" It was never possible to make him understand that since his piano playing was the essence of his person, people *were* showing an intense interest in him personally when they asked and talked about his piano playing. Every single aspect of his talent was a reflection in depth of Shura the person. The few who were privileged to know him intimately saw a man of refinement, who was courtly and mannered, witty, warm, and affectionate. They also saw that if someone crossed him, or if he believed he had been wronged, there could be no reasoning with him. Regardless of the facts, he would turn away never again to resume the offending relationship. Forgiveness did not come easily to Shura Cherkassky. Black was black and white was white.

Solace from this intense loneliness, outside of the hours he spent at his beloved piano, came from the pleasures he found along the way in life, a few of them being travel, fine dining, and staying at five-star hotels as he tirelessly trekked the world playing concerts. One of his favorite establishments was the Pierre Hotel, his home in New York City whenever he performed there.

HYATT REGENCY MAUI
ON KAANAPALI BEACH
200 NOHEA KAI DRIVE
LAHAINA, MAUI, HAWAII 96761-1990 USA

808 661 1234 TELEX 708 667 6030
TELEFAX 808 667 4499

January 4, 1990

My dear Betty,
Got your express letter yesterday for which many thanks.
You are one of the very few people who are sincerely concerned
about my personal satisfaction, and I cherish that more
than anything. I have a feeling (intuition?) that in future
you will be able to help me. It is especially reactions
after concerts, back stage people, etc. But I do not agree
with you about staying longer in places after concerts
when I did that; it wasn't any different. It happens
back stage at once, or, if someone makes a small party
choosing people that might interest me. Mischa Elman
made a remark: "The tragedy of artist is that
people entertain the artist the way they think, but do
not bother to ask the artist". How true it is.

Figure 15.1 Letter, January 4, 1990.

Here until 24th,
then London.

THE LANDMARK
HOTEL · AND · PLAZA
BANGKOK

August 11, 1990

My dear Betty,

I am not
unhappy. as healthwise and careerwise things are
going marvelously well, but I feel personally unfulfilled
(I don't think I spell that word right!). Most people are
interested in me only because of my music,
but for nothing else.

Figure 15.2 Letter, August 11, 1990.

Room 738 was reserved exclusively for his stays, and it was there on his specially delivered Steinway upright piano that he practiced, and there that he received visitors, ordered room service, and spent countless hours on the telephone. With the blinds perpetually drawn, the thermostat turned as high as it could go, mounds of fresh fruit continuously in evidence, a voluminous aluminum suitcase tucked in the corner, and an ever-present clock ticking off the minutes, his meticulous, slow practice filled the days before any recital. An occasional lunch at the Russian Tea Room, his favorite New York restaurant, and an obligatory trip to the East Side office of his ophthalmologist, Dr. Arnett, were the only breaks to the outside world that he permitted himself.

Food was a definite source of interest to Shura, with yogurt and fresh fruit serving as the staples of his diet. Yet he adored many kinds of food, delighting in *borscht* and *blinis* in Russia, salmon quenelles at the White House Restaurant in London, Ben & Jerry's chocolate ice cream in America, and giant steaks before every concert no matter where he played in the world. Evian spring water, milk, and Pocari Sweat, a Japanese libation rich in vitamins and sugar, quenched his thirst, while sumptuous desserts satisfied his sweet tooth. He rigorously observed "juice day" once a week, during which he drank only fruit juice, and which was much more an exercise in willpower than a matter of diet. "Character," he called it. Once while visiting my husband and me on Cape Cod, an outing to a restaurant for a five-course dinner was followed by a trip to a local ice cream cafe where this mature artist, who was then seventy-eight years old, promptly ordered a double hot fudge sundae and a pistachio milkshake, both of which disappeared in a matter of minutes. It was particularly interesting to watch him devour an apple, which went down core, seeds, and all. His food bills were enormous, and on one occasion in the 1980s he telephoned from Japan, wanting to share the news that he had just eaten $175 worth of dinner, a fact that amused him no end. Before retiring, it was his habit to drink a cup of boiling hot water while it was still bubbling.

While food was often a source of solace, alcohol was a forbidden. "Not a drop of alcohol? Not one drop? Are you sure? Are you *absolutely* sure?" Invariably at any restaurant anywhere in the world, these were the questions that he asked about any item on the menu that interested him, from appetizer to dessert. His aversion to alcohol was well founded given the havoc it had wrought in Josef Hofmann's life. It was Hofmann's downfall, his destruction, Shura often said, recounting how the last time he heard Hofmann in concert he found himself crying at the tattered renderings from this once great giant of the piano who had figured so meaningfully in his life. Not that there wasn't a time in Shura's life when he did imbibe. Hungarian-American pianist Gyorgy Sandor told me of performing a concert on a Monday evening in Warsaw in 1938, following which Shura came backstage to congratulate him. They subsequently went out to celebrate, and when Sandor said he was very thirsty, Cherkassky suggested he have some vodka. When the soloist of the evening asked what *vodka* was, his friend replied, "a very good drink." Sandor then had a very large glass of the stuff, which of course didn't quench his thirst, and so he had another and another—five in all. In about an hour he passed out and was taken back to his hotel where he slept the whole next day and woke up on Wednesday. Luckily he had no concert on Tuesday. Sandor, who was introduced to Shura in his youth through the Russian pianist Ray Lev, described him as:

> [a] *formidable* pianist and very attractive but shy human being, who had an all-absorbing mother and whose behavior was rather bizarre and childlike. His interpretations were very different from the standard and his way of practicing would have destroyed many other pianists. Everything was practiced extremely slowly, with the fingers pressed into each key. There was never a wrong note. He played a wonderful *Petrouchka* and a superb Brahms F Minor Sonata.

By the late forties, following years of serious drinking, Shura vowed never again to touch a drop of alcohol, a promise he scrupulously honored. On occasion his obsession with not having alcohol even in his presence produced stories that, while invariably amusing, also drove home the tremendous underlying discomfort he felt in relation to drinking. One such incident took place at the Pierre Hotel in the spring of 1993. A well-intentioned manager sent a bottle of wine, along with some fruit and cheese, to the artist's room. The bottle was promptly removed by Shura and set outside in the corridor for the maid to take away. Thinking the wine had been left undelivered, a conscientious maid returned it to his room while he was out to dinner. When the offending bottle was found in his room yet again, he took it and tried to uncork it, with the intent of pouring the wine down the bathroom drain. Unsuccessful in his efforts and with no corkscrew in sight, Shura took the bottle into the elegant dressing room of his suite and banged it mightily against the marble sink in an effort to break it open. The bottle didn't break—but the marble sink *did* from the force of the blow! The next day a new marble sink was installed by the Pierre's plumbers in room 738. A similar incident occurred in 1989 in Montreux, Switzerland, where the pianist was performing the Schumann concerto at a festival with the Tokyo Philharmonic. Nimbus, his recording company at the time, sent a "fantastic" bottle of champagne with a welcoming note to his hotel room. The following morning the artist asked the waiter who brought him his breakfast to open the bottle and the unsuspecting waiter assumed the hotel guest wanted to drink it. Instead Shura asked the waiter to follow him into the bathroom where he commanded the waiter to pour the champagne down the sink. "I tell you, the thought of pouring it down the sink helped me play exceptionally well that night!"

His aversion to drink was matched by his attraction to heat. Shura loved to be hot. Not warm, *hot*. "It can't be too hot for me. The hotter the better." His contract called for tea backstage with water boiled to 220° F. His rooms at the White House in London were kept at a temperature other guests found intolerable. Maids in hotels complained of near suffocation while tidying his room. Coffee made in a percolator then had to be brought to a boil on the electric range to satisfy his body's need for heat. During a stay in Chicago in the summer of 1987 when the temperature soared daily to well over 100° F, causing major medical problems among the city's elderly, Shura asked for a space heater to be brought to his room. The manager of a hotel in Arizona was stupefied when this distinguished guest insisted on lying by the pool in 110° sun with neither the protection of suntan lotion nor a cover for his head. Astonished as well was the manager of a Miami hotel who observed the world-class artist lying beside the hotel pool in full concert dress taking the sun prior to a performance. When on several occasions Shura stayed in my Cape Cod home, thermostats throughout the house had to be set at 90° and one wool blanket was added to the two down comforters already on his bed. Eccentric? No. Just signs to some that the arrhythmia from which he suffered was causing circulation problems.

This desire and need to be warm was also one of the reasons for his choice of hot, exotic vacation spots with beautiful beaches and luxury hotels that could accommodate his few but very precise needs. For most of his life Shura Cherkassky toured the globe as a performer; he also trekked the world much as a nomad, ever seeking new destinations, new adventures, new stimulations, and liking best to travel with a one-way ticket. How many people have been asked in the most matter-of-fact way, "Tell me, have you ever been to Siberia?" as Shura asked me during one of our earliest conversations. When he was a baby his father showed him travel albums of Paris and Switzerland, whetting his appetite for the travel that would become a passion later in his life. During his adult years he was tireless in seeking out new itineraries, and the Official Airline Guide became his favorite reading matter. Eternally restless, he once asked a doctor about his compulsion to always be on the move and was told that it was simply the way he was and he should do as he felt. As a child in Odessa his great ambition was to be a streetcar conductor, a desire he didn't understand until, as an adult, he realized the attraction to him as a four- or five-year-old child was the fact that a streetcar was always moving. He simply couldn't sit still either as a child or as an adult. He adored big cities and beaches and nothing in between and the time not spent on stage or practicing was devoted to seeking out one new, exotic location after another. Travel agents annoyed him with their uninformed recommendations, and he often cited his trip to Upper Queensland on the Great Barrier Reef in 1990 as an example of their incompetence. Soon after his arrival there, where he had been "guaranteed" there would be no rain, the guests at the Hayman Island Resort Hotel were evacuated to Sydney to protect them from an approaching typhoon!

The pianist's first airplane flight took place in Australia in 1928 when he flew from Brisbane to Toowoomba on tour. When asked about that flight, he wrote me the description in figure 15.3. No matter what the circumstances, he adored flying all his life and had an enviable capacity for willing himself to sleep on flights so that jet lag, until late in life, was an unknown to him.

There wasn't a corner of the earth that eluded him as he pursued his goal of escaping boredom. Between March of 1935 and January of 1936 he had made that famous tour in which he circled the globe (giving concerts in Russia and the Orient), a journey that included three transatlantic trips, one voyage across the Pacific from San Francisco to Yokohama, and the long railroad journey through Siberia from the Chinese border to Paris. Nor did the child in Shura Cherkassky ever die. In December of 1987, at the age of seventy-eight, he boarded the Concorde in London for a one-day trip to the North Pole where he visited Santa Claus, went sledding, and duly sent postcards and letters to his friends from the world's most frigid post office, the correspondence as always written with his signature fountain pen and never a ballpoint (see fig. 15.4).

Just as spontaneity was a hallmark of his playing, so too was it a distinguishing characteristic of his travel plans. Once he was sitting in an airport waiting for a flight to Paris, on which he was already ticketed, when he noticed a blinking red light signaling the imminent departure of a plane to Bangkok. Off he went to Bangkok, which became one of his favorite repeat destinations, with protracted stays at either the Oriental, the Landmark, or

158, The White House,
Regents Park,
London, N.W.1 3UP, England.
March 2, 1993

My dear Betty,

How you know about that plane in 1928 when I flew with my father from Brisbane to Towoomba and back. It wwas about half-an-hour, probably now it is only 10 minutes or so. That is in Queensland,Australia). As far as I reeall iw was almost like helicopter. I never had really a bad experience flying. Only one many years ago taking oof from Madrid to Bordeausas we were starting to go up, one wheel tire came over or something like that, we could land-thank God, lets pray that nothing ever happens to us flying. I hope we meet and talk, and plan few things. So glad now that you saw me in London, and you know how I live here, what name I have, etc., etc. I will never wish to change living anywhere else, especially now that all the legal matters rae fixed up. All my love to you and Richard.

Shura.

Figure 15.3 Letter, March 2, 1993.

the Ambassador Hotel. There he was provided with a comfortable suite, a piano on which to practice, a pool in which to swim, and congenial people with whom he could chat. He was always impressed by the Thai people, who seemed so desirous of pleasing guests and "who never laughed at you, only with you." At precisely five o'clock each afternoon he took tea on the terrace of the Oriental Hotel where he watched the sun set, describing it as one of the most beautiful sights in the world. He often wrote about his feelings for this favorite vacation destination (see fig. 15.5).

Whether he was on vacation or not, swimming and regular massage were faithfully observed rituals throughout his life. Citing his mother's withdrawal from the concert stage because of cramps in her shoulders that left her unable to perform, he feared the same fate might befall him. "In those days they didn't know what massage and physiotherapy was. That's why I'm so fanatical about swimming and massage." While vacationing with my husband and me in Venice, Italy, during the summer of 1988, his venturing into the Adriatic Sea resulted in a near drowning. Wearing plugs to protect his ears, Shura

Suomi-Finland
Rovaniemi-Napapiiri-Polarkreis
Arctic circle - cercle polaire

NAPAPIIRIN MAJA

MERRY CHRISTMAS
HAPPY NEW YEAR

Extraordinary experiency — one day trip on Concord from London. 24-31 December to 1-9 January, I am at Ambassador Hotel, Bangkok, Thailand.
With love,
Shura.

Kustantaja H. Laamanen-Tuonti Import

IM & EX Advertising

21.12.83

PAR AVION
LENTOPOSTI
FLYGPOST

EUROPA
FINLAND 2,20

Mr. and Mrs. Richard Casper
Box 554
Barnstable, Massachusetts
02630
U.S.A.

Figure 15.4 Letter, December 21, 1983.

was unable to hear the frantic shouts of my husband as he tried to warn him away from the massive rocks toward which he was drifting. Swimming furiously, my husband grabbed Shura by the chin in a lifesaving hold, pulling him away from disaster. Finally a *salvataggio* saw the problem and swiftly swam to the pair, escorting Shura back to shore. The captain of the Port of Venice was duly informed of the near drowning, and the famous pianist's blood pressure was checked every hour on the hour by the seaside nurse for the rest of the afternoon. In celebration of his survival the three of us went to dinner that evening at Do Forni, a lively restaurant behind the Piazza San Marco. During the course of the evening a taped version of a Brahms's *Hungarian Dance* was played, becoming the inspiration for one of Shura's most brilliant encores during the upcoming concert season.

Another favored destination was Cape Cod, where he was engaged to play on the Great Artists Series of the Cape Cod Conservatory where I served as director. His first concert there took place on October 30, 1983, but when

June 3, 1989

Dear Betty,

There is so much in my thoughts it would fill pages in writing so I better make it short. And when we next meet, will tell you all sorts of things in detail. Bangkok really never dissapoints. I think I figured out one of the reasons. The Thais' part of their religion is to please, and never say NO to anything, especially to foreigners, so life here is easy, effortless, no inhibitions, etc., etc. This Hotel is fabulous, a suite with "Bach" upright piano, haven't started practicing yet. wonderful swimming pool. although now this is supposed to be the start of rainy season; no rain yet, plenty of marvelous sun. The food at some restaurants are probably even better than in Europe. French, Italian, German, Japanese, they have the best food, and even Thai food is quite delicious, but not too often.

Figure 15.5 Letter, June 3, 1989.

he had arrived at Barnstable Airport the previous morning, he was carrying only a small duffel bag, had no other luggage, and after a very proper greeting, asked to go directly to a supermarket where he rolled a carriage up and down the aisles, selecting yogurt and a large variety of fresh fruit. His shoes were particularly noticeable: a gleaming black patent leather, the mystery of which was solved when he removed the heavy winter coat he was wearing. He was attired in full concert dress. Observing my surprise, he smiled shyly and explained he wanted to save time packing and unpacking by simply wearing what was required onstage. In fact, time was an obsession with the man, so much so that there were moments when I thought early on in life he must have swallowed a clock. His love of precision was one of the reasons he particularly liked visiting Japan where he stayed frequently at the Okura Hotel. It delighted him to order breakfast for 7:23:30 a.m. and have room service knock at exactly 7:23:30 a.m.

Following dinner on the evening prior to this Great Artists Series concert, Shura practiced for the following day's recital. One of the local newspapers had requested an interview that the artist said he would be happy to give but only after he practiced the required four hours. Would the reporter mind meeting him at midnight? All credit to this earnest young man who arrived punctually at midnight to interview the famous visitor. In response to the first question posed, Shura's literal mind revealed itself. When the reporter said, "I am told you never know what you are going to do when you walk onstage and sit down to play. Why is that?" Cherkassky replied with astonishment, "What do you mean? Of course I know what I am going to play. Every artist knows what he is going to play. How could he give a concert if he didn't know what he was going to play?" The reporter, of course, had been referring to my visitor's well-known spontaneity, but Shura's literal mind had missed the point. But that same mind didn't miss a single nuance at his concert the next afternoon. The way he floated out the opening of Beethoven's Opus 27 *Sonata quasi una fantasia* in E-flat made an indelible impression on those who heard him. At the end of the recital, a normally reserved Cape Cod audience shouted its approval.

The overwhelming success of this performance caused an instant invitation for a reengagement. It was settled that another recital would be given in the spring of 1985, but when the time arrived, the weather didn't cooperate and Shura Cherkassky spent eight hours at Nantucket airport instead of a scheduled fifteen-minute stopover on the way to Hyannis. Phone calls went back and forth trying to find a way to get him across Nantucket Sound by any means, but no solution could be found to get through the fog. When Shura finally arrived at his original destination, Hyannis, he was profusely apologetic and seemed genuinely amazed that he was embraced with open arms instead of a sour face. Plans were made to reschedule the concert for the coming November, an engagement that happily went off without complication and was accompanied by the first of several requests to stay in our home. Each visit invariably produced tales to tell, as during a weeklong visit in June of 1994, following another appearance on the Great Artists Concert Series. After the usual celebration dinner and fun conversation until three o'clock in the morning, the three of us went off to bed with at least two of us (my husband and I) delighted at the prospect of a late sleep-in. At one point I was certain that I was dreaming of the *Là ci darem la mano Variations*, which Shura was to perform at Lincoln Center's Mostly Mozart Festival the following week, but the insistent repeated jumps in the fourth variation became clearer and clearer until I opened my eyes and understood the jumps were taking place not in my dream but in my living room. The clock told me it was 6:30 a.m. In the living room I found dear Shura practicing happily away. "Oh, Betty, are you there? Come, come listen to what I might do with the jumps. Tell me what you think." While dutifully listening I became aware that, ever the perfect gentleman, Shura, at 6:30 a.m., was practicing in his gray business suit, which he was wearing over his green silk pajamas.

Although traveling, staying in five-star hotels, and dining all gave him satisfaction, possessions had absolutely no interest for him. He saw them simply as a burden. Shura owned the clothes on his back, of which his favorite item was a fur-lined coat, custom-made in Montreal, the watch on his wrist, a tape recorder, and a much-beloved aluminum suitcase that traveled the world with him. His love of color in piano playing translated itself into a predilection for strikingly patterned and colored shirts, which in the words of one observer "would squint the eyes of a Matisse." He did enjoy shopping in Hong Kong, which he described as "out of this world, two or three times cheaper than in America or Europe, and where one does not have to leave the hotel room as the tailor comes to you with samples, then fitting, even shoes, and in three days' time all is ready, and superb!"

His Steinway piano was rented, as was a tiny flat at the White House, his apartment-hotel off Marylebone Road near Regent's Park in London, where he settled after a stay at the Prince of Wales Hotel in De Vere Gardens. The move to London was made in 1961 following his mother's death. Originally he settled in flat 40 on the ground floor of the hotel, but moved upstairs to flat 156 when the former was converted to an office. In 1972, "for technical reasons," according to Shura, 156 became 158. Cluttered and claustrophobic, flat 158 was dominated by a Steinway grand piano on which piles of well-worn music were stacked, with an ever-present clock, metronome, and tape recorder filling the little remaining space. An unauthenticated early photograph of Chopin given to Shura by Josef Hofmann's wife stood prominently on the battered credenza. And at one time before it disappeared, another gift of Mrs. Hofmann held a place of honor in the White House apartment: a bronze sculpture of the hand of Anton Rubinstein that had belonged to her husband. In 1962 she presented it to her husband's extraordinary pupil with the words, "I want Shura Cherkassky to inherit this memento of Anton Rubinstein because he is Rubinstein's musical grandchild." But of all the objects in flat 158, the most treasured by Shura was a photograph of his dearly beloved mother that was prominently displayed on a tiny desk where also lay an ancient typewriter on which letters and memos to friends and agents were batted out. Separating the piano from the rest of the space was a heavy velvet drape, a concession to a grumpy neighbor. A miniscule kitchen, bath, and bedroom completed the layout, and the entire arrangement suited this multimillionaire pianist just fine. With all the traveling he did, flat 158 fulfilled his needs because he really didn't reside in any one place in particular or have any desire to do so. "What would I do with more space?" he asked. "I can't even boil an egg or make a bed properly." Hotel living was always his preference, for all that really mattered was that he be allowed to practice, which he was at the White House, as long as he didn't start before nine o'clock in the morning or continue after ten in the evening.

> Why don't I have my own flat? The answer is simple—because I have no patience. If I had a place of my own I would feel very isolated—I like to have people around even if I don't say hello to anyone—just that they're there. And if I need anything I just pick up the phone and ask the porter to get it. There is a restaurant. What would I do with my own place? A housekeeper would leave me because I keep the rooms too hot.[2]

Although he was an American citizen, London was his favored city, and he would think of living nowhere else, describing as one of the happiest days of his life the one on which he was granted permanent resident status in Great Britain and received an official stamp in his passport. "London is a *wonderful* city and it grows on you continually." He was even more content when a problem with his personal taxes was resolved through a six-figure settlement in the early 1990s. Indeed, the rejection and near poverty he experienced in his early days in America left a lasting hurt, and in his maturity he candidly expressed his distaste for the country that had paid him so little heed in his youth. In May of 1955 he wrote from Auckland, New Zealand, to his cousin, Sadie Ginsberg in Baltimore, following a trip to California.

> Dearest Sadie,
>
> . . . Wonderful flight from Copenhagen to Los Angeles via Greenland and Winnipeg in 26 hours. But I hated Los Angeles. My dear, it took this little trip of three days for me to realize I could *never* [underlined in original] be happy in America. I just don't belong there and there is no real trying to like it because it's the right thing to do. No, that's final. America is too much against my nature.

Again in 1982 he wrote Sadie:

> Honestly I am not happy coming to America. Altogether the atmosphere in America does not suit me. No use to think logically, it's the feeling. Really I would not shed a tear if I knew I would never see USA again.

And while he prospered later on in America, his feelings never changed.

Although he had no interest in possessions, Shura *did* have an intense interest in earning money since it represented, along with the rave reviews he could read, a measure of success in terms of what he could count. He talked about his earnings quite freely to many people, and when questioned on the wisdom of this he would reply, "Why not? Are people going to steal it from me?" No, his friends answered, but if he really wanted to be sure people liked him for the person he was and not for what they thought they might get from him, perhaps it would be best to keep such matters to himself. Once in fact, in the early 1990s, as we drove to a concert a few hours distant from London, a woman also present in the auto said,

> "Why don't you buy me a car, Shura?"
>
> "Why should I?" he replied.
>
> "Because you're well able."
>
> There was silence for a few minutes before the same woman pointed to a house in the near distance and said, "Why don't you buy me a house like that one?"
>
> Shura replied, "I'm going to sleep now. Don't talk to me until I wake myself!"

As he dozed, the insistent woman was asked how much such a house would cost. "About three hundred thousand pounds," she replied. Whenever we were in that particular person's company, the conversation was somehow always steered to the same topic. Little did she realize how she embarrassed herself, or how Shura would frown after she left and say, "My God! How can anyone talk like that?" The truth is that some people did view Shura as a potential source of income and were not particularly shy about giving not-so-subtle hints or making outright declarations that they should be remembered by him in a significant way, but he was not the least bit influenced by anything they had to say. After such persons left us he would look over to me, shake his head, roll his eyes, and start laughing that wonderful laugh of his.

Shura's method of banking money was anything but conventional. Large sums were left in his apartment, traveled with him in the favored aluminum suitcase, were often girdled about his waist, and could even be found in his wallet as he sat on stage performing. Once coming off a plane in Switzerland at the height of summer he appeared dressed in his winter coat and gave the impression of having gained a lot of weight. Not so. He was transporting money to his Swiss bank, having lined his coat and suit jacket and shirt with the deposit he was about to make. During a stay at the Pierre Hotel he once asked me to count a sum of cash that had been delivered in a paper bag by his New York representative in payment for a concert. Dutifully I sat down at the desk in his suite and fifteen thousand dollars later finished counting. In spite of once being mugged on the back stairs of the White House he never changed his ways. Counting money down to the last penny was an obsession with him, and it had to be absolutely correct, whether the transaction took place between Shura and a bank or Shura and a friend. One such accounting took place in a letter written on May 31, 1967, to Suzanne Rosenbaum, the late chairperson of the Johannesburg Musical Society, following an encounter in Vienna (see fig. 15.6).

At the time Shura Cherkassky entered Royal Brompton Hospital in London prior to his death in December of 1995, he left $300,000 in varying currencies and denominations at his White House flat, and more than $2 million on deposit in a Swiss account. In accordance with the terms of his will, five thousand pounds was given outright to an employee of one of his former management companies. Of the remainder of his English assets, 45 percent went to a then current employee in London; 30 percent to a friend in Germany; and 25 percent to a friend in the Ukraine. The $2 million in

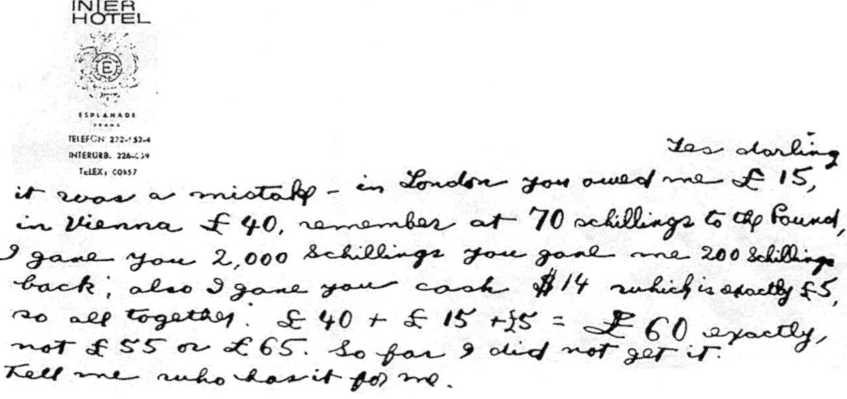

INTER HOTEL
ESPLANADE
PRAHA
TELEFON 272-152-4
INTERURB. 226-C39
TELEX: C0657

Yes darling
it was a mistake – in London you owed me £15,
in Vienna £40, remember at 70 schillings to the Pound,
I gave you 2,000 Schillings you gave me 200 Schillings
back; also I gave you cash $14 which is exactly £5,
so all together: £40 + £15 + £5 = £60 exactly,
not £55 or £65. So far I did not get it.
Tell me who has it for me.

Figure 15.6 Letter, 1967.

his Swiss account was distributed according to instructions left with the bank. His favored charities were the Musicians' Benevolent Union and the Odessa Philharmonic, led by American conductor Hobart Earle.

Throughout his life kindness and generosity were a given with service people. His lonely way of life led him to reach out to porters and waiters and maids and desk clerks as he traveled the world. His contact with them and his use of the telephone were important to his psychological survival. He called frequently from the far corners of the globe, talking for as long as an hour, and would end by saying, "Well, I'd better stop now or this call will cost me one whole concert fee." Then he'd laugh and add, "Oh, I don't give a damn," and continue to chat happily away. The telephone was both his toy and his salvation from loneliness, and in his wisdom he used it unsparingly.

He was also generous when there was a clearly demonstrated need, such as when, during his 1987 concert tour of the Soviet Union, he learned that his critic friend desperately needed new pins for his piano. On another occasion, a Russian member of the staff of the White House apartment-hotel received a significant sum of money from Shura to send to needy family members inside Russia.

Shura was not a religious man in terms of observing rituals. Perhaps the pogroms that took place in Odessa in 1905 and 1906 warned his parents away from formal religious practice. During the 1980s a well-meaning acquaintance coaxed him into attending a Passover Seder that Shura later described in his inimitable way as "very nice, but you know, very boring." However, he did believe in God and at times would refer to the Almighty as having given him a very special gift that it was his responsibility to make not only the most of, but to use with better and better results each time he performed. Sometimes with great reverence he would point his fingers toward the sky, indicating that for him, Someone was there. In a letter to me dated November 27–28, 1993, he wrote of his God-given gifts (see fig. 15.7). This intuition, of which he often spoke, figured prominently in Shura's life, both onstage and offstage. It guided him pianistically, just as it steered him in his relationships with people. It was intuition that bound him to Josef Hofmann in his youth, prompted his acceptance of the Hamburg date in 1949 that turned his career around, and led him to trust or turn away from people. When, year after year, I received a birthday card exactly on my special day, I asked Shura how he always managed to make the greeting arrive exactly on time. He responded as can be seen in figure 15.8.

One area in which Shura *was* religious was the absolute reverence and respect he held for his parents in their life and after their death. He fre-

158, The White House,
Regents Park,
London, N.W.1 3UP, England.

November 27/28 (middle of the night),1993

My dear Betty,

My "intuition" tells me I must write to youright now. Suddenly I see things <u>clearly</u>. I do not care what people say about me personally nor even if they know a bit about me personally . All I care for is that they don't say that I am going down in my piano playing! That is precious, God gave me enormous talent, but that is not enough, I must be faithful to God, grateful, and try outmost to do what I can to constantly go up.

Figure 15.7 Letter, November 27–28, 1993.

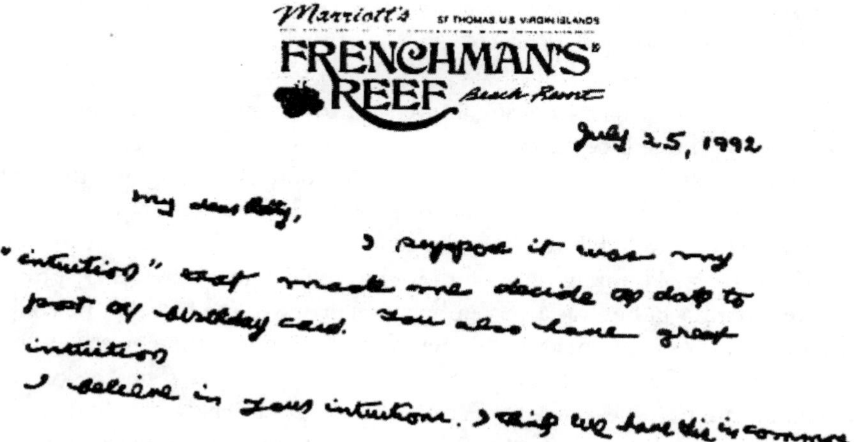

Marriott's ST THOMAS U.S. VIRGIN ISLANDS
FRENCHMAN'S REEF Beach Resort

July 25, 1992

My dear Betty,

I suppose it was my "intuition" that made me decide the date to post a birthday card. You also have great intuition

I believe in your intuitions. I think we have this in common

Figure 15.8 Letter, July 25, 1992.

quently said his parents never exploited him as a child prodigy and that he was absolutely sure of their love. While he didn't particularly enjoy his prodigy days, he was well aware that it was his cherished parents who kept him on the path that led to his world fame. "You know, with so many child prodigies, after a while something happens. They just completely go astray. I'm glad I didn't." Shura's reaction to his prodigy days was different than Ruth Slenczynska's reaction to her days as a wonder child. She knew Shura at the Curtis Institute and also in Paris where she lived just down the avenue from him and his mother at 4 Rue Faraday. She told me she remembered him as the nicest person and as someone whose mother was absolutely driven, always telling him he didn't practice enough, and reprimanding him severely when he went daily to a fair that was taking place in Paris at the time. For her part, Miss Slenczynska said she had always wanted to play like Shura. When asked in what sense, she replied "He always played the way he wanted to. I had to play the way my father told me!"

Shura also often cited their support of his decision not to study with Rachmaninoff, a decision he never regretted:

> I loved Rachmaninoff, but I don't regret the decision not to study with him. Why he wanted to change my technique and study with Rosina Lhevinne has been a puzzle to me all my life. . . . As much as I adored Rachmaninoff—I absolutely worshipped him—I think Hofmann was right in my case. Hofmann himself was a child prodigy. When you're a child and you play for the public, for the rest of your life it becomes second nature.

For his part, Shura had an absolute aversion to listening to so-called child prodigies, with one lone exception. He agreed to hear Daniel Barenboim, as a child, play an early Beethoven sonata. "As soon as he touched the first note, instantly I knew he was a superb player. That was exceptional. Most people play very well, but few can play like that."

While he spoke rarely of his father who died January 26, 1935, Shura allowed that his father was a very unhappy man due to the fact that he could not obtain a license to practice his dental profession and thereby earn a living to provide for his wife and son. After his death Isaak Cherkassky was cremated and his ashes placed at Ferncliff Cemetery in Hartsdale, New York, a village twenty miles north of the city, where many luminaries from music and film are interred, among them Leopold Auer, Béla Bartók, Joan Crawford, Judy Garland, Oscar Hammerstein, Paul Robeson, and Thelonius Monk. Once a year we would drive to Ferncliff where Shura Cherkassky the son would drop on his knees before his father's urn and say a silent prayer.

Following the visit a walk would take place on the cemetery grounds, where on one occasion it was discovered that family members related to the pianist Nadia Reisenberg were buried. Next to Nadia's plaque, another plaque was in place for the time when her sister, Clara Reisenberg Rockmore, the famed thereminist whom Shura knew from his days with Hofmann in Rockport, Maine, would join the group. Since there was only the date of birth on the plaque, it was clear that Clara Rockmore had not yet died. However, there was no convincing Shura that this was the case and he insisted on immediately finding a telephone and making a phone call to reassure himself of the current status. When there was a reply on the other end of the phone, Shura said, "Oh, good, you're not dead. You're sure?"

Just as he visited Ferncliff once a year, so too did he visit Cimetière Caucade at Nice, France, where his beloved and adored mother had been laid to rest in vault no. 7, row 35, section E, following her death April 30, 1961, at the age of eighty-eight. The attachment he held for his mother never diminished throughout his life. He recounted once how he never wanted any brothers or sisters, and that when his mother told him he might be getting a sister he "went into such jealousy" and started crying. Needless to say, he remained an only child, he the focus of her life, and she, and the piano, the focus of his.

Clucking, elderly ladies were a given in Shura's life, often vying desperately with one another for his attention. He handled the inflammatory situations that often arose with delicacy, except when the attention craved by one or another of the ladies would take away from his precious vacations. Henriette Roos, a friend of many years, received the letter shown in figure 15.9 when she suggested *she* should have come before his vacation. Still he could be as compassionate as he was vehement, as is obvious in the message by postcard he sent to Henriette at the time of her beloved cat's death: "I know how upset you are about your cat, but you must understand sixteen years is a lot for a cat. Take heart. Always your friend, Shura."

While he made friendships with women, his sexual preference was for men, a penchant that caused him great conflict. The ambivalence that he felt over his homosexuality is key to understanding Shura Cherkassky's personality. "I want a woman inside a man's body," Shura once told me. This could explain why he was able to make solid, lasting, meaningful relationships with women while he satisfied his physical instincts with men. Yet over the long years of our friendship I often pondered Shura's homosexuality. He was neither proud of it, nor ashamed of it. He neither flaunted it nor hid it. He simply didn't like it, saying over and over again that he had no use for gay men or the gay world (see fig. 15.10).

He often offered the possibility that his proclivity came from his youthful obsession with Horowitz and his desire to be like him in every way. Although he remained sexually active up to the last few months of his life, he repeatedly said that he had never found the kind of satisfying relationship for which he had so desperately searched all his life. Matrimony turned out to

3 AOI-CHO, AKASAKA, MINATO-KU
TOKYO, JAPAN

CABLE ADDRESS: HOTELOKURA TOKYO
TEL: 582-0111

July 22, 1967

My dear Henriette,

I really think you are being most unreasonable. How can you be "hurst" because I don't arrive in Amsterdam on time to see you just as I am in the other part of the world? Do you expect me to cut my trip and see less of the world and skip different places in this world in order to see you in Amsterdam? Don't misunderstand me, of course I'd love to see you and feel sorry that already second time I am missing you in Europe, but you can not be so demanding that I cut my trip (and it's difficult getting here) and you even suggested I skip Acapulco. I do not like at all to mention it here, but it brings back the memories when a few years ago you wanted me not to see my father's urn in Westchester County so I could accomodate seeing you. I really think you should realize yourself how unreasonable, and even how silly you are. Do not be angry with my letter, but surely you are asking too much that I should make my trip around the World shorter in order to see you! Flights from Tokyo to Moscow (new service non-stop) are only once a week, on Thursday. I want to be in Japan until 27th and anyway

15.9 Letter, July 22, 1967.

be a failed solution to his dilemma. His marriage to Mrs. Eugenie Blanc, the widow and concert manager, took place March 21, 1946, in Laguna Beach, California. Shura readily admitted he wasn't the type to compromise, that things for him were black and white with nothing in between, and their marriage was a stormy one by all accounts that ended in an acrimonious divorce

3 AOI-CHO, AKASAKA, MINATO-KU
TOKYO, JAPAN

CABLE ADDRESS: HOTELOKURA TOKYO
TEL: 582-0111

on 20th the plane was completely booked, and my ticket routed that way. anyway I fully explained the circumstances, of course it's a pity I won't see you in Europe again this time. August I was supposed to have been in Greece, resting, but with the new government there I am better off in Spain! I don't remember the name Jaap Duits from Paris. I'll ring Mrs. Muller anyway, ask Mr. Duits to get in touch with Mrs. Muller. If you do not wish to get in touch with Dolfje Hirnon, I can understand the reason.

So write to me. I have only friendly feelings towards you and always wish you the best of everything in life. I hope you understand and believe me.

Best wishes and with love,

Shura.

40, The White House, Regents Park, London, N.W.1, England.

158, The White House,
Regents Park,
London, N.W.1 3UP, England.
March 2, 1993

My dear Betty,

I never since my young days was popular with those people, they always made me feel they don'r acceptme, and always I have a depressing mood afterwards. Individuals yes, but the massaes are to me are like poison.

Figure 15.10 Letter, March 2, 1993.

two years later. Physical abuse was cited by Genia Cherkassky as grounds for the suit. In her pleading for alimony she argued that $27,000 of her money had been used to support Shura and his mother while he pursued his career. In 1948, $27,000 was the equivalent of over $200,000 in 2005. The husband responded he could not provide financial support as he had no net income from his concert fees of $700–$750 (approximately $6,000 in 2005 dollars), due to expenses. Judge Thurmond Clarke granted alimony amounting to 10 percent of Shura Cherkassky's net income for two years, which Genia deemed "not enough. I am destitute."[3]

All Shura would say of Genia was that "She was insanely jealous of mother," and once in Paris when she had torn up a letter he had written to the mother he held so dear there was a furious row, following which he locked his not-so-dear wife in the closet of the hotel room where they were staying. "My wife was very bossy, because she thought she knew all the answers. Mother wasn't bossy though she was unhappy because at that time [1946] I didn't practice as seriously as I do now."[4] The close relationship he had with his mother remained until the end of her days, and he once told a friend, whose mother was very ill, that "your first duty is to your darling mother. Be as good as you possibly can to her, spoil her, no matter what the others say. You know we don't have our mothers too long. Spare nothing but do everything for her even sacrificing your own self. You will *not* regret this later." When asked why he married in the first place he simply shrugged and said in that wonderful voice with its Russian, American, British, and French inflection, "Oh, everybody was doing it." But there is also the possibility that financial opportunism entered the equation. Family life never had any interest for Shura, and in 1994 he told a reporter for the *Straits Times* in Australia that he didn't have much in common with his remaining relatives in America. "They are very nice people. Much nicer than me maybe, but they have their own house and children and those things don't interest me."[5] Among the artists managed by Genia Cherkassky, whose New York office was located at 117 West Fifty-eighth Street, were the baritone Alfred Zega and the pianist Herbert Stessin who remembered her as "a very nice person." Those who knew Genia, among them Gretchen Clumpner who worked for the Little Orchestra Society at the same time Genia was employed there, agreed with Stessin's appraisal. Clumpner added that Lithuanian-born Genia Ganz, who "had the face of ballet great Ulanova," had told her she applied to and was accepted in 1937 to the Stanislawski Theater School in Moscow, but decided to come instead to America. Her first husband died and she subsequently married Shura Cherkassky. Once during the early 1980s, as Shura was walking across Fifty-seventh Street in New York, a woman approached him and greeted him. When there was no sign of recognition, the woman said, "I'm Genia. Don't you remember me?" He didn't. Still, when she died in 1986 he told me, "Although our marriage was not successful I was sad to hear of her death."

What Shura never seemed to understand was that from earliest childhood he had simultaneously had a mistress and a lover that was neither male nor female: the piano. And it was with the piano that he was inextricably joined, psychologically and spiritually. Everything that defined the greatest love affairs revealed itself in his playing: constancy, fidelity, affection, warmth, love, passion. He caressed and he teased; he whispered as softly as he roared; and ultimately from the piano he drew the greatest of sonic orgasms. Could this be the reason why playing the piano was the greatest satisfaction in Shura Cherkassky's life, a satisfaction no person, male or female, could ever replace or surpass?

Liaisons were made over the years but none endured. This can be attributed first to his focus on the piano and his worldwide itineraries, which precluded any semblance of a normal home life, and in an equal degree to his willful personality and insistence on doing things his way (see fig. 15.11). This letter is reminiscent of one written by Josef Hofmann to his wife on the occasion of an "ill-bred indiscretion":

> There is no doubt that I am different from other people, but how else could this be? First, I was born a different animal from others; second, I was brought up differently from others; and third, I've lived a different life from others. Why wonder then and accuse me of certain lacks, when I have so many other qualities, which

158, The White H ouse,
Regents Park,
London, N.W.1 3UP, England.
April 28, 1993

My dear Betty,

Just a few lines before I leave on Friday! It was nice to speak to you on the phone last night. I told you plenty. This morning telephoned me and said he was upset, couldn't sleep because of thinking, so I said I would phone him back later. I might see him, or anyway, will write him from Bangkok, I will explain that we have different lives, and there is no reason to break relationship, but he must have a full understanding of my life, and to know that artists are somewhat different. I'll let yyou know more later.

Figure 15.11 Letter, April 28, 1993.

> average people do not possess? One cannot be perfect in every respect. One quality usually develops at the expense of another.[6]

Unfortunately, Shura never saw how his determination to have things his way set up insurmountable obstacles to the long-term relationship he so desperately wanted: "In the long run I'm the easiest person of all because I never change my mind about what I want. With me everything is yes or no, black or white." Upsets over failed encounters were not uncommon. He often felt he had been set up just to be rejected, with several particularly unfortunate incidents of this ilk occurring in Chicago and New York in the 1980s and 1990s in which no one, not Shura, not the intended companion, nor the facilitator of the liaison came out well. Everyone lost, from start to finish. Still he could not walk away from the outcome and would telephone me repeatedly to ask why, why, such a thing had happened. He felt utterly betrayed, and no words could console him or convince him to stop gnawing over something that was finished (see fig. 15.12).

Finally, in 1993, there appeared to be a change in his reactions to these difficult and unwinnable situations when he appeared to adopt the attitude he expressed to a business manager in South Africa in 1965: "Music is my friend, my *only* friend and I shall *not* allow anything personal to spoil my music—music is a faithful friend." These sentiments were echoed in a letter he sent me (fig. 15.13), written on March 7, 1994.

> My dearest Betty,
>
> You are the only one who really understands me well and I know you would do anything for me if you were able. There is of course a tremendous amount of things to say, I wouldn't even know where to start or when to finish. All in all is well—people everywhere say I am playing better than ever. That is because I live differently and do not waste time with people who mean nothing to me. I try not to think of negative things. My music is everything for me.

In the 1980s a workable friendship, based in part on companionship and mutual understanding, was established with a young German educator. This friendship endured. The two vacationed together once or twice a year traveling to hot, scenic locations such as the Ivory Coast and the Seychelles.

Then a young South American entered Shura's life in 1993 through the prompting of a friend. Meetings ensued in Mexico, Paris, and the south of France, none of which brought the hoped-for happiness. In July of 1995 Shura broke off the relationship, vowing to seek no more.

There would be no need. He died five months later.

158, The White House,
Regents Park,
London, N.W.1 3UP, England.
November 27/28 (middle of the night),1993

My dear Betty,

I want nothing to do with them. I lost (I wonder if rather I "gained") one night of unpleasantness but I am sure they all lost much, much more. Had things turned out well I would have gone out of my wayeven to take a trip inviting to Bangkok for a few days, I love being crazy that way. Have I written enough? I am sure you must find this a compliment that I write to you like this. You are the only one. Of course I have nice friends, even good friends, but they would not quite, quite understand to detail, or perhaps would not wish to know or bother or take seriously my feelings. I admire Mrs. Horowitz, perhaps she is rude, not nice, etc., but she is sincere, I undersand well what she meantwhen she said she would leave money to dogs and cats. Probably noone triend to make her happy, they treated her like the wife of Horowitz, and daughter of Toscanini.

My deepest friendship and love,
Shura

Figure 15.12 November 27–28, 1993.

158, The White House
Regents Park,
London, NW1 3UP, England.
March 7, 1994

My dearest Betty,

You are the only one really who understands me well and I know you would do anything for me if you were able.

There is of course a tremendous amount of things to say, I wouldn't even know where to start or when to finish. All in all is well - people everywhere say I am playing better than ever. That is because I live differently, do not waste time with people who mean nothing to me, try not to think of negative thngs, etc., etc.

Figure 15.13 Letter, March 7, 1994.

Notes

1. *Los Angeles Star News*, 18 November 1987.
2. *Classical Piano*, July 1993.
3. *Los Angeles Star News*, 5 January 1948.
4. *Guardian* (London), 10 October 1981.
5. *Straits Times* (Singapore), 8 February 1994.
6. Nell S. Graydon and Margaret D. Sizemore, *The Amazing Marriage of Marie Eustis and Josef Hofmann* (Columbia: University of South Carolina Press, 1965), 183.

CHAPTER SIXTEEN

Prague, 1995

My trip to Prague in November of 1995 began along the sun-drenched Adriatic coast the previous August. Shura sent one of his wonderfully enthusiastic faxes from the Tel Aviv Hilton where he was vacationing to the Hotel des Bains in Venice where I was vacationing. Would I like to join him in Prague for his concert tour there in the fall? He'd be playing a recital, giving two performances of the Rachmaninoff Third Concerto, along with two rehearsals of the piece, one of them open, all in the space of four days. Of course I would love to be there, I faxed back, and another encounter in this treasured friendship, sadly the last one, was set in motion.

The weeks preceding the Prague trip were a bit of a roller coaster, with Shura in and out of a London hospital for 24-hour stays while doctors aspirated fluid from around his heart. Still he went on tour as scheduled, canceling only a few performances during the autumn months, something that it greatly disturbed him to do. Calls came from Paris and Munich after his concerts there in October in which he said his chest felt very tight and that, on some plane flights, he needed oxygen. Following the Paris recital he telephoned to say how upset he was at having been pushed to attend an après-concert party when he was so tired. "Why can't people understand?" he kept asking. The simple fact was that in the last months of his life many people gave short shrift to the signals of ill health he started sending out in June of 1995. The assumption was that he was simply tired after a long season and that the disturbing symptoms would disappear with rest. Few seemed to notice that a man who had enjoyed extraordinary health all his life was now describing the alarming symptoms of major heart disease. But when people suggested he seek a second opinion, Shura said he had been told in London there was no need for that, as he already had the best doctors. Indeed he had a fine Harley Street physician. In a fax from Tel Aviv on August 13, 1995, he wrote he had talked once again with his doctor:

> I spoke to him. He assures me there is absolutely nothing wrong. It's a reaction from heavy season, which takes some time to "unwind." He also says a bit of it is mental dissatisfaction on my part missing intimate personal life. But this is price one pays for a successful career.

As the weeks went by it became increasingly frustrating for me trying to deal by telephone with Shura's growing concern. Clearly he understood things were not right at all with the body he knew so well and which friends considered a near perfect machine.

While his life forces diminished he was asked why he did not play fewer concerts and save his strength for important dates in larger halls. "No, no, I couldn't do that. You know my management loses money if I don't play." To which many naturally replied, "So what? Shouldn't your health be the overriding consideration here?" It should have been, but for him it wasn't. His persistence in these last weeks of his life gave a whole new meaning to the cliché "The show must go on." In spite of his increasing medical difficulties, he spoke continuously of plans for the future, and described in detail what new inspiration had come to him on stage as he played this or that phrase. He particularly dwelled on the Chopin B-flat Minor Sonata, repeatedly calling attention to how he played the relentless beat of the funeral march each time it was programmed.

The weekend before the Prague tour was to begin Shura entered a London hospital to have fluid drained from around his heart, following which he called to say all had gone well and the trip to Prague was on. Twelve hours later he telephoned to say the most recent x-rays showed the fluid was back and so the trip was off. With the passing of another twelve hours, the telephone squealed with Shura on the other end saying his chest had cleared and the trip was on. "No more calls! I'll see you in Prague."

When my plane landed in Prague, the city offered a muted welcome, shrouded as it was in damp drizzle and fog. Proceeding directly to Shura's hotel, I found him his usual warm, effusive self, but what a shock it was to see him so physically depleted from the enormous amount of weight he had lost over the previous three months. Indeed, when he dressed for his concert that evening a hotel maid spent a good deal of time searching for large safety pins which we then used to attach his shirt to his now baggy trousers for the purpose of holding them up. Still the focus when we met was on my life and not on his very obvious difficulties.

That night his recital included works of Bach, Beethoven, Chopin, Tchaikovsky, and Liszt performed in Dvorak Hall at the Rudolfinum, home of the Czech Philharmonic. Among the finest creations of nineteenth-century Czech architecture, Dvorak Hall was a resplendent setting for what would be the last performances of Shura Cherkassky's life. Backstage before the concert, he went through the usual routine of the mandatory two programs, grapes and hot tea, *very* hot tea. He practiced slowly and softly, his usual way, until it was nearly time to go on stage, when he closed his eyes, counted backwards until he was ready, and then lifted himself with great difficulty from his chair. We then started toward the elevator that would take him to the stage. The backstage reality was that this man could hardly breathe, could barely walk, and he hugged the wall on one side for support while I held him on the other. Yet when he sat down at the piano to play there wasn't a hint that anything was awry. And in spite of his physical condition, he performed with everything known to be the essence of Shura Cherkassky's playing: phenomenal virtuosity, the teasing of a phrase that brought smiles from the audience, the ability to summon any sound he wanted from the piano, and the simple haunting beauty that tugged at the heart. At the end, not unexpectedly, there was the usual torrent of bravos and applause.

Following the performance we returned to his suite at the Intercontinental Hotel for a late supper, something he particularly liked to do after a concert. "Gemütlich—cozy," he called it. And then, tired as he was, a mischievous twinkle came into his eyes, and brilliant raconteur that he was, this very sick octogenarian launched into some of his favorite stories in his inimitable way until we were both laughing and Shura said, "Oh my God, if people could see us now they would think we were mad as two hatters!" Perhaps because he was to perform Rachmaninoff's Third Concerto on this Prague tour, he recounted the following with particular relish:

> Rachmaninoff used to play for all these rich millionaire women, and they liked to show him off at parties. One woman called him to ask if he could play the piano after dinner on a certain evening. She asked what his fee was and he said five thousand dollars—a fortune in those days! She said that was just fine, "but you cannot mingle with the guests."
>
> "In that case, Madame," Rachmaninoff said, "my fee will be only be three thousand dollars."
>
> Isn't that a wonderful story? Shura laughingly asked.

The next morning he practiced the Rachmaninoff concerto and rehearsed it with orchestra that afternoon, an easy run-through for him, much less so for the Czech Philharmonic. After bringing him back to his hotel I decided to take a walk around Prague, and while passing a church with its steeple bell chiming a quarter to five in the afternoon, I slipped and fell on one of Prague's famed cobblestone streets. There was a searing pain in my right ankle, and as I sat crumpled on the ground a very kind Czech woman found a taxi to take me back to my hotel where bellmen put me in a wheelchair and took me to my room. Ice was ordered for my badly swollen ankle, which was assumed to be an inconvenient sprain. Then while I was wondering how to get back to Shura on time the telephone rang, and I was told as gently as possible that my mother had died unexpectedly at a quarter before noon Eastern Standard Time, the exact moment of my fall. As her only next of kin I spent the next hour making appropriate arrangements for her as well as for my return home.

Shura was obviously dying. My mother had died. And, as I was about to learn, my ankle was not sprained, but broken. It was all more than a bit of a mess but there was nothing to do but carry on and make no mention of anything to Shura other than to say an old injury had acted up. And carry on both of us did with the help of Dana Drtinova, the representative from the Czech Philharmonic who was in charge of Shura's concert appearances in Prague. She proved to be exceptional in every way in spite of the burdens placed on her young shoulders. From an artist whose needs would best be met in a hospital rather than backstage on a concert tour, to an accompanying friend who needed an orthopedist and someone in whom to confide her grief, Dana rose to the occasion mightily. She even suggested canceling Shura's remaining concerto performances after realizing how very sick he was. Another hero of this Prague trip was Mr. Homulka, a chauffeur with the Czech Philharmonic who, when not driving us about, alternately held Shura's arm and pushed my wheelchair. Right before my departure from Prague Mr. Homulka presented me with, from the Czech Philharmonic's library, a copy of a score of Beethoven's *Coriolan Overture* with the markings of Gustav Mahler. Goodness radiated from these two people.

On the morning of November 9 an open rehearsal of the Rachmaninoff concerto took place to a house packed with conservatory students and faculty. During the performance Shura took off his coat and dropped it in front of the piano. When he was finished playing a young child ran to the front of the stage and lifted the coat to give it to him, and he in turn bent down and warmly shook her little hand, gaining yet another ovation from the audience.

Too tired to go back to the hotel, he stayed at the Rudolfinum practicing until late afternoon. Although clearly exhausted he refused to give in for even a second to the thought of not going on, and unlikely as it might seem, his performance that night was a triumph, with orchestra and audience alike erupting in frenzied approval. Eighty-six-year-old Shura went back to his hotel a very sick but happy man, already musing over what he might do differently at the performance the next evening.

The following morning he took an obvious turn for the worse, which prompted an urgent telephone call to his doctor on Harley Street in London. After explaining his breathing was labored and he had trouble staying awake, the London doctor increased one of his medications, decreased another, and said to give him lots of coffee. No words could persuade Shura to stay in his room and rest, and with tremendous effort he went to the hall to rehearse. When I begged him to return to the hotel and not practice anymore he said, "Oh, no, no, morally I could never do that. *Never!*" Right before going on stage that evening Shura turned to me and said, "I love this concerto," and then with absolute glee he added, "There are notes and notes and more notes." Shura Cherkassky's final performance of his life given that night in Prague should be ranked as one of the personal and pianistic triumphs of all time. Has anyone else ever performed Rachmaninoff's Third Concerto, with its stupendous difficulties, at age eighty-six or even seventy-six? When he walked offstage he came to me and said, "You know, Betty, I *am* a miracle," and in that moment I realized that Shura Cherkassky knew he was dying.

On November 11 he returned to London and we spoke frequently by phone during the next days. While his breathing was labored and the coughing even heavier than in Prague, he still worked at his beloved piano, practicing the Liszt B-minor Sonata, and planning future programs. He also spoke repeatedly of $300,000 in cash that he kept at the White House flat, saying over and over again, "Remember that it's there." No amount of talking could convince him to place the money in a proper bank. At the end of the week he entered Royal Brompton Hospital for what was supposed to be a thirty-six-hour stay. Instead, he never returned to his flat at the White House. He suffered greatly over the next six weeks going in and out of crisis situations. Daily calls to London produced updates from very kind nurses at the hospital or from the stream of friends who visited him. Indeed, one of the nurses allowed that "There is a positive queue waiting to see him."

On Christmas day we spoke and Shura asked "When . . . can . . . you . . . come?" I told him I would be well enough to limp around by the first week of January and that I was booked on a British Airways flight for the seventh.

"Good," he said. But on December 27 the phone rang and I learned that the dearest of my friends had slipped peacefully away that morning. On January 7 I was ticketed to fly to London for Shura's funeral the following day at St. George's Church in Hanover Square. Instead, I was one of thousands of passengers stranded at Boston's Logan airport, closed by the great blizzard of 1996, which paralyzed America's northeast corridor. Perhaps it is just as well for my last memory of Shura Cherkassky will always be of a valiant and courageous man who, sick as he was, gave his all to his audience in one last great roar of sumptuous piano playing. No written epitaph could speak more eloquently of Shura Cherkassky than his own performances in Prague in November of 1995.

CHAPTER SEVENTEEN

Final Tributes

On April 12, 1996, friends and relatives and admirers of Shura Cherkassky gathered from many points in the United States and Europe to listen as Harold Shaw, his American manager, Judith Arron, executive director of Carnegie Hall, Elizabeth Carr, friend and confidante, and Charles Cumula, his personal representative in America, spoke of the legend and the legacy of Shura Cherkassky, man and artist. Prior to this American tribute the scheduled funeral service had been held on January 8 in London followed by burial at Highgate Cemetery in North London. In lieu of flowers, donations were to be sent to the Musicians' Benevolent Union and the American Friends of the Odessa Philharmonic.

During February of 1996 Shura Cherkassky had been scheduled for a month-long tour of Japan, a country where he had played in 1935, 1971, 1976, 1981, 1983, and 1988, with the latter appearance greeted with such success that it precipitated an invitation for annual tours there. Instead of the planned recital for February 12, 1996, Cherkassky's manager in Japan, Masa Kajimoto, arranged a moving and impressive memorial service, which took place in Tokyo's 2,600-seat Suntory Hall. A program booklet, which was created for the occasion, was given to each member of the capacity audience. At stage left, a piano and bench were placed and set atop the Steinway was the bouquet of flowers that would have been presented to the artist at curtain call.

Above the stage a 300″ screen was mounted, onto which Shura Cherkassky's 1990 Suntory Hall performance was projected via high-definition TV, one of the first pieces of film to use this technology. As soon as the lights went down the video began, continuing without interruption for ninety minutes. The visual clarity and the amplification of sound through two precision speakers created a mood so real that some members of the audience commented that they felt the artist they had so dearly revered was actually there with them. Following the showing of the video the audience moved to the lobby outside the auditorium where photos tracing Shura Cherkassky's life and career had been mounted. The simple atmosphere allowed people to reflect on their feelings as they stood in front of the photos for up to thirty minutes. Many in attendance expressed their thanks for this opportunity to "meet" Maestro Cherkassky, while others said it gave them a much-needed opportunity to say goodbye.

Most fittingly, America's final tribute to Shura Cherkassky took place at New York's Carnegie Hall in beautifully refurbished Weill Hall. A reception at Steinway Hall on West Fifty-seventh Street followed. Harold Shaw, who made the arrangements, spoke first, telling the story of Shura Cherkassky's life and career and documenting the chronology with a series of compelling and evocative photos. At the conclusion of the memorial a 1993 video was played, introduced by Charles Cumula, of Shura performing the last movement of the Tchaikovsky G-major Concerto with the NHK Symphony under the direction of Evgeny Svetlanov. Before the showing of the video, Harold Shaw introduced Judith Arron who spoke of Shura Cherkassky's relationship with Carnegie Hall and also shared some of her own fond memories of the man.

> Shura Cherkassky performed his first recital at Carnegie Hall on December 7, 1927, and we were holding the date of December 7, 1997 for him to perform his 70th anniversary concert on our Main Hall Stage. Sadly his last concert at Carnegie Hall was February 13, 1995. During his sixty-eight years of performances at Carnegie Hall, he performed twenty-one times in spite of taking two hiatuses of many years. Those performances included concerts with the New York Philharmonic as well as his solo recitals.
>
> I will never forget the day in December, slightly more than ten years ago, when I went to the Cincinnati Airport for an early morning flight to New York. There were six other passengers on the plane that Sunday morning, and one of them was Shura, he had just performed a concert with the Cincinnati Symphony the night before. He was anxious to sit next to me, and all the way to NY, kept asking, "My dear, tell me why you are going to New York," and I kept answering, "Shura, I often go to New York on Cincinnati Symphony business." When we arrived in New York, he asked if I would ride with him to the Pierre and then his driver would take me on to my hotel. That afternoon it was announced that I would be moving to New York to become General Manager and eventually Executive Director of Carnegie Hall. A few weeks later I received a wonderful letter from Shura remind-

ing me of all of the concerts he had played while I was in Cincinnati and then reminding me that he had delivered me to Carnegie Hall. Over the last ten years Shura Cherkassky has been a regular performer at Carnegie Hall, and on every occasion he reminded me that he brought me to Carnegie Hall. "Yes, Shura, you did bring me to Carnegie Hall and I did bring you to Carnegie Hall . . . and I will miss you.

I then recounted the last months of Shura's life as I knew them, told of the Prague trip, and concluded with the following remarks:

Shura Cherkassky sparkled. On stage, backstage, offstage. There is no other word to describe the infectious effervescence he radiated to his audience and his friends. Never have I seen greater commitment on the part of anyone to his art. It would not be trite to say that Shura had a lifelong love affair with the piano, which became the total reason for his being, the destiny from which he had no desire to escape, the karma that would determine his next life.

Shura was a man of great qualities—integrity, balance, common sense, courage, and perhaps, above all, simplicity. He was a person endowed with a keen mind and extraordinary imagination, someone who had a passionate and unending love for music. To those to whom Shura extended a hand in friendship, he was unwavering in his loyalty. A warmer or bigger heart I have never known. Through his enormous talent he built a better world for all of us who love the arts, casting new lights and shadows and brightening and bettering that which we thought we knew, until he showed us we really didn't.

He was also great fun, with a delicious sense of humor. A brilliant raconteur, those who knew him intimately would be regaled with one hilarious tale after another until the wee hours of the morning. He had a fierce aversion to sentimentality and I can see that mischievous twinkle in his eye as he merrily recounted one of his favorite stories: "Shortly after Bellini's death, his nephew, a would be composer, decided to write a work in Bellini's memory. He sent the work to Rossini to get the reaction of the great Maestro who finally responded, saying, 'It would have been *much* better if *you* had died and *he* had written the memorial!'"

Our beloved friend recognized that it is not only the horizon, which is fascinating but the expectation of finding a world beyond it, a world discovered through vision and unending hard work, great expectations and even greater generosity of spirit. He understood more clearly than anyone I have ever known that while it is the absence of darkness that helps us to see, we have to know what it is we want to recognize if we are to bring others with us on a wonderful voyage of discovery in which we find hope, joy and refreshment. These were the three priceless commodities Shura Cherkassky offered his audiences through his playing. Hope, because he stressed that which springs from men's souls; joy, because he allowed the spirit of man to transcend the machinations of men; refreshment, because through his playing he brought us respite from care and anxiety and allowed us to lose ourselves in something greater than ourselves, in emotions that caused us to transcend ourselves and feel liberated and sustained. Who among us here today can ever forget how this deeply feeling gentleman touched us in our innermost core with his precious talent?

Shura Cherkassky played a remarkable role in my life bringing me hope and joy and refreshment. It is the memories of Shura which cause me, and should cause all of us here today to celebrate, to feel joyous, to be uplifted. He was for life and for living it to the fullest. At least once in his lifetime, William Shakespeare found himself as hard put as I am now, to find the words to respond to Shura's life. Shakespeare wrote, "I can no other answer make but thanks, and thanks and *ever* thanks." Sentiments, to be sure, shared by each of us here today.

The phone calls from around the globe have stopped, as have the faxes and letters and postcards. So too the dazzling concerts and the fun meetings between two friends who became soul mates. Still, inside of me, Shura Cherkassky lives on, *for memories make a paradise from which one can never be evicted.*

Our much beloved friend now rests, in peace, at Highgate Cemetery in North London.

Shura Cherkassky: A Discography

Compiled by Donald Minaldi

The following introductory section, Cherkassky's Recorded Legacy, was compiled by Donald Manildi (Curator, International Piano Archives, University of Maryland).

Shura Cherkassky was barely fourteen years old when he made his first recordings at the Camden, New Jersey, studios of the Victor Talking Machine Company on October 31, 1923. His final recording session took place almost seventy-two years later in London on May 17, 1995. All available information indicates that Cherkassky can thus claim the longest recorded career of any pianist.

The listing that follows encompasses all of Cherkassky's commercially issued audio recordings as of January 2005. Reproducing piano rolls are not included. A significant quantity of additional material exists, taken mainly from broadcasts and in-house tapings of his concerts. It is hoped that more of this material will be released, not only to further document the spontaneous quality of his playing before an audience, but also to make available the repertoire that Cherkassky did not record commercially.

Space limitations prevent the inclusion of all formats and issue numbers for these recordings. Therefore I have only provided the catalog number(s) under which each item was most recently, or most widely, available. All recordings may be assumed to be digital compact discs unless the designation [LP] or [45 rpm] appears. These refer to analog vinyl discs playing at 33.3 or 45 revolutions per minute, respectively. The symbol # before the date of recording identifies a public performance.

There is one Cherkassky recording that appears to have been announced but never released; no copy has been traced, and it is mentioned here for the sake of completeness. I refer to a Vox 78-rpm set (624) from the late 1940s, ostensibly containing Prokofiev's Sonata No. 3 and Toccata.

For their assistance in providing necessary information, I wish to thank Ruth Edge and Greg Burge of EMI, Jon M. Samuels, Michael Gray, Tim S. Cole, and Farhan Malik.

Albéniz, Isaac

Tango in D, Op. 165, No. 2 (trans. Godowsky)

(5/1974)	L'Oiseau-Lyre DSLO 7 [LP]
#(12/9/1974)	Desmar DSM 1005 [LP]
#(3/23/1975)	Decca 433 653
#(9/27/1985)	Decca 433 651

Bach, Johann Sebastian

Partita No. 6 in E Minor, S. 830

#(8/3/1968)	Orfeo 431 962

Chaconne (Violin Partita No. 2 in D Minor, S. 1004, trans. Busoni)

(3/23/1956)	HMV ALP 1574 [LP]
(3–4/1984)	Nimbus 5021
#(12/2/1991)	Decca 433 654

Toccata, Adagio and Fugue in C, S. 564 (trans. Busoni)

#(2/3/1985)	Decca 433 655

Fantasy and Fugue in G Minor, S. 542 (trans. Liszt)

#(11/22/1979)	Decca 433 656

Balakirev, Mili

Islamey

(1968)	ASV 6096
#(2/20/1982)	Decca 433 651
(2/1982)	Nimbus 45016 [45 rpm]

Tarantella in B
(2/1982) Nimbus 45016 [45 rpm]

Bartók, Béla

Sonata
(1968) ASV ALH 965 [LP]

Beethoven, Ludwig van

Bagatelle in G Minor, Op. 119, No. 1
(3/21/1956) HMV ALP 1527 [LP]

Ecossaises (trans. Busoni)
(10/31/1923) Biddulph LHW 34
(5/2/1928) Biddulph LHW 34

Sonata No. 13 in E-flat, Op. 27, No. 1
(3–4/1984) Nimbus 5021

Sonata No. 32 in C Minor, Op. 111
(c. 1963) World Record Club T271 [LP]; Imperial 534 [LP]

Variations and Fugue in E-flat, Op. 35 (*Prometheus* or *Eroica*)
(c. 1963) World Record Club T271 [LP]; Imperial 534 [LP]

Bennett, Richard Rodney

Five Etudes
(1968) ASV ALH 965 [LP]
#(8/3/1968) Orfeo 431 962

Berg, Alban

Sonata, Op. 1
#(12/5/1963) Ermitage 133; Aura 143

#(9/1/1983)	Decca 433 657
(3–4/1984)	Nimbus 5021

Bernstein, Leonard

Touches

(4/30/1987)	Nimbus 5091

Brahms, Johannes

Intermezzo in B-flat Minor, Op. 117, No. 2

(3/24/58)	HMV 7ER5113 [45 rpm]

Sonata No. 3 in F Minor, Op. 5

(c. 1949)	Ivory Classics 72003
#(8/3/1968)	Orfeo 431 962
#(11/7/1968)	ASV ALH 948 [LP]

Variations on a Theme of Paganini, Op. 35

#(9/1/1983)	Decca 433 655 (Book II only)
(3–4/1984)	Nimbus 5020

Britten, Benjamin

Holiday Diary, Op. 5

#(5/7/1973)	Decca 433 657

Chaminade, Cécile

Autrefois, Op. 87, No. 4

(6/1/1950)	Ivory Classics 72003
(5/1974)	Decca 448 063

Chasins, Abram

Three Chinese Pieces

(3/22/1956)	HMV ALP 1527 [LP]
(3–4/1984)	Nimbus 5020 (No. 3 only)

Cherkassky, Shura

Prélude Pathétique

(3/20/1924) Biddulph LHW 034
(8/2/1928) Biddulph LHW 034
#(2/20/1982) BBC Legends 4160
#(3/6/1982) Decca 433 651

Chopin, Frédéric

Andante Spianato and Grand Polonaise, Op. 22

(6–10/1985) Nimbus 5044

Ballade No. 1 in G Minor, Op. 23

(10/1976) Tudor 720
(2/1981) Nimbus 45021 [45 rpm]

Ballade No. 2 in F, Op. 38

(3/22/1956) HMV ALP 1489 [LP]
(10/1976) Tudor 720

Ballade No. 3 in A-flat, Op. 47

(1/28/1958) HMV 7ER5120 [45 rpm]
#(3/23/1975) Decca 433 653
#(5/9/1987) BBC Legends 4057

Ballade No. 4 in F Minor, Op. 52

(2/1982) Nimbus 45021 [45 rpm]
#(5/9/1987) BBC Legends 4057

Barcarolle in F-sharp, Op. 60

(c. 1963) Philips 456 742
(10/1976) Tudor 720

Concerto No. 2 in F Minor, Op. 21

(4/18–20/1966) Menuet 160 013 (Kempe/Royal Philharmonic)

Etudes, Op. 10

(3/1953–4/1955) Philips 456 742 (Nos. 1–12)

#(9/28/1970)	BBC Legends 4057 (No. 3)
(6/1/1950)	Ivory Classics 72003 (No. 4)
#(3/23/1975)	Decca 433 653 (No. 4)
(c. 1969)	ASV 6109 (No. 12)

Etudes, Op. 25

(3/1953–4/1955)	Philips 456 742 (Nos. 1–12)
#(3/23/1975)	Decca 433 653 (Nos. 7 and 10)

Etudes, Trois Nouvelles

(11/19/1954)	Philips 456 742

Fantasy in F Minor, Op. 49

(6/1/1950)	Philips 456 742; Ivory Classics 72003
(4/29/1966)	Menuet 160 013
#(5/7/1973)	Decca 433 650
(10/1976)	Tudor 720

Fantasy-Impromptu in C-sharp Minor, Op. 66

(8/2/1956)	Ivory Classics 72003

Impromptu No. 2 in F-sharp, Op. 36

(8/2/1956)	Ivory Classics 72003

Mazurka in F Minor, Op. 7, No. 3

(3/21/1956)	HMV ALP 1489 [LP]

Mazurka in D, Op. 33, No. 2

(6/1/1950)	Philips 456 742; Ivory Classics 72003

Mazurka in B Minor, Op. 33, No. 4

(6–10/1985)	Nimbus 5044

Mazurka in F-sharp Minor, Op. 59, No. 3

(2/1981)	Nimbus 45021 [45 rpm]

Mazurka in C-sharp Minor, Op. 63, No. 3

(6–10/1985)	Nimbus 5044

Mazurka in C, Op. 68, No. 1
(8/2/1956) Ivory Classics 72003

Nocturne in E-flat, Op. 9, No. 2
#(5/29/1980) BBC Legends 4057

Nocturne in B, Op. 9, No. 3
(2/1981) Nimbus 45021 [45 rpm]

Nocturne in D-flat, Op. 27, No. 2
(3/22/1956) HMV ALP 1489 [LP]
#(9/1/1983) BBC Legends 4057
(6–10/1985) Nimbus 5044

Nocturne in C Minor, Op. 48, No. 1
#(1/31/1988) BBC Legends 4057

Nocturne in F Minor, Op. 55, No. 1
(c. 1963) Philips 456 742
#(5/4/1975) Decca 433 653
(2/1981) Nimbus 45021 [45 rpm]
#(5/9/1987) BBC Legends 4057
#(12/2/1991) Decca 433 654

Nocturne in E, Op. 62, No. 2
(6–10/1985) Nimbus 5044

Nocturne in E Minor, Op. 72, No. 1
(5/31/1950) RCA Victor LBC 1066 [LP]
#(9/1/1983) BBC Legends 4057
(6–10/1985) Nimbus 5044

Polonaises, Op. 26, Nos. 1 and 2; Op. 40, Nos. 1 and 2; Op. 44
(1969) DG 445 433; DG 429 516

Polonaise in A-flat, Op. 53
(1949) Pearl GEM 0138; Ivory Classics 72003
(1/29/1958) HMV 7ER5120

(1968)	ASV 6109
(1969)	DG 445 433; DG 429 516

Polonaise-Fantasy in A-flat, Op. 61

(1969)	DG 445 433; DG 429 516
#(4/18/1982)	Ivory Classics 70904

Preludes, Op. 28

(1968)	ASV 6109; Philips 456 742 (Nos. 1–24)
#(8/3/1968)	Orfeo 431 962 (Nos. 1–24)
#(5/4/1975)	Decca 433 653 (Nos. 4, 6, 7, 10, 13, 17, 20, 23)
(10/1976)	Tudor 720 (No. 15)

Scherzo No. 1 in B Minor, Op. 20

(10/1976)	Tudor 720
(5–6/1985)	Nimbus 5043

Scherzo No. 2 in B-flat Minor, Op. 31

(10/1976)	Tudor 720
(2/1981)	Nimbus 45021 [45 rpm]
#(1/31/1988)	BBC Legends 4057

Scherzo No. 3 in C-sharp Minor, Op. 39

(c. 1963)	World Record Club T247 [LP]
(10/1976)	Tudor 720

Scherzo No. 4 in E, Op. 54

(1968)	ASV 6109
(10/1976)	Tudor 720
#(10/7/1991)	BBC Legends 4057

Sonata No. 2 in B-flat Minor, Op. 35

#(3/6/1982)	Decca 433 650

Sonata No. 3 in B Minor, Op. 58

#(2/3/1985)	Decca 433 650; Philips 456 742
(6–10/1985)	Nimbus 5044

Tarantelle in A-flat, Op. 43

#(12/2/1991)	Decca 433 654

Variations on Mozart's *Là ci darem la mano*, Op. 2
(8/10/1955) HMV ALP 1489 [LP]
(2/11/1987) Nimbus 5091

Waltz in E, Op. Posth.
(c. 1963) World Record Club T247 [LP]

Waltz in E Minor, Op. Posth.
(8/25/1925) Biddulph LHW 034
#(11/22/1979) Decca 433 651

Waltz in E-flat, Op. 18
(3/22/1956) HMV ALP 1489 [LP]
#(5/9/1987) BBC Legends 4057

Waltz in A-flat, Op. 42
#(4/18/1982) Ivory Classics 70904

Waltz in C-sharp Minor, Op. 64, No. 2
(c. 1969) Classics for Pleasure CFP 157 [LP]
#(12/18/1978) BBC Legends 4057

Clementi, Muzio

Sonata in B-flat, Op. 24, No. 2
(c. 1963) World Record Club T247 [LP]

Copland, Aaron

El Salon Mexico (trans. Bernstein)
#(3/20/1989) Decca 433 657

Daquin, Louis-Claude

Le Coucou
(c. 1969) ASV 6096

Debussy, Claude

Arabesque No. 1 in E
(2/1981) Nimbus 45018 [45 rpm]
#(1/31/1988) Decca 433 651

Clair de lune (from *Suite bergamasque*)
(c. 1969) ASV 6096

L'isle joyeuse
#(12/5/1963) Ermitage 133; Aura 143

Falla, Manuel de

Ritual Fire Dance (from *El amor brujo*)
(c. 1969) ASV 6096

Franck, César

Prelude, Chorale and Fugue
(4/30/1987) Nimbus 5090

Gershwin, George

Three Preludes
(3/17/1958) HMV 7ER5131 [45 rpm]

Glazunov, Alexander

Waltz in D, Op. 42, No. 3
(5/1974) Decca 448 063

Glinka, Mikhail

Tarantella in A Minor
(1946) Pearl GEM 0138; Ivory Classics 72003

Godowsky, Leopold

Alt Wien (from *Triakontameron*)
(5/1974) Decca 448 063

Symphonic Metamorphosis of *Wine, Women and Song* by Johann Strauss Jr.

(1968) ASV 6096; Philips 456 745
(5/1974) Decca 448 063
(5–6/1985) Nimbus 5043

Waltz Poem No. 4 (for the left hand)

(5/1974) Decca 448 063

Gould, Morton

Boogie-Woogie Etude

(1949) Pearl GEM 0138; Ivory Classics 72003
(12/6/1955) DG 445 433
(1968) ASV 6096
(2/1981) Nimbus 45018 [45 rpm]
#(12/2/1991) Decca 433 654

Prelude and Toccata

(1949) Pearl GEM 0138; Ivory Classics 72003

Gounod, Charles

Waltz from *Faust* (trans. Liszt)

(3/22/1956) Testament SBT 1033

Grieg, Edvard

Concerto in A Minor, Op. 16

(11/17–22/1965) Eurodisc 87690 [LP]; World Record Club ST559 [LP]; Music for Pleasure 57002 [LP] (Boult/London Philharmonic)

Sonata in E Minor, Op. 7

(4/30/1987) Nimbus 5090

Hindemith, Paul

Sonata No. 3
(8/10/1955) HMV ALP 1574 [LP]

Hofmann, Josef

Kaleidoskop, Op. 40, No. 4
(5/1974) L'Oiseau-Lyre DSLO 7 [LP]
#(4/18/1982) Ivory Classics 70904
(3–4/1984) Nimbus 5020
#(6/2/1988) Classical 1001
#(12/2/1991) Decca 433 654

Ives, Charles

Three-Page Sonata
#(12/2/1991) Decca 433 654

Khachaturian, Aram

Toccata
(1946) Pearl GEM 0138; Ivory Classics 72003

Liadov, Anatoly

Musical Snuff Box, Op. 32
(1946) Pearl GEM 0138; Ivory Classics 72003
(3/21/1956) Testament SBT 1033

Liszt, Franz

Concerto No. 1 in E-flat
#(unknown) Rococo 2057 [LP] (Gielen/orchestra)
(4/10–15/1952) Testament SBT 1033 (Fistoulari/Philharmonia)

(6/1964)	Denon COCO 78571 (Wallberg/Bamberg Symphony)

Consolation No. 3 in D-flat

(5/31/1950)	RCA Victor LBC 1041 [LP]
(c. 1963)	World Record Club T247 [LP]

Funérailles

(3–4/1984)	Nimbus 5021

Gnomenreigen

(1949)	Pearl GEM 0138; Ivory Classics 72003

Grand Galop Chromatique

(c. 1960)	World Record Club T58 [LP]

Hungarian Fantasy

(12/12–13/1960)	DG 445 433; DG 447 415 (Karajan/Berlin Philharmonic)

Hungarian Rhapsody No. 2

#(10/7/1984)	Decca 433 656
(6–10/1985)	Nimbus 5045

Hungarian Rhapsodies Nos. 5, 6, and 11

(1949)	Pearl GEM 0138; Ivory Classics 72003

Hungarian Rhapsody No. 12

(10/1982)	Vox 7210; Vox CDX 5139
#(10/7/1991)	Decca 433 656

Hungarian Rhapsody No. 13

(3/21/1956)	Testament SBT 1033
#(12/18/1978)	Decca 433 656

Hungarian Rhapsody No. 15

(1949)	Pearl GEM 0138; Ivory Classics 72003
#(11/1/1970)	Decca 433 656

Liebestraum No. 3 in A-flat

(3/24/1958)	Testament SBT 1033; Ivory Classics 72003
(10/1982)	Vox 7210; Vox CDX 5139
#(12/10/1982)	Decca 433 656

Paganini Etude No. 3 (*La Campanella*)

(c. 1963)	World Record Club T247 [LP]

Polonaise No. 2 in E

(1968)	ASV 6109
#(8/3/1968)	Orfeo 431 962

Réminiscences de Don Juan (after Mozart)

(1/14–16/1953)	Testament SBT 1033

Rigoletto Paraphrase (after Verdi)

(1968)	ASV 6109

Sonata in B Minor

(9/25/1951)	HMV ALP 1154 [LP]
(6–10/1985)	Nimbus 5045
#(9/27/1985)	Decca 433 656

Tarantella (Venice and Naples)

(10/1982)	Vox D-VCL 9048 [LP]

Totentanz

#(unknown)	Rococo 2092 [LP] (Horvat/orchestra)
(6/1964)	Eurodisc 72581 [LP] (Wallberg/Bamberg Symphony)

Litolff, Henry

Concerto symphonique No. 4: Scherzo

#(5/27/1958)	HMV ASD 536 [LP] (Sargent/BBC Symphony)
(1/5–7/1967)	Philips 456 745 (Boult/London Philharmonic)

Lully, Jean-Baptiste

Suite de pièces (Allemande, Air tendre, Courante, Sarabande, Gigue)
#(4/18/1982) Ivory Classics 70904

Mana Zucca (Augusta Zuckermann)

Fugato-Humoresque on *Dixie*
(c. 1969) ASV 6096

Prelude
(8/25/1925) Biddulph LHW 034

The Zouaves Drill
(12/6/1955) DG 445 433
(c. 1969) ASV 6096

Medtner, Nikolai

Fairy Tale in E Minor, Op. 34, No. 2
(1946) Pearl GEM 0138; Ivory Classics 72003

Mendelssohn, Felix

Fantasy in F-sharp Minor, Op. 28
(10/1982) Vox 7210; Vox CDX 5139

Prelude and Fugue in E Minor, Op. 35, No. 1
(10/31/1923) Biddulph LHW 034 (Prelude only)
(4/4/1928) Biddulph LHW 034 (Prelude only)
(2/1981) Nimbus 45018 [45 rpm]
#(10/7/1984) Decca 433 655

Rondo Capriccioso, Op. 14
#(12/5/1963) Ermitage 133; Aura 143
(10/1982) Vox 7210; Vox CDX 5139

Scherzo à capriccio in F-sharp Minor
#(4/18/1982) Ivory Classics 70904
(10/1982) Vox D-VCL 9048 [LP]

Scherzo in E Minor, Op. 16, No. 2
(10/31/1928) Biddulph LHW 34
(4/4/1928) Biddulph LHW 34

Song without Words, Op. 19, No. 3 (*Hunting Song*)
(7/29/1925) Biddulph LHW 34

Songs without Words, Op. 38, No. 5 and Op. 53, No. 2
(3/24/1958) HMV 7ER5113 [45 rpm]

Messiaen, Olivier

Ile de feu I and II
#(5/7/1973) Decca 433 657
(2/9/1987) Nimbus 5090

Moszkowski, Moritz

Caprice espagnole, Op. 37
(5/1974) Decca 448 063

Liebeswalzer, Op. 57, No. 5
#(5/5/1991) Decca 433 651

Mozart, Wolfgang Amadeus

Sonata No. 11 in A, K. 331: Rondo alla Turca
#(10/13/1986) Decca 433 651

Mussorgsky, Modest

Pictures at an Exhibition
(2/1/1981) Nimbus 1416
#(2/20/1982) BBC Legends 4160

Okumara, Hajime

Ondo No Fuma Uta; Otemoyen

(c. 1969)	ASV 6096

Pabst, Paul

Paraphrase on Themes from *Yevgeny Onegin* by Tchaikovsky

(5/1/1985)	Nimbus 5091
#(12/2/1991)	Decca 433 654

Paderewski, Ignace Jan

Minuet in G, Op. 14, No. 1

#(11/22/1979)	Decca 433 651

Poulenc, Francis

Toccata

(1949)	Pearl GEM 0138; Ivory Classics 72003
(3/23/1956)	HMV ALP 1527 [LP]
#(12/5/1963)	Ermitage 133; Aura 143

Prokofiev, Sergei

Concerto No. 2 in G Minor, Op. 16

(11/15–16/1954, 4/5/1955)	HMV ALP 1349 [LP] (Menges/Philharmonia)
#(5/2/1991)	BBC Legends 4092 (Nagano/London Philharmonic)

Suggestion diabolique, Op. 4, No. 4

(1946)	Pearl GEM 0138; Ivory Classics 72003

Rachmaninoff, Sergei

Barcarolle in G Minor, Op. 10, No. 3

(5/17/1995)	Decca 448 401

Concerto No. 3 in D Minor, Op. 30

#(12/11/1957)	BBC Legends 4092 (Schwarz/BBC Symphony)
(11/1994)	Decca 448 401 (Temirkanov/Royal Philharmonic)

Elegy in E-flat Minor, Op. 3, No. 1

#(5/1/1991)	Decca 433 651

Melody in E, Op. 3, No. 3 (1892 version)

(5/17/1995)	Decca 448 401

Polka de W. R.

(1949)	Pearl GEM 0138; Ivory Classics 72003
(c. 1969)	ASV 6096
#(5/4/1975)	Decca 433 653
#(11/22/1979)	Decca 433 651
#(3/28/1993)	BBC MM206

Prelude in C-sharp Minor, Op. 3, No. 2

(5/17/1995)	Decca 448 401

Prelude in B-flat, Op. 23, No. 2

(1/28/1958)	HMV 7ER5131 [45 rpm]

Prelude in G Minor, Op. 23, No. 5

(3/17/1958)	HMV 7ER5131 [45 rpm]
(5/17/1995)	Decca 448 401

Prelude in G-sharp Minor, Op. 32, No. 12

(5/17/1995)	Decca 448 401

Rhapsody on a Theme of Paganini, Op. 43

(5/9–10/1953)	HMV ALP 1616 [LP]; RCA Victor LBC 1066 [LP] (Menges/Philharmonia)

Sonata for Cello and Piano in G Minor, Op. 19

(12/27/1934, 10/1/1935)	Biddulph LHW 034 (Marcel Hubert, cello)

Variations on a Theme of Corelli, Op. 42
#(10/13/1986) Decca 433 655
(2/9/1987) Nimbus 5090

Rameau, Jean-Philippe

Tambourin (trans. Godowsky)
(6/26/1925) Biddulph LHW 034
(5/1974) L'Oiseau-Lyre DSLO 7 [LP]

Ravel, Maurice

Pavane pour une infante défunte
(c. 1969) ASV 6096

Sonatine
#(3/20/1989) Decca 433 657

Rebikov, Vladimir

Christmas Tree, Op. 21: Waltz
(1946) Pearl GEM 0138; Ivory Classics 72003
#(3/20/1989) Decca 433 651

Rimsky-Korsakov, Nikolai

Flight of the Bumble Bee (trans. Rachmaninoff)
(2/1981) Nimbus 45018 [45 rpm]
#(2/20/1982) BBC Legends 4160

Rubinstein, Anton

Concerto No. 4 in D Minor, Op. 70
(12/1994) Decca 448 063 (Ashkenazy/Royal Philharmonic)

Melody in F, Op. 3, No. 1
(5/1974) Decca 448 063
#(5/4/1975) Decca 433 653

Saint-Saëns, Camille

Prelude and Fugue in F Minor, Op. 90, No. 1
(6/1/1950) Ivory Classics 72003

The Swan (trans. Godowsky)
(3/22/1956) Testament SBT 1033
(c. 1969) ASV 6096
(5/1974) Decca 448 063

Schubert, Franz

Impromptu in E-flat, Op. 90 (D. 899), No. 2
(5–6/1985) Nimbus 5043
#(5/5/1991) BBC MM99

Impromptu in G-flat, Op. 90 (D. 899), No. 3
(5–6/1985) Nimbus 5043
#(5/5/1991) BBC MM99

Impromptu in A-flat, Op. 90 (D. 899), No. 4
(3/21/1956) HMV ALP 1574 [LP]
#(5/5/1991) BBC MM99

Moment Musical in F Minor, Op. 94 (D. 780), No. 3 (trans. Godowsky)
(5/1974) Decca 448 063
#(5/23/1975) Decca 433 653

Sonata in A, Op. 120 (D. 664)
#(11/7/1968) ASV ALH 948 [LP]
#(5/4/1975) Decca 433 653
(2/29/1987) Nimbus 5091

Sonata in A, Op. Posth. (D. 959)
(c. 1960) World Record Club T58 [LP]

Schumann, Robert

Carnaval, Op. 9
#(unknown) Rococo 2119 [LP]
#(1/31/1988) Decca 433 652
#(6/2/1988) Classical 1001 (*Chopin* and *March of the Philistines* only)

Concerto in A Minor, Op. 54
(11/17–22/1965) Eurodisc 87690 [LP]; World Record Club ST559 [LP]; Music for Pleasure 57002 [LP] (Boult/London Philharmonic)
(c. 1974) Pye TPLS 13063 [LP] (Morris/London Symphonica)

Der Contrabandiste, Op. 74, No. 10 (trans. Tausig)
(c. 1963) World Record Club T247 [LP]
(c. 1969) ASV 6096
(2/1981) Nimbus 45018 [45 rpm]

Fantasiestücke, Op. 111
(c. 1960) World Record Club T58 [LP]
#(5/10/1986) Decca 433 652

Kreisleriana, Op. 16
(5–6/1985) Nimbus 5043; Philips 456 745

Sonata No. 1 in F-sharp Minor, Op. 11
#(12/5/1963) Ermitage 133; Aura 143

Symphonic Etudes, Op. 13
#(3/23/1975) Philips 456 745
#(2/6/1984) Decca 433 652
(3–4/1984) Nimbus 5020
#(12/1/1991) Decca 433 654

Scriabin, Alexander

Etude in C-sharp Minor, Op. 2, No. 1
#(2/12/1982) Decca 433 651

Prelude in C-sharp Minor, Op. 9, No. 1 (for the left hand)
(1946) Pearl GEM 0138; Ivory Classics 72003

Prelude in D, Op. 11, No. 5
#(5/4/1975) Decca 433 653

Sonata No. 4 in F-sharp, Op. 30
#(12/20/1982) Decca 433 657

Shostakovich, Dmitry

Concerto No. 1, Op. 35
(11/16/1954) HMV ALP 1349 [LP] (Menges/Philharmonia)

Polka from *The Golden Age*, Op. 22
#(2/20/1982) Decca 433 651

Preludes, Op. 34, Nos. 5 and 10
(1946) Pearl GEM 0138; Ivory Classics 72003

Sibelius, Jean

Romance in D-flat, Op. 24, No. 9
#(10/7/1991) Decca 433 651

Sinding, Christian

Rustle of Spring, Op. 32, No. 3
#(2/3/1985) Decca 433 651

Strauss, Johann, Jr. (*see also* Godowsky)

On the Beautiful Blue Danube (trans. Schulz-Evler)
(1968) ASV 6096; Philips 456 745

Strauss, Richard

Burleske in D Minor, Op. 11
#(unknown) Rococo 2119 [LP] (Horvat/orchestra)

Stravinsky, Igor

Circus Polka
(8/10/1955) HMV ALP 1527 [LP]

Petrouchka: Three Scenes
(9/19, 20, 25/1951) HMV ALP 1616 [LP]
#(12/5/1963) Ermitage 133; Aura 143
(1968) ASV ALH 965 [LP]
#(11/22/1979) Decca 433 657
(2/1981) Nimbus 45018 [45 rpm]
(6–10/1985) Nimbus 5045

Tchaikovsky, Peter Ilyich (*see also* Pabst)

Concerto No. 1 in B-flat Minor, Op. 23
(11/13/1951) DG 455 433; Philips 456 745 (Ludwig/Berlin Philharmonic)
(1/5–7/1967) World Record Club T796 [LP] (Boult/London Philharmonic)
#(1/30/1968) BBC Legends 4160 (Solti/London Symphony)

Concerto No. 2 in G, Op. 44 (Siloti edition)
(1946) Concert Hall CHC 3 [LP] (Rachmilovich/Santa Monica Symphony)
#(4/1946) Pearl GEM 0138 (mvts. 2 and 3 only) (Stokowski/Hollywood Bowl Symphony)
(12/3–5/1955) DG 455 433; Philips 456 745 (Kraus/Berlin Philharmonic)
(1981) Vox 7210; Vox CDX 5139 (Susskind/Saint Louis Symphony)

Nocturne in C-sharp Minor, Op. 19, No. 4
(5/1974) Decca 448 063

None But the Lonely Heart (trans. Nagel)
#(11/22/1979) Decca 433 651

October, Op. 37a, No. 10 (from *The Months*)
(1946) Pearl GEM 0138; Ivory Classics 72003

Sonata in G, Op. 37
(2/1982) Nimbus 45016 [45 rpm]
#(4/18/82) Ivory Classics 70904

Theme and Variations, Op. 19, No. 6
#(9/27/1985) Decca 433 655

Selected Bibliography

Adler, Larry. *It Ain't Necessarily So*. London: Collins, 1984.

Barber, Charles. *Lost in the Stars: The Forgotten Musical Life of Alexander Siloti*. Lanham, Md.: Scarecrow Press, 2002.

Barenboim, Daniel. *A Life In Music*. New York: Scribner's, 1991.

Bertensson, Sergei, and Jay Leijda. *Sergei Rachmaninoff*. New York: New York University Press, 1956.

Bie, Oscar. *A History of the Pianoforte and Pianoforte Players*. London: J. Dent and Sons, 1899. Reprint, New York: Da Capo, 1966.

Bowers, Faubion. *The New Scriabin: Enigma and Answers*. New York: St. Martin's, 1973.

Brendel, Alfred. *Music Sounded Out*. New York: Farrar Strauss Giroux, 1990.

———. *Musical Thoughts and Afterthoughts*. Princeton, N.J.: Princeton University Press, 1976.

Burton, Humphrey. *Leonard Bernstein*. New York: Doubleday, 1994.

Busoni, Ferruccio. *The Essence of Music and Other Papers*. Translated by Rosamond Ley. New York: Philosophical Library, 1957. Reprint, Westport, Conn.: Hyperion, 1979.

Chasins, Abram. *Speaking of Pianists*. New York: Knopf, 1967.

Columbo, Francesco Maria, and Hans Fazzari. *Per un omaggio a Shura Cherkassky*. Milan: Nuovi Edizioni, 1998.

Cooke, James Francis. *Great Pianists on Piano Playing: Study Talks with Foremost Virtuosos*. Philadelphia: Presser, 1913.

Costa, Bice Horszowski. *MIECIO: Remembrances of Mieczyslaw Horszowski*. Genoa, Italy: Erga Edizioni, 2002.

Crimp, Bryan. *Solo: The Biography of Solomon*. Hexham, UK: Appian Publications and Recordings, 1994.

Dubal, David. *The Art of the Piano: Its Performers, Literature and Recordings*. New York: Summit Books, 1994.

———. *Evenings with Horowitz*. New York: Birch Lane, 1991.

———. *Reflections from the Keyboard: The World of the Concert Pianist*. New York: Summit Books, 1984.

———. *Remembering Horowitz: 125 Pianists Recall a Legend*. New York: Schirmer Books, 1993.

Fay, Amy. "Hoffmann's Playing and Composition." *Music Journal* 19 (1901): 566.

———. *Music Study in Germany*. New York: Dover. 1965.

Figes, Orlando. *Natasha's Dance: A Cultural History of Russia*. New York: Picador, 2002.

Foster, Sidney. "David Saperton." LP sleevenote. IPA 118/19 (1977).

Freeze, Gregory, ed. *Russia, A History*. Oxford: Oxford University Press. 2nd ed. 2002.

Friedheim, Arthur. *Life and Liszt: The Recollections of a Concert Pianist*. Edited by Theodore L. Bullock. New York: Taplinger, 1961.

Friskin, James, and Irwin Freundlich. *Music for the Piano*. New York: Holt, Rinehart and Winston, 1954.

Gerig, Reginald. *Famous Pianists and Their Techniques*. Newton Abbot, UK: David and Charles, 1976.

Godowsky, Leopold. Foreword to 53 *Studies on the Chopin Etudes*. Berlin: Schlesinger, 1914.

Graffman, Gary. *I Really Should Be Practicing*. New York: Avon, 1981.

Graydon, Nell S., and Margaret D. Sizemore. *The Amazing Marriage of Marie Eustis and Josef Hofmann*. Columbia: University of South Carolina Press, 1965.

Hinson, Maurice. *Guide to the Pianist's Repertoire*. Bloomington: Indiana University Press, 1973.

———. *The Pianist's Guide to Transcriptions, Arrangements and Paraphrases*. Bloomington: Indiana University Press, 2001.

Hofmann, Josef. *Piano Playing with Piano Questions Answered*. Reprint, New York: Dover, 1976.

Holcman, Jan. *Pianists: On and Off the Record*. College Park: International Piano Archives at Maryland, 2000.

Horowitz, Joseph. *Conversations with Arrau*. New York: Knopf, 1982.

Hosking, Geoffrey. *Russia: People and Empire*. Cambridge: Harvard University Press, 1997.

———. *Russia and the Russians*. Cambridge: Belknap Press, 2001.

Hughes, Lindsey. *Russia in the Age of Peter the Great*. New Haven, Conn.: Yale University Press, 1998.

Huneker, James G. *Chopin, the Man and His Music*. London: W. Reeves, 1903.

Hurok, Sol, and Ruth Goode. *Impresario*. Westport, Conn.: Greenwood, 1975.

Husarik, Stephen. *Josef Hofmann: The Composer and Pianist*. Thesis, Ann Arbor, Mich.: University Microfilms, 1983.

Hutcheson, Ernest. *The Literature of the Piano*. New York: A. A. Knopf, 1948.

Jablonski, Edward. *Gershwin*. New York: Doubleday, 1987.

Kaiser, Joachim. *Great Pianists of Our Time*. New York: Herder and Herder, 1971.

Kehler, George. *The Piano in Concert*. Metuchen, N.J.: Scarecrow Press, 1982.

Kenneson, Claude. *Musical Prodigies: Perilous Journeys, Remarkable Lives*. Portland, Oreg.: Amadeus Press, 1998.

Kirk, Elise K. *Music at the White House*. Urbana: University of Illinois Press, 1986.

Kolodin, Irving. *The Musical Life*. New York: Knopf, 1958.

Landowska, Wanda. *Landowska on Music*. London: Secker and Warburg, 1965.

Lassimone, Denise, and Howard Ferguson, eds. *Myra Hess by her Friends*. London: Hamish Hamilton, 1966.

Lehmann, Stephen, and Marion Faber. *Ruldolf Serkin: A Life*. New York: Oxford University Press, 2003.

Leinsdorf, Erich. *Cadenza: A Musical Career*. New York: Houghton Mifflin, 1976.

Lhevinne, Josef. *Basic Principles of Piano Playing*. New York: Dover, 1972.

Loesser, Arthur. *Men, Women, and Pianos: A Social History*. New York: Dover, 1972.

Long, Marguerite. *At the Piano with Debussy*. London: Dent, 1972.

Lyle, Wilson. *A Dictionary of Pianists*. London: Robert Hale, 1985.

Mach, Elyse. *Great Pianists Speak for Themselves*. Vol. 1. New York: Dodd Mead, 1980.

———. *Great Pianists Speak for Themselves*. Vol. 2. New York: Dodd Mead, 1988.

Marcus, Adele. *Great Pianists Speak with Adele Marcus*. Neptune, N.J.: Paganiniana, 1979.

Martyn, Barrie. *Rachmaninoff: Composer, Pianist, Conductor*. London: Scolar Press, 1990.

Methuen-Campbell, James. *Chopin Playing: From the Composer to the Present Day*. New York: Taplinger, 1981.

Milstein, Nathan, and Solomon Volkov. *From Russia to the West*. New York: Holt, 1990.

Mohr, Franz. *My Life with the Great Pianists*. Grand Rapids, Mich.: Baker Book House, 1992.

Monsaingeon, Bruno. *Sviatoslav Richter: Notebooks and Conversations*. Princeton, N.J.: Princeton University Press, 2001.

Montefiore, Sebag. *The Life of Potemkin*. New York: St. Martin's, 2001.

Neuhaus, Heinrich. *The Art of Piano Playing*. New York: Praeger, 1973.

Nicholas, Jeremy. *Godowsky: The Pianists' Pianist*. Northumberland, UK: Appian Publications and Recordings, 1989.

Noyle, Linda J., ed. *Pianists on Playing*. Metuchen, N.J.: Scarecrow Press, 1987.

Paderewski, Ignace Jan, and Mary Lawton. *The Paderewski Memoirs*. London: Collins, 1939.

Paperno, Dmitry. *Notes of a Moscow Pianist*. Portland, Oreg.: Amadeus Press, 1998.

Plaskin, Glenn. *Vladimir Horowitz*. New York: William Morrow, 1983.

Reich, Howard. *Van Cliburn*. Nashville, Tenn.: Thomas Nelson, 1993.

Revesz, G. *Psychology of a Musical Prodigy*. Westport, Conn.: Greenwood, 1999.

Rezits, Joseph. *Beloved Tyranna: The Legend and Legacy of Isabelle Vengerova*. Bloomington, Ind.: David Daniel, 1995.

Roberson, Steve. *Lili Kraus*. Fort Worth, Tex.: TCU Press, 2000.

Rubinstein, Arthur. *My Many Years*. New York: Alfred A. Knopf, 1980.

———. *My Young Years*. New York: Alfred A. Knopf, 1973.

Sachs, Harvey. *Rubinstein: A Life*. New York: Grove, 1995.

Saerchinger, Cesar. *Artur Schnabel*. London: Cassell, 1957.
Said, Edward W. *Musical Elaborations*. London: Vintage, 1992.
Schnabel, Artur. *My Life and Music*. New York: Dover, 1988.
Schonberg, Harold C. *The Great Pianists*. New York: Simon and Schuster, 1963.
———. *Horowitz: His Life and Music*. New York: Simon and Schuster, 1992.
Seroff, Victor I. *Rachmaninoff*. New York: Simon and Schuster, 1950.
Sitwell, Sacheverell. *Liszt*. London: Faber and Faber, 1934.
Slenczynska, Ruth. *Forbidden Childhood*. New York: Doubleday, 1957.
Slonimsky, Nicholas. "Musical Children: Prodigies or Monsters?" *Etude* 66 (October 1945): 592.
Smith, Cecil. *Worlds of Music*. Philadelphia: J. B. Lippincott, 1952.
Smith, Julia. *Master Pianist: The Career and Teaching of Carl Friedberg*. New York: Philosophical Library, 1963.
Steuermann, Edward. *The Not Quite Innocent Bystander*. Edited by Clara Steuermann, David Porter, and Gunther Schuller. Lincoln: University of Nebraska Press, 1989.
Walker, Alan. *Franz Liszt: The Final Years 1861–1886*. New York: Alfred A. Knopf, 1996.
———. *Franz Liszt: The Virtuoso Years 1811–1847*. New York: Alfred A. Knopf, 1983.
———. *Franz Liszt: The Weimar Years 1848–1861*. New York: Alfred A. Knopf, 1986.

Special Collections

Edith Evans Braun collection, 1916–1976. New York Public Library. Lincoln Center Research Libraries. JPB 91–96.
Robinson Locke Scrapbook, Volume 275, Reel 24. New York Public Library. Lincoln Center Research Libraries. ZZ-Z617.
Hulda Lushanka Papers, 1908–1971. New York Public Library. Lincoln Center Research Libraries. JPB 93–92.
Marcella Sembrich collection, 1790–1988. New York Public Library. Lincoln Center Research Libraries. JPB 91–94.

Periodicals

In my opinion. *Musical Opinion* 74 (January 1951): 133.
In my opinion. *Musical Opinion* 75, (May 1952): 456.
London Musical Events 8 (July 1953): 26.
In my opinion. *Musical Opinion* 76 (February 1953): 265.
In my opinion. *Musical Opinion* 76 (June 1953): 520.
In my opinion. *Musical Opinion* 76 (July 1953): 583.
In my opinion. *Musical Opinion* 77 (December 1953): 136–37.
In my opinion. *Musical Opinion* 77 (March 1954): 329.
Struth, S. "Ein moderner virtuose fasziniert." *Musikleben* 8 (January 1955): 30–31.
In my opinion. *Musical Opinion* 78 (May 1955): 456–47.

London Musical Events 10 (May 1955): 50.
In my opinion. *Musical Opinion* 79 (May 1956): 455.
Rutland, H. "Henry Wood Promenade Concerts." *Musical Times* 98 (September 1957): 503.
London Symphony Orchestra. "Cherkassky and Edouard van Remoortel." *Musical Opinion* 80 (May 1957): 457.
"Shura Cherkassky." *Musical Opinion* 80 (June 1957): 520.
"Shura Cherkassky." *Musical Opinion* 81 (December 1957): 154.
Chissell, J. "Shura Cherkassky." *Musical Times* 98 (May 1957): 268.
Zofingen. *Schweiz Mus* 97 (December 1957): 484.
"BBC Symphony concert." *Musical Times* 94 (February 1958): 94.
"Shura Cherkassky." *Musical Opinion* 81 (May 1958): 367.
Chapman, E. "Musical Survey." *London Musical Events* 13 (May 1958): 29.
Emery, J. "Bournemouth Symphony Orchestra Easter Festival." *Musical Times* 99 (June 1958): 329.
Philharmonia Orchestra. *Musical Opinion* 81 (June 1958): 567.
Royal Academy of Music. *Musical Opinion* 82 (December 1958): 152.
"Shura Cherkassky." *Musical Opinion* 82 (June 1959): 584.
London Symphony Orchestra. *Musical Opinion* 83 (December 1959): 155.
London Symphony Orchestra. *Musical Opinion* 83 (January 1960): 233.
Carmichael, J. "Shura Cherkassky." *Music and Musicians* 8 (January 1960): 21.
"Shura Cherkassky." *Musical Opinion* 83 (March 1960): 385.
Jacobs, A. Passing notes. *Gramophone* 37 (April 1960): 543.
"Triumphal Cherkassky return." *BB* 72 (November 1960): 39.
Recital, New York. *Musical America* 81 (January 1961): 79.
Recital, New York. *Musical Courier* 163 (January 1961): 25.
Recital, London. *Musical Opinion* 84 (May 1961): 471.
Carmichael, J. "Magical Chopin." *Music and Musicians* 10 (January 1962): 43.
"Krips and Cherkassky in Philharmonic debuts." *Musical America* 82 (January 1962): 238.
Weissmann, J. Music survey. *Music Events* 17 (30 July 1962): 29.
Spero, C. "Burning Berlioz." *Music and Musicians* 11 (November 1962): 52.
Editorial notes. *Strad* 73 (November 1962): 235.
Sigmon, C. Recitals in New York. *Musical America* 88 (January 1963): 150.
Cizik, V. "Koniec vsetko nenapravi." *Hudební Slov* 8, no. 7 (1964): 217–18.
Sefl, V. "Prazsti symfonikove." *Hudební Rozhledyz* 17, no. 3 (1964): 546.
Recital, Bucharest. *Muzsica* 14 (July 1964): 46–47.
Recital, Budapest. *Muzsika* 7 (May 1964): 33.
Popisil, V. "Tri klaviriste." *Hudební Rozhledyz* 17, no. 13 (1964): 564.
Payne, A. "Exceptional Appassionata." *Music and Musicians* 13 (May 1965): 95.
Curten, C. W. "Ein portrait auf platen." *Photoprisma* no. 3 (May–June 1965): 87.
"Spotlight on Shura Cherkassky, pianist." *Music Events* 21 (January 1966): 12.
Blyth, A. "Shimmering sea." *Music and Musicians* 15 (April 1967): 44.

"Shura Cherkassky, biography." *Music Events* 21 (September 1967): 12.
Holzknecht, V. "Pet muzu za klaviaturou." *Hudební Rozhledyz* 20, no. 13 (1967): 409–10.
Brown, P. "Almost orchestral." *Music and Musicians* 16 (February 1968): 51.
Tschculik, N. "Aus den Wiener Konzertsalen." *Osterreichische Musikzeitschrift* 28 (February 1968): 98.
Crankshaw, G. "Concerto for quartet." *Music and Musicians* 16 (May 1968): 48.
Holzknecht, V. "Diference s Cerkaskym." *Hudební Rozhledyz* 21, no. 1 (1968): 29–30.
Editorial notes. *Strad* 79 (November 1968): 265.
Cizik, V. "Komone koncerty." *Hudební Slov* 12, no. 2 (1968): 65.
Crankshaw, G. "New Tchaikovsky for old." *Music and Musicians* 16 (April 1968): 42.
Gill, D. Pianists. *Musical Times* 109 (May 1968): 449–50.
Orchester 16 (June 1968): 290.
Jehne, L. "Trochu soli do Ostravy." *Hudební Rozhledyz* 21, no. 1 (1968): 30.
Simmons, D. London Music. *Musical Opinion* 92 (December 1968): 120.
Gill, D. Music in London. *Musical Times* 110 (January 1969): 54.
Blyth, A. "Cheeky Traditionalist." *Music and Musicians* 7 (April 1969): 30.
Dinolov, L. "Kamerni Kontserti." *Bulgarsko Muzikozanie* 20, no. 7 (1969): 72.
Crankshaw, G. "Towering Bartok." *Music and Musicians* 18 (February 1970): 171.
Muenchner konzerte. *Oper U Konzert* 8 (December 1970): 22–23.
Orga, A. Piano. *Music and Musicians* 19 (February 1971): 59.
Richards, D. Pianists. *Music and Musicians* 20 (September 1971): 74.
Lawrence, R. Orchestra. *Music and Musicians* 20 (December 1971): 80.
Scharnazi, A. Muenchner konzerte. *Oper U Konzert* 10, no. 3 (1972): 32.
Bowen, M. Pianists. *Music and Musicians* 20 (February 1972): 76.
Greenbaugh, J. Pianists. *Music and Musicians* 21 (May 1973): 78–79.
"How do you like your Chopin?" *High-Fidelity and Musical America* 23 (June 1973): 75.
Morrison, B. Pianists. *Music and Musicians* 22 (April 1974): 58–60.
Kuntze, G. W. "Beethoven aus Cherkassky's haenden." *Orchester* 23 (March 1975): 193.
New York. *Music Journal* 34 (May 1976): 30–31.
New York. *Music Journal* 35 (April 1977): 40.
Morrison, B. Pianists. *Music and Musicians* 25 (June 1977): 53.
Nesteva, M. "Shura Cherkassky." *Soviet Muzyczny* 25 (July 1977): 53.
Thackeray, R. Recitals. *Musical Times*, 118 (May 1977): 410.
Morrison, B. Pianists. *Music and Musicians* 26 (January 1978): 52.
Morrison, B. Pianists. *Music and Musicians* 27, no. 42 (September 1978).
Morrison, B. Pianists. *Music Journal* 37 (January 1979): 43.
Morrison, B. Pianists. *Music and Musicians* 27 (April 1979): 58.
Morrison, B. Pianists. *Music and Musicians* 27 (July 1979): 63.
Kimelkis, G. "Shura Cherkassky." *Soviet Muzyczny* 12, no. 1 (December 1979): 88–89.
Morrison. B. "In My Opinion." *Musical Opinion* 103 (February 1980): 193.
Music and Musicians 28 (February 1980): 52.
Sale, E. Pianists. *Music and Musicians* 28 (August 1980): 52.
Keener, A. Review. *Music and Musicians* 25 (September 1980): 52.

Review. *Bulgarsko Muzikozanie* 32 (March 1981): 58.
Review. *Oper U Konzert* 20, no. 2 (February 1981): 42.
Review. *Musical Times* 123 (April 1982): 72.
Kanski, J. "Jak uczyl Hofmann?" *Ruch Muzyczny* 28, no. 1 (September 1984): 11.
Konzerte. *Oper U Konzert* 22, no. 3 (March 1984): 26–27.
Marks, A. J. Recitals. *Musical Times* 125 (July 1984): 803.
Marks, A. Recitals. *Musical Times* 127 (December 1986): 700.
Goldsmith, H. "Cherkassky and Horowitz: Russian romantics." *Opus 3* no. 3 (1987): 29–31.
Konzertnoe obozenie. *Soviet Muz* (December 1987).
Hall, G. "Cherkassky." *Musical Times* 129 (March 1988): 48.
Montparker, Carol. "Shura Cherkassky: Sprightly sage of the piano." *Clavier* 29 (1990): 10–14.
Keene, C. "Shura Cherkassky in Training." *Key Classics* 10, no. 3 (1990): 12–13.
Kerner, L. "Squeeze Play." *Village Voice* 35 (11 September 1990): 82.
Morrison, B. "The Grange de Meslay Festival." *Musical Times* 131 (November 1990): 615–16.
"[International Brighton] Festival." I 114 (September 1991): 337–38.
Harrison, M. "Who Needs an Orchestra?" *Musical Opinion* 114 (October 1991): 358–59.
Hough, S., and B. Morrison. Pianist to Pianist. *Gramophone* 69 (October 1991): 64–65.
Concerts [eightieth birthday recital]. *Musical Opinion* 111 (January 1992): 32.
Ehrlich, C. "Pianists good and great." *Musical Times* 133 (Jan 1992).
Keller, J. M. "A seat on the aisle: The old and the new." *Piano Quarterly* 40, no. 157 (1992): 48.
Goldsmith, H. *American Record Guide* 58, no. 4 (1995): 50–51.
Obituary. *Neue Musikzeitung* 45 (February–March 1996): 2.
Obituary. *Opernwelt* no. 2 (February 1996): 76.
Obituary. *Das Orchester* 44, no. 3 (1996): 87.
"Hommage: Adieu Shura!" *Diapason* [France] no. 423 (February 1996): 9.
Obituary. *American Organist* 30 (March 1996): 87.
Obituary. Notes 52, no. 4 (1996): 1121.
Obituary. *American Record Guide* 59, no. 2 (1996): 21.
Obituary. *Gramophone* 73 (March 1996): 12.
Obituary. *Mens en Melodie* 51 (February 1996): 98.
Obituary. *Ruch Muzyczny* 40, no. 1 (1996): 5.
Obituary. *Musical Opinion* 118 (Spring 1996): 4.
Jack, A. "The Master of Surprise" *Classic* CD no. 71 (March 1996): 42.
Tashiro, M. Obituary. Notes 53, no. 4 (1997): 1118.
CD Reviews. *International Piano Quarterly* 1 (Spring 1998): 93–95.
Albeson, A. T. "Eccentric genius." *International Piano Quarterly* 6 (May–June 2002): 42–45.
Stewart, A. "Inspiration and intuition." *International Piano Quarterly* 8 (March–April 2004): 68–69.

Index

About the Author

A native New Yorker, **Elizabeth Carr** won numerous scholarships and awards for study at some of the most prestigious music institutions in New York and Europe. She holds degrees in piano performance, history of music, and musicology. Her piano studies took place in New York with William Harms, a close friend and contemporary of Shura Cherkassky at the Curtis Institute, where Harms was a protégé of Josef Hofmann and Moritz Rosenthal. Following four years of study with Harms, she pursued graduate work at the Cherubini Conservatory in Florence, Italy, with Rio Nardi, a student of Busoni, and again with Nardi at the Mozarteum in Salzburg, Austria. Upon her return to the United States, she studied at Juilliard and New York University and coached with Raymond Lewenthal, the world-renowned protagonist of the music of Alkan, who in his youth studied extensively with Lydia Cherkassky, mother of Shura Cherkassky.

Following her career as a college professor, pianist, concert presenter, and director of the Cape Cod Conservatory in Massachusetts for twenty-six years, Elizabeth Carr received the President's Award from the National Guild of Community Schools of the Arts for "outstanding commitment and lasting achievement in the field of the arts and arts education." She is now an arts and education consultant, and with her husband she divides her time between New York City, the Virgin Islands, Italy, and Cape Cod.